NORWAY

BY

G. GATHORNE HARDY

AUTHOR OF "NORSE DISCOVERY OF AMERICA"

WITH AN INTRODUCTION BY

THE RIGHT HON. H. A. L. FISHER, M. P.

NEW YORK

CHARLES SCRIBNER'S SONS

1925

Printed in the United States of America

EDITOR'S FOREWORD

NORWAY is a country with no enemies and many friends. Some are attracted to Norway by sport; others by the stern beauty of its rockbound coast; others, again, have come under the spell of the old Norse literature, and are thus led on to take interest in the fabric and growth of Norse society. The merit of Mr. Gathorne Hardy is that, quite apart from his exact and well-proved Norse scholarship, he writes with a hearty enjoyment of every side of Norway—of its fishing, its scenery, its literature old and new—and is, besides, thoroughly instructed in its political and economic history. He is thus able, in the short space allotted to him by the editor of this series, to present a balanced view of Norwegian civilisation founded on intimate knowledge and inspired by a lively recollection of delightful hours spent among the fiords and fells of his favourite land.

H. A. L. FISHER.

THE MODERN WORLD
A SURVEY OF HISTORICAL FORCES

Edited by
The Right Hon. H. A. L. FISHER, M. P.

The aim of the volumes in this series is to provide a balanced survey, with such historical illustrations as are necessary, of the tendencies and forces, political, economic, intellectual, which are moulding the lives of contemporary states.

Already published:

GERMANY	by G. P. Gooch
IRELAND	by Stephen Gwynn
NORWAY	by G. Gathorne Hardy
RUSSIA	by Valentine O'Hara and N. Makeef

In preparation :

TURKEY	by Arnold Toynbee
IRAQ	by Gertrude Bell
INDIA	by Sir Valentine Chirol
CHILE	by His Excellency Don Augustin Edwards
ENGLAND	by the Very Rev. W. R. Inge
ARGENTINA	by Clarence H. Haring
AMERICA	by John Finley

THE MODERN WORLD

NORWAY

INTRODUCTION

I DO not think that I am giving too free a rein to my enthusiasm for the country and its inhabitants in claiming that Norway is rightly accorded an independent place in this series. If we lay the stress on the first word of the expression " Modern World," we may plead that the renaissance of Norwegian independence dates from the present century—1905; that, though not directly engaged in the late war as a belligerent, Norway has been economically affected by it to an extent not traceable in the case of any other neutral; and that, apart from this, she is at present undergoing a most interesting period of transition in spheres as apparently distinct as those of industry and religion. But besides all this, it may be urged that a country which has achieved so large a measure of world-wide distinction in proportion to her scanty population deserves special and individual consideration. The great literature of the Eddic poems and the prose sagas is not the common heritage of Scandinavia; it was the achievement of Norwegians, whether at home or in colonies which they had founded does not greatly affect the question. Names such as Holberg, Ibsen, and Björnson in literature, or Amundsen and Nansen in other fields of activity, are known and respected all over the world, and, while other names might be added to the list, this is no bad showing for a nation whose total population, even at the present day, is not much more than $2\frac{1}{2}$ millions.

One is nevertheless perpetually confronted by the fact that Englishmen as a whole think in terms of Scandinavia rather than of Norway, Sweden, and Denmark. When remonstrated with, they invariably demand a comparison, and wish to know what, after all, are the essential differences between the three nations. The question is rather embarrassing, not because great differences do not in fact exist, but because comparisons are proverbially odious, and apt to sound invidious. Conscious as I am of the fine qualities possessed in common by the whole of Scandinavia, I am reluctant to pursue the matter deeply, and would rather leave the reader of this book to make his own deductions from it. A few of the factors which tend to distinguish Norway from her neighbours may, however, be indicated.

Geography makes of Denmark a continental, and of Sweden a Baltic, nation. The backwardness of Russia has turned the interests of Sweden also to the continent of Europe, where, in the past, she attained a great reputation. Norway is naturally the most isolated of the three. She has been less subject to external influences than either of her neighbours, and, in so far as she has been susceptible to these, the country with which she has had the closest relations has been Great Britain. There is, in fact, a remarkable sympathy between Norway and ourselves; so much so that Norwegians have assured me, with every appearance of sincerity, that they can more easily appreciate the point of view of an Englishman than that even of a Swede or a Dane.

But Norway remains predominantly Norway. While Sweden has taken pride in a cosmopolitan outlook, and Denmark has continuously been exposed to German influences, Norway has developed on more national lines. The historical fact that, in union with each of the other two countries, she was forced into a subordinate position has accentuated nationalist sentiment to an exceptional degree. Fortunately, the physical circumstances which rendered her inaccessible to alien influences have conduced to the formation and preservation of peculiarly fine characteristics. Her people have always, even under the most adverse circumstances, been able to retain an exceptional measure of freedom, while they have learned, in isolation, to think and act for themselves. In Denmark, a country of short distances and relatively easy communications, tyranny, in various forms, had greater scope. The peasantry there were little better than serfs until nearly the end of the eighteenth century. An all-powerful though effete aristocracy was only superseded, in 1660, by an autocratic monarchy which lasted almost to living memory. Bjerregaard's panegyric on Norway as *frihedens tempel* could never have been applied to Denmark without irony. In spite, therefore, of their long political subordination to Denmark, Norwegians seem always to have felt a certain measure of proud superiority to their masters. Molesworth records this attitude as long ago as 1692, and I am afraid that, however little it may be justified at the present day, the average Norwegian's sentiment towards the Dane would still be fairly expressed by the Scotsman's phrase, " Puir wee bodies." His feelings may be as affectionate, when he is not annoyed by some legacy of the old régime such as the Greenland question or the retention of Norwegian archives, as those of a man for a woman or a child, but they usually retain, I think, a trace of subconscious superiority. Possibly the disproportion between the size of the respective countries, considered apart from their populations, to some extent contributes, however illogically, to the persistence of this attitude.

As between Sweden and Norway, the boot has hitherto tended to be on the other leg. Four hundred years of Danish domination, while it left the Norwegian still personally free and independent, levelled the classes of Norway into a homogeneous mass with a superficial resemblance to peasantry. To the Swede, who prided himself upon courtly manners and fine social distinctions, the Norwegian population seemed rather boorish and uncivilised. Though this impression was in fact unjustified, and based on a misunderstanding of the superficial appearances, there was in reality, until recently, a very marked and fundamental difference between the social organisation of Norway and of Sweden. In Sweden, as elsewhere, democracy has of late made its influence felt, but within living memory the situation was pretty much that described by a character in Newland's *Forest Scenes in Norway and Sweden*—a book, by the way, which is on the whole distinctly pro-Swedish. " We in England don't care much about precedence, as you know. . . . But it is not so here ; they all know their places, like schoolboys, and fight for them like dogs at a feeding-trough if you happen to make a mistake about them. . . . Half the people you meet with here are counts and barons . . . but, besides this, there were their confounded orders of knighthood : there are knights of the Cherubim and Seraphim, and knights of the Elephant and Castle, and knights of the Goose and Gridiron, and Heaven knows what besides. Then came the officials, from the Prime Minister down to the postmaster, and their sons and grandsons. Why, there was not a tradesman I dealt with, hardly a beggar I gave a skilling to, who had not a clear right to go before me—aye, and showed every disposition to exercise it, too ! "

This, needless to say, was a caricature, even at the time when it was written, but it embodied a substantial truth. Norway, on the other hand, was at this time and even earlier almost completely free from class distinctions : there, the raw material for a democracy was present even before such a form of government was established. It is easy to see, therefore, how such conflicting ideas as to the proper organisation of society were bound to lead to misunderstanding and friction under any form of union between the two countries. The Norwegian to the Swede seemed rustic and uncouth ; the Swede to the Norwegian artificial and arrogant. The Union broke for more tangible reasons, but differences in the national character of the two nations prevented it from ever being really harmonious.

But enough of this subject, upon which I have only entered reluctantly and under pressure. No one would dream of expecting three cousins, each born in a different environment, educated in a different school, and engaged in a different profession, to be exactly alike, especially if they had notoriously quarrelled during the greater part of their past lives. They would still preserve some strong resemblances, the separate achievements of each would be a source of some pride to all, and all would feel a certain amount of family solidarity, but it would be unscientific simply to lump them together as "the Browns" or "the Robinsons." The indiscriminate use of the convenient expression "Scandinavia" is open to the same objection, and now that every variety of union tried since 1319 has finally broken down, it is time that we began to think and speak of Norway, Sweden, and Denmark.

Of these three nations, Norway should be to Englishmen the most interesting and the most intelligible. Interesting, as the least affected by continental influences, and therefore the best fitted to illustrate racial characteristics, in so far as it differs from ourselves; particularly interesting now, when it is undergoing a period of rapid transition, the ultimate effects of which are very difficult to forecast. Intelligible because through centuries of almost unbroken and generally friendly intercourse the Englishman and the Norwegian have developed a very similar mentality. Even the Norwegian antagonism to us during the South African War was animated by a fundamentally British sentiment, sympathy with the little man who puts up a plucky fight against a big one. In studying Norway we are not only learning something about an interesting and attractive foreign nation, but throwing fresh light upon our own development, habits, and character. It is a study which deserves far more elaboration than the present volume can hope to provide, but if it directs attention to the subject and encourages a more general interest, it will not have been written in vain.

For the unstinted help which Norwegians have given me I can never be sufficiently grateful : I fear that they may feel ill-repaid when some topic into which they have entered deeply has had to be dismissed in a few words. I can only plead the necessity for observing some proportion, and assure them that my thanks are not to be measured by the space which I have been able to accord to their respective subjects. Above all, I would have their friends to know that the opinions expressed are in all cases not theirs but mine. I would not have them held accountable for heretical historical theories or dubious political views. At our next meeting, I can assure them that they will find it all too easy to convert me, at least for the time being, since all my Norwegian acquaintances exert a charm which completely anæsthetises the critical faculty. I take this opportunity of adding that the translations, metrical and otherwise, to be found in the book are also mine. Since the Norwegian language is not very generally understood in this country, some attempts of this kind seemed necessary, especially in dealing with the literature.

The names of all who have helped me with information are too numerous to be recorded, though selection seems invidious. Yet I think I must mention my friend Rolv Laache, Dr. Jakob Worm-Müller, Professor Seip, Professor Paasche, and Mr. Vidnes of the Press section of the Utenriks-Departement. In this country the help which I have received has also come from one who is a Norwegian by birth, though now a naturalised British subject, Sir Karl Knudsen, K.B.E. To all of these, and others whose kindness is no less appreciated, I beg to tender my most grateful thanks.

G. G. H.

July 1925.

CONTENTS

CHAPTER I

THE COUNTRY

THE topographical characteristics of Norway have been so often described, since the twelfth-century author of the *Historia Norwegiæ* prefaced his work with some vivid remarks on the subject, that they may be taken to be generally known in this country. Great numbers of Englishmen, since the days when Sir Hyde Parker thought the practice overdone, have visited its valleys annually as salmon fishers, or climbed its fjelds or roamed its forests in pursuit of reindeer or elk. An even greater though more transient body of observers has toured its fjords and gazed at its midnight sun; while even the residue, who have never actually been to Norway, have characteristic landscapes forced upon their attention in the posters of travel-bureaux and steamship companies. In these circumstances it would be folly and presumption to imagine that any description could add materially to the sum of knowledge: the most that can usefully be done is to emphasise certain features which have had, and continue to have, a close bearing upon the political, social, and economic development of the country. "History," says Buckle, "is the modification of man by nature, and of nature by man"; and whatever objection may be raised to a sweeping generalisation so characteristic of this author, it is certainly true that the history of Norway has been very materially influenced, and even controlled, by the situation and physical conformation of the country. It is probably for this reason that the national songs and poetry of Norway abound, to a degree not to be met with elsewhere, in allusions to its scenery. Nature has been a rough nurse, but she has made the people what they are, and they know it and love her for it.

Norway is a large country, and a generalised description cannot therefore be true of the whole of it. Even in calling it mountainous one must make an exception in favour of the level and treeless plain of Jaederen in

the south-west. The kingdom extends over more than
thirteen degrees of latitude, a difference approximately
the same as that separating the Skager Rak from the
Gulf of Genoa ; it would be unreasonable, therefore,
to expect uniformity of climatic conditions, though
there is, in fact, far less variation than might be anticipated. Norway is commonly advertised as the Land
of the Midnight Sun ; but of course this phenomenon
is only to be seen in the districts north of the arctic
circle—that is to say, in the *fylker* or counties of Nord-
land, Tromsö, and Finmarken. One is accustomed,
again, to think of Norway as a timber-producing
country, which indeed it is, but the districts draining
into the Trondhjem and Oslo Fjords—the latter region,
as will presently be shown, is a large one—account for
the most important forests. As it would be beyond
the scope of this work to go into topographical details,
what follows must therefore be read in the light of this
necessary warning.

The tool with which Providence has engineered communications, excavated harbours, and carved out a
home for the population has been mainly the ice of
prehistoric glaciers. Norway still contains the largest
area of glaciers in Europe, and over nearly 2000 square
miles of its surface the ice-cap is still to be seen ; but,
except for the peaks of the mountains, the whole of
the country was once covered by an enormous glacier,
which has scored the elevated plateau of the high
fjeld with deep, straight-sided channels. Along what
is now the west coast, the plateau descended abruptly
nearly to sea-level ; here the lower lands and isolated
projections beyond it have been divided, by a network
of such channels, into the archipelago of the *skjaergaard*, or sheltering island wall so welcome to the sea-
sick traveller after his voyage over the North Sea.
Into the ice-cut valleys which debouch from the mainland the sea has rushed for enormous distances, to form
the fjords which so indent the coastline that the shore
of Norway, straightened out, would reach nearly half-

way round the globe. Other countries may boast higher mountains, but few can rival the impressiveness of the cliffs which here descend, practically sheer, from snow-line to sea-level, dwarfing the villages beneath to an insignificance which startles afresh each time they are visited. Pent between cliffs of almost equal magnificence, the valley runs far back into the interior, its level floor enriched with a closely ground detritus, the dust and shavings from Nature's mighty saw and plane. This fertile valley-floor was itself part of the fjord at a comparatively late geological epoch —indeed a large proportion of the cultivable soil of Norway consists of land formerly submerged, which has since risen some hundreds of feet above its former level. The result is such an abrupt differentiation between fell and dale, that as a broad generalisation it may be said that the Norwegian lives and moves and has his being exclusively in the clefts of his country, and leaves the mountains to themselves. His cattle, indeed, visit the higher tributary valleys during the summer, under the care of women residing temporarily in the rude châlets known as *saeters*, and the hunters, of course, will climb and wander anywhere in pursuit of game. But it is broadly true that human life is restricted to the coasts and the cliff-enclosed channels which seam the elevated barrens of the high fjeld.

> " There's a land lying close to perpetual snow,
>   Where life only blooms in the crannies below,"

sings the national poet, Björnson, and though his words are intended to apply to vegetable life, they are equally true of his countrymen. So it has been from the earliest times. " Est autem Norwegia," writes the author of *Historia Norwegiæ*, " regio vastissima, sed maxima ex parte inhabitabilis præ nimietate montium." The cultivated land is less than 4 per cent. of the total area of the country, and more than 75 per cent. is altogether uninhabitable.

It follows from what has been said that there is but

little intercommunication between the inhabitants of
the western valleys. I have passed from one to another
and found native companions complaining of a difficulty in understanding a dialect quite different from
their own, and one can readily understand, in the light
of such an experience, the tardiness of the Norwegian
race to find national unity. Except by the use of sea
communications, the inhabitant of a western valley is
largely restricted in the line of his movements. His
nearest neighbours across the mountains he may never
see. He is walled in. To describe Norway as a
mountainous country gives, in fact, in some respects
a misleading idea of the situation. A mountainous
country suggests to most people a region like Switzer-
land, with habitations and even important villages at
extremely high altitudes. But western Norway always
suggests to my mind a cake with slices cut out of it,
standing upon a plate, the plate representing the inhabited regions, the cake the barren fjeld. In most
countries it is the free life of the mountain-dweller
which strikes the literary imagination. In Norway it
is often this notion of an impassable barrier which is
voiced in poetry ; for the Norwegian is really not so
much a mountaineer as a valley-dweller. Thus Björnson's Arne, in his song *Over de höie Fjelde*, is oppressed
by the enclosing "wall" (*mur*). Thus Brand warns
Agnes in Ibsen's drama :

> " Maiden, ah ! bethink thee well ;
> Closely crushed 'twixt fell and fell,
> Pent, where crags their shadows throw
> On the twilit cleft below,
> Life must now be grim and grey
> As the close of autumn day."

Yet these conditions, gloomy and unattractive as
they may sound, have developed some of the finest
elements in the Norwegian character. The dweller by
the fjord looked to the sea and across it for his livelihood, with the result that the Norse sea-rover became
the embodiment of maritime enterprise ; while the folk

who lived inland, separated by imperfect communications from external sources of wealth, gained a sturdy independence and self-reliance, turned their hands to every necessary craft, from house-building to shoe-making, and developed the industry essential to make a closely restricted area produce everything necessary to subsistence.

There is another, and less satisfactory, side to this divergence of outlook between coast and interior. The coast alone has been subjected to any material extent to foreign influences, and owing to the facility of maritime and the difficulties of inland communication, it is to the coast that the towns are, almost without exception, confined. Indeed, one of the points which strikes the visitor most forcibly is the isolated life led by the inhabitants of the country districts. It is seldom that one sees anything approximating to our idea of a village ; the agricultural population is scattered in separate farms. Our villages, in fact, were the result of a different system of land tenure. But the result in Norway has been so wide a separation between the urban and rural populations that they are almost like two different nations, with distinct ideals and objectives, and actually speaking, at the present day, what are practically two different languages. From this fact have followed effects of great political and historical importance, which will fall to be discussed later, and must throughout be borne in mind.

There is also a marked difference, even a sort of mutual jealousy, between the natives of east and west. The mountain barrier which separates Sweden from Norway operates to some extent to isolate the western inhabitants from their own countrymen, and an Englishman who finds the characteristics which endear the Norwegian to him common to both sides of the plateau will be rather astonished to hear Eastlander and Westlander insisting upon a fundamental difference, and indulging in constant, and at times intemperate, criticism of each other's shortcomings.

To the east and south the plateau slopes down more gently, and conditions are more normal. But even here communications and inhabited districts are largely confined to the valleys. This is partly due to the fact, already referred to, that the soil suitable for cultivation is largely confined within the bounds of the ancient shore-line. A map showing rivers and lakes would sufficiently indicate most of the principal routes from time immemorial. Along these, in early days, rode on the periodical visits of inspection a man with a sixteen-foot pole held across the saddle. An osier ring dangled from each end, and if a branch grew near enough to knock it off, penalties impended for those responsible for road maintenance. Close round, on both sides, but for here and there a marshy opening, grew primeval forest. It is true that some ancient roadways climb out of the cultivated valleys and seem to prefer a mountain route where less clearing of trees was necessary, but if we examine the course of such a well-known example as the Dovre road from Gudbrandsdalen to Trondhjem, we shall find that it follows the course of rivers almost throughout, and is in fact a valley-road in relation to the surrounding fjeld, whatever it may appear to be from the point of view of those who dwell at a still lower level. On the same track where the gradually developing railway system of Norway moves to-day, or where the pony and cariole, now to a great extent superseded by the motor-car, are still the only methods of travel, advanced, in the ninth century, the forces which were to make the country's scattered *fylker* into a united nation. These ancient highways, laid out by Nature for the people of Norway, will well repay the attention of the student of her history.

To the north of Namdalen the conditions need not detain us. Here were, and are, practically no important roads ; communication is maintained by sea. A railway now runs across Sweden from the Gulf of Bothnia to Narvik, but for the most part the intervening ranges are unvisited save by wandering Lapps. Namdalen itself may be visited from Namsos, or by way of the Trondhjem Fjord, the Snaasen Vand (lake), and so to Grong. A railway threatens here, too, and has already reached the shores of the Snaasen Vand.

Near Trondhjem itself the northern and southern plateaux are divided by an interval of lower ground, over which, long before the dawn of Norway's history, passed from Sweden those who were possibly the oldest inhabitants of the country. But it is in the district south of Trondhjem where, if we compare the form of the Scandinavian peninsula to a couchant lion, Norway occupies the head, that the most interesting points relative to the communications are to be noticed. Practically none of the river-valleys along which these routes have developed run into Sweden ; all tend to focus in the Oslo Fjord, mostly within but a short distance of the capital. Norway is thus self-contained ; true, there is now easy access from Sweden to Oslo in the south, but in old days, when Scania was Danish, and the power of Sweden was concentrated north of Lake Vener and the other great lakes, the easiest route to the heart of Sweden was by sea, through a sound exclusively under the control of Denmark.

Many of the routes may be readily traced across the country from the Oslo Fjord to the north and west. A very short distance separates the source of the Gula, which empties into the Trondhjem Fjord, from that of the Glommen, the largest river of Norway, which enters the sea in the neighbourhood of Frederikstad, and is navigable for a considerable distance. The Rauma, flowing into the Romsdal Fjord, rises at the west end of Lesjeskogens Vand, while from the east end flows the Laagen, to join the Glommen near Eidsvold, by way of the Mjösen Lake. South-west of this line Norway is technically an island, according to the definition of our schooldays. Near Otta, the river of that name joins the Laagen after flowing over a distance which places its source within striking distance of the head of the Nord Fjord. The valley of the Baegne suggests a natural line of communication with Aardal, at the head of the long Sogne Fjord. The Bergen Railway, that triumph of Norwegian engineering, makes great use of Hallingdal, whose river also connects with the Oslo Fjord. Another route, following chiefly the course of a river, brings the Hardanger and Bukken Fjords in touch with that on which Oslo stands. " All roads lead to Rome," says the old proverb, but it is far more true to say that all natural Norwegian highways focus in the neighbourhood of the capital.

Oslo, until this year known as Christiania, has been called the capital, but of course was not so in early days. Yet it is easy to see why under the union with Denmark it gained its present status, and why at an earlier date the old town, which stood on approximately the same site, was also of exceptional importance. At the dawn of Norwegian history, however, it is rather the neighbouring districts which claim our attention.

At the head of the fjord lay Vingulmark and Vestfold, and it was from the latter district that the power which was to unify Norway was destined to spring. Between Vestfold and Denmark there was, from early times, a close connection, and we know that as late as the beginning of the ninth century the district owed allegiance to the Danish Crown. On the coast of Vestfold stood an important market and trading port, named Skiringssal, which is mentioned by the Norseman Ottar (or Othere) in the report preserved to us by King Alfred. As Ottar hailed from Haalogaland in the north, the place must have been of exceptional importance to have been so well known to him. First in all probability to hear of the fame of Charlemagne, the kings of Vestfold were not only the most likely to develop an early ambition for wider rule, but they were, as has been indicated, in a geographical position exceptionally favourable to the consummation of their dreams of conquest.

In the earliest historical times, however, the heart of Norway was situated farther north. Vestfold, however well endowed with communications over the southern districts of Norway, was too remote from the coastal region to the north of Trondhjem to be a desirable centre of government. Its inhabitants were also too closely connected with Denmark, from whose rule they had only recently been delivered, to develop at first a distinctively Norwegian civilisation. The cradle of such a civilisation had, however, been prepared by a providential Nature.

As has already been pointed out, the districts round the Trondhjem Fjord are formed by a depression in the general level of the high fjeld, utilised at the present day by the railway entering Sweden by way of Storlien, and dividing the plateau centrally into two divisions, known nowadays as the Nordenfjeldske and Sönden-fjeldske districts. Here a group of fertile river-valleys, radiating from the landlocked meanderings of the Trondhjem Fjord, tends to form a self-contained microcosm which, from its central position, is well suited to provide the nucleus of a national civilisation. At the north-eastern extremity of the fjord lies the valley occupied by the Snaasen Lake and the stream connecting it with the sea. Southwards from this point towards Trondhjem we meet in order the Vaerdal and Stjördal Rivers and the Nid, on which the city stands and from which it derived its ancient name of Nidaros. Beyond these, and providing the natural means of communication with the south of Norway, are the valleys of the Gula and the Orkla. On the opposite side of the fjord a landlocked branch, running roughly parallel to its main course, washes the shores of another habitable district.

At the dawn of Norway's history, the *fylker* or districts occupying this area formed a sort of federation, with common meeting-places for legislation, legal proceedings, and worship. Fortunately, perhaps, for the future consolidators of the Norwegian monarchy, they differed from the rest of the country in having no kings, and, while characterised by a spirit of pride and

independence, their inhabitants seem on the whole to
have been more peaceably inclined than the rest of
Norway. They were well-to-do and content in their
surroundings, and appear to have taken little, if any,
part in the viking movement. Here, then, was a
position marked out by Nature for the seat of centralised
government, as soon as the task of consolidation had
been accomplished, which the natural communications
of the country, making of it a self-contained unit, both
suggested and facilitated.

At this stage, it is hoped that the reader will begin
to see the fallacy of the common notion that Sweden
and Norway are arbitrary divisions of a homogeneous
natural unit. It is quite true that there is for the most
part no clearly defined strategic or national boundary,
capable of being neatly indicated on the map. But a
barrier is no less, but rather more, a barrier if its breadth
is too great to be delineated by a single line, and it
should be clear from what has been written that the
conditions are such as to impede, to a marked degree,
any close and continuous intercourse between the
peoples of Norway and Sweden. While the spurs of the
plateau have isolated the western valleys of Norway
from one another to an extent clearly perceptible at the
present day, and of great historical importance at an
earlier stage, its whole mass intervenes to separate, if
not the territory, at least the inhabitants of the two
countries. Each on his own side of an inhospitable
wilderness, Norwegian and Swede have developed distinct interests, policies, points of view. Towards a
sympathetic understanding of one another the absence
of a strong and definite strategic frontier has been far
from contributing. Those whose outlook is so different
are, perhaps, better situated when they can agree to
differ each on his own side of a satisfactory party-wall.
There have been territorial disputes in plenty in the
course of the history of the Peninsula ; there has been,
as will be seen, a chronic tendency to take the superficial
view of the geographical and ethnological facts and unite

the two countries; but all this has only led in the end
to increased and inevitable friction. The tragic mistake
resembles, in fact, that of young couples who argue
that a mother-in-law is one of the family, and introduce her into the home with disastrous results; neither
kinship nor proximity are reasons for closer *rapprochement* where individuals, or nations, have grown up
completely out of touch with each other's point of
view. While Norway has in the main looked out across
the North Sea towards the Faroes, Iceland, and the
British Isles, with the last of which her commercial
relations have throughout her history been of the
closest description, and her political relations sympathetic and almost uniformly friendly (since as early
as Harald Fairhair there was much trade and amicable
intercourse), Sweden has faced Russia and Germany,
and has developed her policy on corresponding lines, so
that the two countries have seldom come into contact
except on the not infrequent occasions when they were
engaged in mutual hostilities. With this state of affairs
geography, rightly understood, has had much to do.

The conditions already described, however, suggest
that the welding of the scattered elements of the
population into a national unit might prove a slow and
difficult process. District was separated from district
and valley from valley, and strung out along the
imperfectly cleared strips of those narrow dales even
the individuals of the sparse population were thrown
largely on their own resources, and were likely to
become a law to themselves. The coast-dwellers,
indeed, found a common highway and means of intercommunication in the sea, but this provided a ready
means of escape from unwelcome control, and once
aboard his ship the Norseman was in a position to be
even more independent and individualistic than on the
most isolated farm of the interior. This highway, too,
as the more venturesome spirits soon discovered, led
to lands where wealth, far beyond anything that could
be wrung from Norway's restricted cultivable area,

lay unguarded at the mercy of the spoiler, demanding at first no greater accumulation of naval force than a ship or two manned by resolute and courageous seamen. A child, with no previous knowledge of history, could read the viking movement plainly indicated on the map of Norway. And this movement, as the event was to prove, provided an easy refuge, and a life after their own hearts, to all whose spirits were impatient of interference.

The consequence is that, in endeavouring to picture the development and prevailing characteristics of the Norwegian people, one is haunted continually by the wish that the English language had a satisfactory array of synonyms for the word " independent." Naturally enough, the Norwegians themselves are richer in this respect than we, being able to use the word *selvstaendig* to express the positive, and *uavhaengig* for the negative associations of the idea. But even this is short measure for a writer anxious to escape monotonous repetition. Independence pervades, and has always pervaded, every department of life in Norway, individual, local, and national, and the reader will, we fear, become tired of the word by the time he has reached the end of this book.

As might be expected of a nation which in a sense has certainly adopted the motto of Peer Gynt's trolls, *Vaer dig selv nok*—" to yourself be sufficient," the natural resources of the country have, almost down to the present day, sufficed the sparse population as means of subsistence. Indeed, even the industrial develop-ment which now, at last, promises to revolutionise Norway's future depends on a characteristic natural feature—the waterfalls. But this change is a matter of yesterday. Two of the old sources of wealth, fur-trading and the export of live falcons, have become obsolete, the latter entirely, the former substantially. The export of timber, on the other hand, now so import-ant, was less so in the early stages of Norwegian his-tory, when almost every country had a sufficiency of wood for its own needs. Otherwise, conditions have been more or less constant ; the coast-dweller has always been a fisherman and a sailor, the rest of the inhabitants in the rural districts self-supporting farmers. In spite of modern developments, fisheries, shipping, and agriculture, with the timber trade, remain of paramount importance.

Whaling should, perhaps, be specially mentioned. Wherever this industry is carried on in any part of the world, it will be found to a very large extent in the hands of the Norwegians.

The mineral resources of the country have been exploited for a long time, the royal silver-mines of Kongsberg having just celebrated their tercentenary. At present, mining is in rather a bad way, copper being, perhaps, the most important of the ores extracted. Iron - mining began in the sixteenth century, and numerous iron-works flourished down to the nineteenth, when the old method of smelting with wood instead of coal proved unremunerative. There may yet be a revival of this ancient industry if the process of electric smelting attains the requisite perfection.

The absence of coal has been, indeed, the chief cause of the remarkable delay in Norwegian industrial development, and is the main reason for the satisfaction felt by Norwegians at the limited sovereignty granted to them over Spitzbergen by the Treaty of 9th February 1920. This, however, is not the place to go into economic questions. They are merely mentioned here to show in how many departments of national life the physical facts of the country have played a decisive part.

The climate, especially near the coast, is of course remarkably mild for the latitude, and the harbours keep open throughout the winter. Otherwise Norway would be as unfitted for cultivation as Labrador, which in many respects it closely resembles. The long winter, during which farming operations are impossible, only serves to let the peasant combine other occupations, such as fishing and forestry, with the pursuit of agriculture, and the fact that the same people follow

at different seasons many and varied sources of livelihood has contributed in no small degree to the versatility to which we shall have occasion to make frequent
reference. The length of the summer day is no doubt
responsible for a less admirable characteristic of the
rural population—their lack of a sense of time and
indifference to punctuality ; this, however, is a trait
also observable in many Englishmen who have spent
much time in the country.

I ought not, I suppose, to close this chapter without
a reference to sport. But though it was through hunting and fishing that I first fell in love with Norway and
its inhabitants, the numbers of the English works dealing with this side of the subject make me hesitate.
All the same, I think its importance difficult to over-
estimate. The foreigner connected by commercial relations with a country sees little but the coast and the
towns, and where town and country life are so isolated
from one another as they are in Norway, this means a
very partial and one-sided intercourse with the inhabitants. Again, the literature of a foreign country,
if that is the attraction, can be studied at home. The
mere tourist, one fears, is often not the representative
of England through whom one would wish her to be
judged. But the hunter and the angler, let humani-
tarians say what they will, are the Englishman at his
best. And, thanks to the natural formation of the
country, these ambassadors penetrate to the heart of
the people. The rural population, as already stated,
is strung out along the floor of enclosed valleys. In
almost everyone of these valleys there runs a salmon
river, and along its banks moves the English angler,
who is thus brought into intimate and daily touch
with the people. Or the hunter roams the reindeer
fjeld, where the sport is open to all ; and at evening,
in some *saeter*, as well, perhaps, as on less welcome
occasions throughout the day, he meets the Norwegian
peasant on a footing of intimate equality. Or, if the
elk is his quarry, he hires his ground, thanks to the

law which allows but one beast to be killed on each scheduled property, from a number of farmers, with whom he stays and makes friends. Whatever his objective, he probably has with him at least one native hunter or gillie, a man, in Kipling's phrase, " who knows his naked soul." Thinking of all these things, one feels inclined to wonder whether the close friendship between England and Norway, or the ready understanding which exists between natives of the two countries, would have been anything like what they are had it not been for sport. For this reason, much is to be hoped from the recent interest in recreations hitherto left almost exclusively to the foreigner and the peasant, which has grown up in the Norwegian towns. The exodus which I witnessed from Christiania in August of last year (1924), the train crammed with Norwegians with their guns and dogs, is a most welcome sign. Such a movement, however much it may be regretted by the thoughtless Englishman who sees his former monopoly threatened, will probably do more than anything else to break down the barrier hitherto existing between town and country, and to unite the scattered and severed elements of the nation as they have never been united before. Indeed, this seems by far the most promising line of approach to this important problem. The movement must be from town towards country, not *vice versa*. For the countryman who is attracted to town life is lost as a countryman : go back a few generations, and you will find *bonde* blood in the vast majority of those who from the heights of urban civilisation look down upon the agricultural peasantry and fail to understand them. But one who leaves the town for recreation has his home and his interests there ; he remains a townsman, but brings himself into familiar touch with the alternative way of life. He meets the peasant on common ground, drops his superiority, and finds he has something to learn from him. Thus he begins at last, quietly and without friction, to understand and to be understood.

CHAPTER II

ACCORDING to the general plan laid down for the guidance of contributors to this series, the past is to be subordinated to the present, and under these circumstances the space available for the treatment of the earlier history of a country cannot be as large as some could wish. At the same time, a balanced survey of the tendencies and forces which are moulding the lives of contemporary Norwegians cannot be complete if the influence of the past is neglected or slurred. Speak to a Norwegian of the influence of party upon the political situation, and he will inevitably refer to the spirit of *Birkebeiner* and *Bagler*; criticise his fear of domination by foreign capital, and he will recall the mediæval supremacy of the Hansa. Norwegian literature is crammed with historical allusion; whether in the hands of a Björnson, who deliberately appealed to the glories of the past, or of an Ibsen, who condemned a backward-looking tendency in a nation which he regarded as degenerate, the subject calls for repeated reference; while the Grundtvigians made historical and cultural tradition the keystone of their educational system. A current topic, such as the language question, depends for its existence upon historical circumstances, and the influence of the remoter past has not been less, but more, from the fact that for some four centuries the national genius suffered eclipse under the union with Denmark. The complete independence of modern Norway is not yet twenty years old, but the developments of the present century are quite unintelligible, apart from their historical background. Some broad and general sketch of the circumstances under which the nation was born and grew must therefore be attempted, together with some description of the factors by which its growth was arrested.

Political society, like charity, begins at home. Primitive communities start with the family, and, if left undisturbed, would usually take some time before they

progressed to a wider confederation than the tribe or
clan, which is, after all, merely the family with fictitious
accretions. War, and the necessity for defence, are
responsible for the next steps—the local kingdom and,
ultimately, the national state. The final or international stage which we seem to be approaching is to
a great extent the result of modern industrial conditions ; it is not, therefore, surprising that Norway,
which has only recently begun to develop an industrial
existence, is still inclined to be national. But it was
long before even this stage was reached, and the leading
interest in Norwegian history is the struggle between
the national and centralising force represented by the
monarchy, and the centrifugal tendencies of the local
aristocracy. At the outset, the family was still the
all-important unit, and so firmly rooted was this
primitive conception that traces of it are perceptible
at the present day, in the persistence of *odel* tenure,
of which more will be said later (see Chapter XI),
and in the individualism and love of independence
which have characterised the Norwegian from first
to last.

The influence of the viking movement in evoking
a national sentiment in Norway has, I think, usually
been exaggerated. It was primarily the expression of a
desire for individual independence incompatible with
national solidarity. The consolidations effected by
such men as Thorgils and Olaf the White in Ireland,
and doubtless facilitated by the conflicts with the
Danes in that country, failed to benefit Norway. They
were directed to the formation of a separate Irish
kingdom, and it is significant that Olaf the White
seems to have been among those who fell in the sea-
fight in Hafursfjord in 873, in uncompromising resistance to the centralising ambitions of Harald Fairhair.
No doubt something was learnt, and more ought to
have been learnt, from personal experience of the
tendency to more national groupings to be observed
at the time in England and other countries, as well as

from the deplorable object-lesson which the mutual jealousies of the native rulers of Ireland provided. At the same time, it is probably true to say that before the time of Harald Fairhair, about the middle of the ninth century, the influence of the family was supreme, and anything like a national consciousness practically non-existent. It is true that individual families owed a loose allegiance to the local kings of the different *fylker*, but their authority was almost entirely confined to military exigencies, and was, even so, strictly territorial. " The King is right," said Kveldulf in Egil's saga, " to consider it my duty to go with him if he has to defend his own land, and is harried in Firdafylke, but I regard it as quite beyond my duty to go north to Möre and fight there." For the rest, the King and his free subjects stood in a position of strict equality before the *things* or meetings at which judicial and legislative business was transacted. There was, in any case, not much of the latter. In primitive communities of this kind, legislation, in the modern sense, is almost unknown, the whole weight of public opinion being in favour of the retention of ancient established law and custom. In practice, therefore, each family enjoyed an extraordinary measure of independence. The fact that the odel system treated the family rather than the individual as the legal owner of an estate strengthened this independence, by giving to the confiscation of landed property for the crimes or disloyalty of the actual occupier the complexion of injustice.

As against external aggressors, the same conception strengthened the position of the local kings. For the title of a fylke-king to his kingdom was regarded as an odel, just as much as that of a private family to its ancestral estate. Probably, as I have elsewhere suggested, the whole question is connected with the prevalence of ancestor-worship, and the dispossession of a family, whether private or royal, from its odel was subconsciously regarded as impiety.

It was, in fact, the ideas associated with family ownership and the odel system which presented the most formidable obstacle to the task of consolidating the kingdom of Norway. The immediate predecessors of Harald Fairhair had succeeded in establishing a temporary overlordship over neighbouring districts, but the process had stopped at this stage. In other countries, the merging of local principalities into national kingdoms had been carried much further, and was, in fact, characteristic of the age. Denmark and Sweden were by this time, to some extent at any rate, centralised monarchies. In England the same result had been substantially achieved by Egbert in 828; while, above all, there was the recent example of Charlemagne, who before his death in 814 had done more than anyone else to stimulate the ambition of lesser potentates.

It is probably to examples such as these, especially the last, that Harald's action must largely be attributed. He began his reign in those southern regions which, as has been pointed out at an earlier stage, were in closest touch with the trend of events in Europe. It is clear that the young King was strongly influenced by the career of Charlemagne; his Court borrowed features from that of the great Emperor, *e.g.* Harald was the first recorded King of Norway to employ a professional jester, and, while the extent to which his later policy was framed upon the same model may be open to question, there can be little doubt that some connection may properly be traced. The picturesque story of the sagas, which makes the incentive the taunts of a girl named Gyda, who refused to throw herself away on any mere local king, must probably be abandoned as fictitious, though we may still believe in the vow registered by the King not to cut or comb his hair till his ambition had been realised. This was fully in keeping with the practice of the age, and is confirmed by the appearance in a contemporary poem of his earlier name of Lufa or Shockhead, as well as

by the later and more complimentary nickname of
Hárfager or Fairhair.

But to achieve a permanent conquest necessitated a
revolutionary change of policy. The ties of a common
country and common faith only served to render
ancestral thrones or ancestral homesteads an inviolable
possession. Up to the time of Harald Fairhair, it
seems to have been an unheard-of thing to depose a
vanquished fylke-king or to make him swear allegiance.
Oaths of fealty were confined to a ruler's personal
followers. There was plenty of precedent for sub-
jugating neighbouring principalities, but the effect of
such a triumph was limited and short-lived. The vanquished king, if he lived, or his heir if he died, paid
a share of his revenue as tribute to the victor till he
felt strong enough to desist; otherwise, things went on
exactly as before. The apparent exceptions which are
occasionally referred to turn out, on examination, to
be nothing of the kind. Halfdan Whitelegs is stated
in the *Ynglinga Saga* to have set jarls in authority over
Vermeland, and Harald's father, Halfdan the Black,
adopted the same procedure in the case of Sogn. But
in both cases the claim to these districts was by way of
inheritance rather than conquest. Halfdan Whitelegs
took over Vermeland upon the death of his brother,
the former king, and in the other case Halfdan the Black
was peacefully accepted as the heir of his deceased son,
Harald, who had been adopted as King of Sogn by a
childless predecessor. The jarls, therefore, in these
instances were merely discharging the ordinary duties
of viceroys, responsible for the collection of the royal
revenues and for the defence of the district during the
King's absence. The fact that such an annexationist
as Halfdan the Black only adopted this course in this
special instance gives us strong reason to believe that
the rule of letting a member of the vanquished dynasty
remain as a tributary king (*skattkonung*) was regarded
as practically inviolable.

The whole weight of the odel-born classes thus stood

on the side of the existing régime : the kings because
they owed no allegiance at all, but merely paid a tribute,
and the others because such duty as they owed to the
existing under-king was extremely limited, and went
no further than the boundaries of the fylke. They
were untaxed, they made their own laws, and their
relations to a higher authority were in the nature of a
loose and local defensive alliance. Beyond that, they
were their own masters.

Conquest of foreign races outside the boundaries of
Norway was carried out in a very different spirit.
Here is the description of the Norse rule in subjugated
Ireland in *The War of the Gaedhil and the Gael* (Rolls
edition, p. 51) :

" Such was the oppressiveness of the tribute and rent
of the foreigners over all Erinn at large, and generally,
that there was a king from them over every territory,
and a chief over every chieftainry, and an abbot over
every church, and a steward over every village, and a
soldier in every house, so that none of the men of
Erinn had power to give even the milk of his cow, nor
as much as the clutch of eggs of one hen, in succour
or in kindness to an aged man, or to a friend, but
was forced to preserve them for the foreign steward, or
bailiff, or soldier. And though there were but one
milk-giving cow in the house, she durst not be milked
for an infant of one night, nor for a sick person, but
must be kept for the steward, or bailiff, or soldier of
the foreigners. . . . And an ounce of silver *Findruni*
for every nose, besides the royal tribute afterwards
every year ; and he who had not the means of paying
it had himself to go into slavery for it."

Here was real subjugation, complete control ; land
held on sufferance, at the victor's disposition, taxation,
tribute, and thraldom. In the fighting scenes in the
Lay of Helgi Hundingsbane, which is the *locus classicus*
for the word *nef-gild*, or nose-tax, we catch something
of the same spirit in the taunt hurled by one of the
invaders at a leader of the opposing force :

"Tell it, feeding the swine at even,
Leading along to their swill the bitches,
That from the east are come the Wolfings,
Eager for battle from Gnipa-Lund."

Here again defeat is equivalent to thraldom. The
direction from which the Wolfings have come—by sea
—clearly indicates an attack on a foreign country.

These extracts are not irrelevant to a proper understanding both of Harald's policy and the way in which
it was received. In Norway, by Norwegians, such
things simply were not done, but they were possible,
and the application of any of these methods was closely
associated, in the Norseman's mind, with the treatment
of an enslaved people.

The futility of the old system was clearly brought
home to Harald in the first years of his reign. On the
death of Halfdan the Black there was an immediate
rising on the part of the subjugated under-kings.
The greater part of Harald's boyhood was occupied
in regaining, with the assistance of his uncle Guttorm,
the territory which his father had won. There could be
no hope of ruling peaceably over the whole of Norway
without a revolutionary change of policy.

As the actual methods adopted by Harald in order
to maintain his position have been the subject of much
discussion and dispute, it will be best to take them
step by step.

In the first place, he substituted for the existing
fylke-kings his own jarls. Snorre's statement that he
put a jarl in every fylke is not to be understood too
literally ; as the same authority goes on to show, in
many cases one and the same jarl was entrusted with
several fylker. In exceptional cases, where the existing
king was retained, as in Namdalen, he had to swear
fealty to Harald, and ranked as a mere jarl. In other
words, the King extended to conquered districts the
system of viceroys, bound by oaths of allegiance,
which had long been employed, in the King's absence,
in regions to which he was entitled by succession.

The remuneration of the jarl was a fixed proportion—one-third—of the royal revenues collected, and, as the jarl had no title beyond the King's appointment, he had every inducement to remain loyal. But it is to be noticed that in this very first step, wise as it was, a severe blow had been struck at the principle of independent odel rights. For the most important of all these was the right of a king to rule his ancestral dominions, and the kings were now ousted, or at best no longer kings. It is important also to observe, in view of what is often said, that this system was not feudalism. The jarl did not receive land on terms of service; he was merely a collector of the royal revenues, paid by a share of the proceeds.

The next innovation which Harald introduced was to take a personal oath of fealty from all defeated enemies as a condition of quarter. This again was merely an extension of the old Norse custom which bound the King's *hird* or personal following to a duty of military and other service. Snorre's account of each of Harald's early battles invariably terminates with the statement that all those who failed to escape and were granted quarter " became his men." This benefited the Crown in two important ways. In the first place, it enabled the King to prosecute all those who subsequently rebelled, in legal form before a *thing*, for treason (cf. *Heimskringla*, Harald Fairhair's Saga, c. xiv: " This greatly displeased King Harald; he immediately summoned a *thing* there with the bonders at Folden, and prosecuted them for treason against himself "). In the second place, it laid the foundation of a system of general military service (*ledingspligt*) throughout the realm, which gave him an immense advantage over the fylke-kings, who, as we have seen, were hampered in concerted action by the fact that their subjects would not follow them beyond the limits of their own dominions.

The third step in Harald's centralising policy has given rise to more disputes than all the rest put together. It will be useful, therefore, to give the exact words in which this branch of his innovations is described by the earliest authorities. The *Heimskringla* (Harald Fairhair's Saga, c. vi) puts it tersely as follows :

" Harald the King set that law in every place where he subdued a realm, that he took possession of all the odel, and made all the bonders, both rich and poor, pay him rent (*landskyldir*)."

In the Saga of Egil Skallagrimson, c. iv, 13, the statement is somewhat extended :

" Harald the King took possession in every fylke of all the odel, and all the land, inhabited and uninhabited, and seas and lakes as well, and all the bonders were to be his tenants : those also who worked in the forests, and salt-gatherers, and all hunters both by sea and land, they all owed him allegiance."

In *Laxdaela Saga*, c. ii, Harald's policy is thus referred to :

" In the later days of Ketil the reign of King Harald Fairhair began, so that no fylke-king or other great man throve in the land unless he (Harald) alone decided their title (*nafnbót*)."

From all these sources we seem to have a very explicit and consistent statement. Harald claimed the whole land as his property by right of conquest, according to the custom hitherto confined to foreign wars, and illustrated his claim by exacting rent from the odel classes and a fee from all those who made use of unclaimed lands and waters. The passage in *Laxdaela Saga* reinforces this view by suggesting that Harald treated all previous landowners, from kings downward, as tenants at will in cases where he allowed them to remain. According to this view, Harald's policy was a further blow struck intentionally at the principle of inviolable odel, which had already been shaken by the deposition of the local kings. But, according to what seems to be the prevalent opinion among recent historians, this view was a mere contemporary misunderstanding. Harald, they say, simply imposed a land-tax, and the various other dues which have been referred to, but his contemporaries were unable to distinguish between this expedient and the more familiar ideas of rent for land and payment for the use of private property. Now the first thought that is suggested by such a contention is this : if none of Harald's contemporaries could distinguish between land-taxation and rent, why is it to be assumed that Harald was in any better case ? In a land where the idea of a land-tax was unknown, even if Harald's main object was the collection of revenue, why should he not have based his claim upon conquest of the land, and a consequent right to rent and dues ? Even if he had heard of such a foreign expedient as a land-tax, would it not be simpler for him to say, instead of purporting to introduce a foreign custom, " the land is mine, and you must all pay me for it " ? To impose a land-tax was to change the law, and, as we have seen, the Norse Kings possessed no legislative power whatever. To charge rent for one's own land was, on the other hand, a practice commonly employed and universally understood.

But the argument in favour of the accuracy of the contemporary view is considerably strengthened if we consider what was the primary object of Harald's policy. Being already in possession of two-thirds of the royal revenues of every fylke, he was, for his time, inordinately wealthy and in no want of money. The real obstacle to complete and permanent control was, as has been shown, the independence of the odel estates. To break down the pride and undermine this independence of the odellers was an objective beside which the importance of increased sources of revenue sank into insignificance.

I feel, therefore, that not only is there an overwhelming probability that the statements of the Icelandic sources are technically correct, but that Harald must have taken pains to make it clear that he claimed the whole land by right of conquest. The lesson which Harald obviously desired to teach was— you and your lands and the whole country are mine ; not—I am a greedy, grasping man who has already amassed unheard-of wealth and yet does not know where to stop. The accepted view seems to be that Harald produced, by sheer accident, an impression which in the interests of centralised government it was vital for him to produce deliberately. I suggest that the impression produced corresponded to the true facts of the case.

In addition to the exaction dealt with above, Harald is reported in *Fagrskinna* to have imposed a *nef-gild*, a nose-tax, or poll-tax as we should term it to-day. This again, as we have already seen, was a form of tribute already in use in those foreign countries where Norsemen established their dominion. Compared with the treatment of odel, it appears to have aroused but little resentment—a fact which leads one to suspect that it was imposed, if at all, merely upon the otherwise unaffected lower classes of the community. When, to the immense joy of the people, their odel was freed by Haakon the Good, the *nef-gild* was allowed to continue without protest.

Harald's policy may therefore, as it seems to me, be summed up in the words, *he applied for the first time in Norway methods already in existence for dealing with a subjugated people in foreign lands*. This view is strengthened if we hold, with Professor Bugge, that the innovations were only introduced in the case of conquered districts, and did not apply to Harald's inherited dominions. This, it will be seen, is in strict accordance with the statement in *Heimskringla*.

Whatever view may be adopted as to the nature of Harald's policy, there can be no doubt that its effects, at home and abroad, were immediate and far-reaching.

The kind of unconditional surrender and complete submission demanded by the King was everywhere stigmatised as " thraldom," and a large proportion of the most high-spirited men in the country openly declared that exile or even death were preferable alternatives. The first result, accordingly, was an immediate exodus of these independent spirits, principally to conquered regions such as the Orkneys, Shetlands, and Hebrides, where they established winter bases, returning in the summer, in reversal of their previous practice, to harry the coasts of Norway with viking raids. This led to a successful expedition by the King to the Scottish islands, which brought about a second exodus, of more permanent importance, to Iceland, which had recently been discovered by the Norsemen, and which speedily became peopled by these malcontents, with their captured Celtic thralls, while permanent settlement in the Faroe Islands dates from the same period and was brought about by the same cause.

Harald's policy in suppressing the practice of independent viking raids was naturally welcome to England, and relations with this country throughout his reign were uniformly friendly. A flourishing and important trade was carried on between the two countries, and it was doubtless as a result of such an amicable understanding rather than, as represented in the sagas, an insulting joke, that Harald entrusted the upbringing of his son Haakon to King Athelstan of England. Haakon was educated in the Christian faith, and thus a further stage in the development of Norway was brought distinctly nearer.

Meanwhile, in the internal conditions of Norway, the departure of so many prominent families had produced important developments. Primarily the effect was to put into the King's hands an enormous accretion of Crown lands. As a result, we now begin to hear a great deal more of those important but frequently misunderstood institutions, *veizla* and *lén*. The most illuminating treatment of these matters is to be found

in the writings of the late Ebbe Hertzberg, to which
the present writer is largely indebted for the explanation
which follows.

Veizla was a technically gratuitous and unconditional grant of Crown property by the King to a trusted
follower. As employed by Harald, it usually amounted
to no more than was sufficient to enable such of the
local *hersar* as he entrusted with duties of district
administration to keep up the status and surround
themselves with the number of retainers appropriate
to their increased responsibilities. For the remuneration of such local administrators recourse was had to
the institution of the *lén*. Of this we have already
seen one example in the conditions under which the
viceroy jarls were appointed to the different fylker.
Though the word itself is foreign, the principle underlying it was not, and indeed, in early times, the native
spelling *lan* is not infrequently to be found.

The holder of a *lén* or *lán* was a person entrusted
with the collection of some part of the royal revenue,
of which he was to retain a fixed proportion as remuneration, while delivering the balance to the Crown. The
lén was not confined to revenues derived from land ; it
might be the privilege of exercising a royal monopoly,
such as that of trading with the Lapps, or of collect-
ing the tribute which that people had in earlier times
delivered to the local nobility. The grant of a *lén*
was technically personal and revocable, but naturally,
with the development of feudal ideas in neighbouring
nations, some confusion of thought arose, and the *lén*,
when its emoluments were derived from land, tended
to be popularly described as a *riki* or realm, and
to be regarded by the holder as hereditary. This
point of view was, however, strenuously contested by
the earlier kings, especially by Olaf the Holy, whose
policy, as will be seen, was largely affected by the growing importance and independence of the *lendermaend*,
as the *hersar* or local nobility in enjoyment of *lén* and
veizla had come to be termed. *Veizla* was thus a

natural development of the old practice of distributing portions of conquered territory among influential followers, while *lén* was a means of remunerating the collectors of royal revenues, derived from the system under which viceroy jarls and the earlier tributary kings had exercised their functions.

After having, in the manner described, laid apparently solid foundations for the establishment of a centralised monarchy, Harald, in his later years, proceeded to destroy what he himself had constructed. The old idea that every son of a king was entitled to share the succession as an odel was too strong for him. The sons of a fylke-king, indeed, had been better able to appreciate the impracticability of subdivision, and no doubt the formality of acceptance at the *fylke-thing* had also done something to keep the numbers of rival or joint claimants within reasonable bounds; but there was as yet no central body to decide the claim to the whole kingdom, and Harald's sons could see no reason whatever why each of them should not rule more or less independently over a district which had formerly sufficed for the holder of a royal title. It would be unfair to accuse the old man of blindness to the interests of the kingdom which he had created. He was probably more or less powerless, and he at all events did his best to keep the supreme sovereignty in a single hand. What he did was to divide his territory between his numerous sons, conferring upon each the title of a king, while reserving the general overlordship for his favourite child, Eric Bloodaxe, whose mother was of more exalted rank than the other wives of the polygamous monarch, from nine of whom he is said to have separated on the occasion of his marriage with her. In 930, three years before his death, Harald definitely appointed Eric to his throne, and retired in his favour.

Eric Bloodaxe, and his masterful and unscrupulous queen Gunhild, were just as much set upon controlling the whole kingdom as Harald Fairhair. But there seemed small prospect of uncontested supremacy so long as Harald's other sons survived. Before his father's death Eric had accordingly managed to kill two of his half-brothers, while another had died under suspicious circumstances, his death being attributed to poison administered by Gunhild. In the year following Harald's death he accounted for two more—Olaf, grandfather of the future king Olaf Tryggvason, and Sigröd. This drastic policy naturally alienated public sympathy, and when, therefore, the young Haakon, Harald's son, who had been fostered by King Athelstan, came over to Norway as a rival claimant to the kingdom, Eric found he could not muster a sufficient force to resist him, and fled from the country. Haakon's popularity, we are told, was much enhanced by the offer which he made to surrender the odel to which his father had laid claim ; " the news flew like fire in dry grass," and he at once attained so large a measure of popular support that his surviving half-brothers seem to have been at once reconciled to taking a subordinate position. The alternative to being sooner or later killed by Eric Bloodaxe was to make common cause with any claimant who could command general sympathy, and it would have been difficult to vie with Haakon's bid for popularity without surrendering all real sovereignty over the nation.

But though Haakon enjoyed a period of undisturbed supremacy, the consolidation effected by Harald Fairhair was soon in process of dissolution. The influence of Haakon was purely individual : there was as yet no trace of any consciousness of national unity. The sons of Eric Bloodaxe felt no hesitation in calling in the assistance of the Danish king, and in submitting to his technical overlordship after regaining the kingdom. The authority subsequently exercised in Norway by their great enemy, Haakon, jarl of Lade, was a case of sheer usurpation, based on force and his own personal influence, and did not go very deep. Olaf Tryggvason, who brought back the kingdom into

the line of Harald Fairhair, during his short but
brilliant reign, was too much engrossed in missionary
projects to institute political changes, and, after his
death at the battle of Svolder, Norway was divided
between the sons of Haakon Jarl, Eric and Svein, and
the Kings of Denmark and Sweden, who exacted tribute,
though they left the actual government of the country
in the hands of the Norwegians. How little the
establishment of a national monarchy had been maintained from the death of Harald Fairhair to the accession of Olaf the Holy, is shown by the fact that during
all this period petty kings of Harald's race continued
to exist in the central Upland districts.

So remote from the thoughts of that time was a
sense of nationality, that the overlordship of the foreign
Kings of Sweden and Denmark was not only not resisted or resented, but was in some quarters actually
preferred to the more intimate control of a native ruler.
Subject to the payment of a tribute, this system gave
free scope to the independence of local sovereigns.
King Rörek's speech in the Saga of Olaf the Holy
expresses a point of view which, no doubt, was widely
shared. Foreign lords, he pointed out, were further
off, and could be trusted not to interfere so long as
they received the tribute to which they were entitled.
With a native king like Olaf Tryggvason there was less
individual independence; indeed a man might not even
decide for himself what God he should believe in. For
his part, Rörek was well content to leave things as they
were, under the easy-going suzerainty of a foreign king.

It was not until the reign of Olaf the Holy, or, to
give him the name by which he was known in his lifetime, Olaf the Stout, that any real statesmanship was
applied to the problem of national consolidation.
Like his predecessor and namesake, Olaf Tryggvason,
he pursued the double task of establishing a national
monarchy and a national Christian Church. The two
projects went hand in hand. A national Church,
with a code applicable to the whole country, such as

Olaf induced the various *things* to accept, had little chance of permanence if the kingdom itself were to fall to pieces. There is also an evident connection between monotheism and monarchy, while the influence of the local aristocracy, the chief obstacle to the attainment of Olaf's political objects, was not unconnected with the priestly functions of these chieftains. The Christian clergy introduced by the King must of course have looked to the central power for their authority, and the establishment in every district of priests ultimately dependent on the Crown was a sound stroke of policy as well as the act of a religious enthusiast.

Where Olaf Tryggvason had failed was in organisation. He had been content to impose loyalty to his person and conformity to his religion superficially, by the force and attractiveness of his personality ; he did not even attempt, in either case, to lay any enduring foundations. He left Norway to a large extent professedly Christian, but deplorably lacking both in clergy and churches. Similarly, the kingdom over which he had succeeded in enforcing a temporary supremacy in his lifetime was organised throughout on the old lines, and fell to pieces immediately after his death. It was this lack of organisation which Olaf the Holy, in many ways a far less brilliant and attractive figure, made it his business to remedy.

The missionary side of his work is outside the scope of the present chapter. As elsewhere stated, he secured the acceptance of a common Christian code, and when he effected the conversion of a district he did not leave it without a church and clergy. In this branch of his work he was, indeed, uniformly successful. It was his effort at political centralisation which ultimately brought about his fall.

Harald Fairhair had aimed, so far as was possible, at using the natural leaders of the people in the various districts for purposes of local administration. They had been enriched with *veizla* and entrusted with *lén* ; through them the royal revenues had been collected,

under a system which was extremely remunerative to
the collectors ; to them the maintenance of order had
been largely delegated. There was much to be said
for such a policy, under the conditions in which it was
inaugurated, but the vicissitudes through which the
kingdom had passed in the years which followed the
death of Harald had permitted the power of these
lendermaend to grow unchecked to an extent which
no king who aimed at strong centralised government
could allow to pass unchallenged. That which in its
origin was quite distinct from feudalism was by this
time growing confused with it ; the districts administered by a local chieftain of the type of Erling Skjalgson
had come to be regarded as his by hereditary right,
for *lén*, in popular parlance, the word *riki* or realm
was beginning to be substituted. Against this point
of view Olaf set himself to fight relentlessly—perhaps
with more vigour than tact.   " I will not permit," he
said to Erling, " that *lendermaend* should treat themselves as entitled by inheritance to my land."   Accordingly, the tasks of administration and of collection of
revenue were transferred more and more into the hands
of men of meaner birth who were undisguisedly mere
royal officials, and in so far as the old state of things
was allowed to continue, it was made clear that a *lén*
was not the *riki* or realm of the holder, but a *sýsla* or
office held at the royal pleasure, and subject to such
restrictions or modifications as might from time to time
seem advisable. Olaf's court entourage consisted in
the main of men of comparatively undistinguished
descent, as well as of Icelanders whose personal loyalty
could be shaken by no rival interest. These last,
though for the most part primarily court poets of the
type of which Sigvat the skald was an outstanding
example, were entrusted with important diplomatic
missions and invested with a personal importance far
beyond that which had formerly been enjoyed by any
member of the King's personal retinue. This policy
of antagonism to the old local nobility was doubtless

forced by circumstances upon any king who aimed at exercising anything more than the merest shadow of power, but it had its manifest disadvantages. Age-old tradition had made the local chieftains the natural leaders of popular opinion in their respective districts; for the most part they commanded the unquestioning obedience of the surrounding *bönder*, almost after the fashion of the head of a Scottish clan. To supplant these natural leaders by entrusting many of their former functions to bailiffs who were little better than the royal thralls, was to court misunderstanding and unpopularity. No self-respecting freeman was likely to obey the behests of such as these with goodwill or alacrity. Little by little the great families of Norway fell into open opposition. The situation was complicated by the fact that most of them were connected by intermarriage. Across the sea, in England, Knut the Mighty was ready to welcome them with rich gifts and richer promises, and to impress the nobility of Norway with a regal bearing and unprecedented magnificence calculated under any circumstances to put the unconciliatory Olaf and his Court of nobodies into the shade. In 1025 Knut felt himself strong enough to lay claim to the overlordship of Norway. Olaf curtly refused to content himself with any subordinate position, and having concluded an alliance with the Swedish king Anund, embarked on an ill-considered offensive against Denmark, but after an inconclusive naval battle with Knut at Helgeaa, off the Scanian coast, was compelled to withdraw to Norway. Here, in 1028, he fell upon the greatest of all the old nobility, Erling Skjalgson, who had thrown in his lot with the Danish King. The old chieftain was defeated, captured, and brought before the King. Olaf would have offered him quarter, but an over zealous follower sprang forward and gave Erling his death-blow. The significance of the act was not lost upon the King. " Ill betide thee for thy blow," he said ; " thou hast struck Norway from my hand."

The situation was correctly judged. At the news of Erling's death the whole country turned against Olaf, who was forced to fly from the kingdom, and it passed into Knut's hands without a blow.

Norway was now governed for a time by the last of the jarls of Lade, Haakon, who acted as viceroy for the Danish King. This was an arrangement which Knut, with memories of the treatment of Harald Gormson of Denmark by an earlier Haakon, jarl of Lade, could hardly acquiesce in without some misgiving. In 1029 he summoned his viceroy to England, probably on account of suspicions which he had begun to entertain, and on the return voyage Haakon was drowned. On learning the news that Norway was now leaderless, Olaf grasped at the forlorn hope which seemed to be offered him. He managed to collect a force of by no means contemptible size, though its quality left much to be desired. There seems to have been a considerable element of truth in the speech of the Danish bishop, Sigurd, who described Olaf's army as consisting of outlaws, footpads, and banditti. Certainly many of the men were heathens, a circumstance which Olaf must have regarded as a somewhat bitter irony. But in such desperate straits he had to be content with such support as he could obtain.

The historic battle which followed lives in saga in a vivid description worthy of the importance of the issues which seemed to hang on it. But success was not to be ; indeed, Olaf seems hardly to have expected it. After a heroic struggle the King fell, covered with wounds, and it must have seemed at the time that the cause of nationality and the hopes of Harald Fairhair's race had perished with him. But in fact the tide was already turning, national consciousness was already stirring in the hearts of the Norwegian people, and the man who fell at Stiklestad, apparently despised and rejected by his countrymen, was destined within a few years to take his place as the nation's hero and its patron saint.

Politically, however, the reign of Olaf the Holy

was a failure. At his death the kingdom had passed
to Denmark, and the power rested incontestably in the
hands of the local nobility. The credit for creating a
national sentiment is usually conceded to him, and it
is true that after his day there were no more fylke-
kings, but a united Norway. Yet it would be nearer
the truth to recognise that this result was less due to
the virtues of Olaf than to the shortcomings of his
successor, Svein Alfivason, whom, with his even more
detested mother, Alfiva or Aelgifu, Knut the Mighty
had introduced into the country as his viceroy.

The Norwegians soon found that Danish rule was
not this time to be so formal and tolerable a matter
as it had been in the days preceding Olaf's accession ;
the country was subjected to many strange new
customs, originating in Denmark, and to a new and
burdensome system of taxation. Particularly unpopular was a new provision that estates of those guilty
of homicide should be forfeited to the Crown, and that
the property of outlaws, instead of passing to their
heirs, should also be confiscated. This law was obviously inconsistent with the Norwegian view of odel
rights, and likely, in consequence, to cause much discontent. The evidence of Danes was also given a pre-
ponderating weight. One Dane, it was said, was
regarded as a witness worth ten Norwegians. This
was naturally regarded as intolerable. A common
resentment united the nation which Olaf had left
factious and disloyal. There was at once a violent
revulsion of feeling, and the hated Olaf the Stout who
had fallen at Stiklestad became, by a swing of the
pendulum, Olaf the Holy, whom succeeding generations
were to regard as the patron saint of the country.
This transformation was engineered by the very men
who had brought Olaf to his death, as well as by Einar
Tambarskjaelve, the greatest noble of all, who at the
time of the battle had remained neutral. Stories of
miracles wrought by the late King in death and in life
were industriously circulated, and the sceptical objec-

tions of Alfiva were curtly and peremptorily silenced. While Knut was alive and powerful little more was done, but a deputation of the leading men of Norway had meanwhile got in touch with Olaf's young son Magnus, in Russia, and when Knut died, in 1035, the foreign rulers were expelled from Norway without further delay, and the Crown came back to the old dynasty. Svein died almost immediately afterwards, but Knut's son Haardeknut, who had succeeded to Denmark, threatened to take up the struggle. As Magnus and Haardeknut were both boys, however, the nobles of both nations speedily arranged an agreement between the two, by the terms of which each should reign in his own country till his death, when the survivor, in the absence of a direct heir to the deceased, should succeed to the vacant throne in addition to his own. On the death of his half-brother, Harald Harefoot, Haardeknut came into possession of the Crown of England, where, in 1042, he died suddenly, apparently from an apoplectic stroke. Magnus thereupon succeeded to Denmark, but made the great mistake of appointing as his viceroy in that country, Svein, son of Knut's sister Estrid, who almost at once threw off all pretence of loyalty and reigned as an independent sovereign.

The situation was soon complicated by the arrival of a new claimant to royal honours in the person of King Olaf's half-brother Harald, surnamed Haardraade. He is said to have taken part in the battle of Stiklestad, but had afterwards attached himself to the Byzantine Emperor's Varangian guard, where he had attained considerable military distinction. Harald seemed at first inclined to attach himself to the cause of Svein, to prevent which Magnus consented to share the kingdom of Norway with his uncle. Further possible complications were prevented by the death of Magnus in the following year (1047).

Though his nephew, shortly before his death, had conceded to Svein Estridson the title to Denmark,

Harald continued to dispute it, but without success. His chief ambition, however, was to obtain possession of England, an achievement of which Magnus had also dreamt, though affairs nearer home had prevented him from trying his fortune by invasion.   In 1066 a suitable opportunity seemed to present itself, in the efforts of Tostig, the exiled Earl of Northumbria, to re-establish himself in England.   After an unsuccessful attempt to land on the shores of the Humber, Tostig retreated to Scotland, where he was joined by the Norwegian king. On the 20th of September the Norwegian forces won a considerable victory over the Northumbrian earls in the neighbourhood of York, but within a week Harald was confronted with a more formidable antagonist, his namesake of England, who defeated and slew him at Stamford Bridge.

From the date of the accession of Magnus there could no longer be any doubt that Norway was a united and indeed a powerful nation.   It was no longer a question of welding the scattered districts of the country into a whole ; the ambition of the Norwegian Kings was now fired with dreams of foreign conquest. It is probably fortunate that the fall of Harald Haardraade at Stamford Bridge put an end to these schemes. Such a dissipation of energy must have proved disastrous to so thinly populated a country.   But in a sense Norway was already in possession of no inconsiderable empire.   The Norwegian who crossed the North Sea found almost everywhere men of his own race and speech, and everywhere scenes recalling the exploits of his countrymen.   If he sailed as far as to Iceland or Greenland, there were those there who could tell him of even more distant lands which had been visited by men of his own stock.   That the fame of the discovery of America, the Wineland of Leif Ericson and Karlsefni, had reached even to Denmark in the reign of Svein Estridson, we know from the writings of Adam of Bremen.   Passing south from Iceland by the Faroes, to the Shetlands, the Orkneys, and the Hebrides, to Man and to Ireland, wherever he went the Norseman found those who, though they might originally have sailed from different fjords and from different districts, shared at least with him a common nationality. Under such stimulating influences his conceptions expanded, and Norway and *Noregs-veldi*, rather than any mere *herred* or *fylke*, claimed his affection and his loyalty.

CHAPTER III

NATIONAL ECLIPSE

THE subordinate position which Norway occupied during the period between the Union of Kalmar in 1397 and the final separation from Denmark in 1814 has always presented a painful problem to the national historians. At the death of Haakon V, in 1319, no one could have prophesied that Norway would soon be little better than a dependency or province of Denmark, still less that she would tamely submit to such humiliation for a period of more than four centuries. At this date, under the misrule of Christopher II, the fortunes of Denmark were at their lowest ebb, but from the death of Valdemar II in 1241 a period of decline had set in, " for from that time onwards," in the words of the contemporary annals, " (the Danes) became, through their civil wars and internal havoc, a mockery to all the peoples around them." Simultaneously, a long and exhausting period of civil war in Norway had just come to an end, with the suppression of Skule's insurrection in 1240 by King Haakon Haakonson, and under a strong and centralised monarchy the prestige of the kingdom was destined to rise steadily for more than another century. In 1282, when the growing power of the Danish nobility found expression in the first of a series of charters exacted from the Crown, the Norwegian aristocracy was so weakened that less than thirty years later the old titles of jarl and lendermand could be abrogated by royal ordinance without a symptom of opposition. Norway appeared to be a strong, centralised monarchy, without a sign or a possibility of internal discord ; and when, on the death of Haakon V in 1319, his heir and grandson, Magnus, united under his sceptre the two kingdoms of Norway and Sweden, the future appeared as promising in these northern regions as it seemed dark and hopeless in Denmark.

Yet the seeds of the decay which was to affect the fortunes of Norway are to be traced in this period of apparently unexampled prosperity, and, in order to understand the collapse which eventually took place, it is necessary to go back to the stage reached at the end of the last chapter, and examine the various elements on which the strength of the nation at that time depended.

The expulsion of the foreign rulers, and the restoration of Magnus, the son of Olaf, in 1035, on the death of Knut the Mighty, was the work of the old local aristocracy of the lendermaend. The policy which St. Olaf had pursued towards this class had only succeeded in consolidating the alliance between nobles and people which from time immemorial had made the great local magnates the natural leaders of popular opinion. Such an aristocracy, left unchecked, is apt to become tyrannous and independent of the class below it ; but the attempts which Olaf, in pursuance of his centralising policy, had made to weaken the influence of the lendermaend, by the appointment of royal officials, had united the local nobility and the free yeomanry of the country, with the results which led to his defeat and death at Stiklestad. The power of the Crown was still subject to popular control in judicial and legislative matters, exercised at the *things*, while the position of the aristocracy was strengthened by the fact that the restoration of Harald Fairhair's dynasty had been their work.

In these circumstances, the struggle for supremacy between the nobles and the Crown was destined to continue for a long time. The latter was seriously handicapped by the accepted rules of succession. The conception of the kingdom as an odel made it, as was shown as early as the death of Harald Fairhair, not an individual, but a family inheritance, to a share in which all the sons of the late King were equally entitled. It is true that after the death of King Olaf there was no longer any question of subdivision of the inheritance into small kingdoms. The national consciousness had now advanced beyond that stage ; henceforth the

kingdom of Norway was one and indivisible, but the
system of succession led, one may almost say normally,
to the joint rule of several claimants over the whole.

In the days of the fylke-kings, the worst effects of
this system were to some extent held in check by the
obvious necessity for some limitation to the number of
rulers over so small a territory, while the necessity of
the formal recognition of the King by the local *thing*
no doubt provided a further safeguard. But the consolidation of the kingdom of Norway had been accompanied by no corresponding centralisation of the
assembly, whose recognition was a necessary element
in the right to succeed ; the old local *things* persisted
with but little modification in their scope, while the
size of the country prevented the recognition of the
undesirability of a plurality of rulers. The principle
of succession to the Crown was, moreover, odel with
a material difference. While, in the case of private
property, right to succession was primarily confined to
legitimate heirs, in the case of the monarchy there was
no such restriction, and legitimate and illegitimate issue
stood upon exactly the same footing. Hence, while
there would have been in any case a risk of civil disturbance arising from the existence of several claimants to sovereignty, this disadvantage was enormously
increased by the opportunities afforded to pretenders
of uncertain origin. Since the only recognised means
of testing the *bona fides* of such claims was the ordeal,
this circumstance manifestly tended to place the ultimate decision in the hands of the Church, upon the
collusion of which, as all must now recognise, the
successful issue of the trial by hot iron depended. As
early as the canonisation of Olaf, the clergy had given
proof of their ability in matters of this kind, when the
bishop had contrived to provide a fire in which the hair
of the late King could not be burnt, while the luckless
Alfiva's plea for " ordinary fire " had, for obvious
reasons, been disregarded. Thus the rules governing
the succession to the throne of Norway were calculated

to provide both nobles and clergy with a powerful instrument for the promotion of their own importance.

Though the worst effects of this system of joint rule were delayed until after the death of Sigurd the Crusader in 1130, there were disquieting developments as early as the reign of Magnus Barefoot in 1094, when the first of the pretenders made his appearance. After the death of Magnus, the kingdom was shared between three sons, Eystein, Sigurd, and Olaf, and the situation would in all probability soon have been critical, had it not been for the early death of Olaf, and the protracted absence of Sigurd on a crusade. After his return in 1111 till the death of Eystein in 1122, the joint Kings managed to keep the peace, though their relations were not always of the most cordial description. An amusing passage in their saga represents them as bickering over their respective accomplishments, and in the famous lawsuit which Sigurd launched against the powerful lendermand Sigurd Raneson, the two Kings took opposite sides. Eystein seems to have been of a conciliatory and peace-loving disposition ; otherwise the arrangement under which the country was governed could hardly have been carried on without an open breach.

After Eystein's death, the kingdom of Norway reverted to a single hand. Sigurd, though subject towards the close of his reign to fits of insanity, was extremely popular, and internal dissension was confined to rivals among the nobility, and was never directed against the Crown. But it could not be denied that divided rule suited the ambitions of the lendermaend, as Sigurd himself seems to have recognised, when in his own lifetime he made his subjects swear to take his son Magnus as his successor. Probably at the time he did so he had already heard of a rival claimant, whom many were prepared to support.

Norwegian nobles, trading with England, had met in Grimsby a lean, dark man of Celtic appearance and dress, who in broken Norse claimed to be a son of

Magnus Barefoot. The name by which he was known was Harald Gilchrist, or Gilli for short. It seems probable that he was what he proclaimed himself, for, if the lendermaend had been on the look-out for a plausible impostor, they would hardly have selected a man so little likely to commend himself to Norwegian sympathies. Their choice, if free, would at least have fallen on someone who could speak their language fluently. Be that as it may, Harald was brought over to King Sigurd's Court, where, after solemnly swearing to lay no claim to kingly rank, either in Sigurd's life or in that of his son Magnus, he was allowed to prove his title by ordeal, which was satisfactorily arranged. He was thereupon taken into high favour at Court, and up to the date of Sigurd's death in 1130 he strictly observed his pledge.

After this date, however, Harald was prevailed upon by a strong party of the nobles to break his oath, on the plea of duress, and to lay claim to a share in the kingdom. Thus began a state of civil war which continued almost uninterruptedly for 110 years, and strengthened the power of the nobles at the expense of the Crown. It is probably a mistake to regard this result as being altogether the fruit of a deliberate and calculated policy. Private quarrels between different great families led in many cases to the support of rival claimants, and the process, once started, was difficult to stop : on the death of one leader, motives of self-protection forced his adherents to set up another, whose pretensions might be genuine or spurious. But the effect was none the less to place the real power in the hands of the aristocracy, rather than of the young puppet Kings and pretenders who depended upon their support, and in 1161 the nobles were strong enough to set up as King Magnus, son of the lendermand Erling Skakke, though his claim through his mother was unrecognised by Norwegian law and custom.

This step was not calculated to increase the power of any great family but that of Erling ; on the contrary, in deliberately promoting Magnus out of their own class, the nobles were showing a self-sacrificing spirit in the general interests of the kingdom. Erling, too, seems to have been uninfluenced by considerations of personal interest; the general aim seems to have been to put an end to the civil wars by selecting a sovereign whom the overwhelming majority were prepared to support. As regent for his son, Erling ruled Norway wisely and well, while his policy in procuring the support of the Church and regularising a weak title by the ceremony of coronation (see p. 201), though it tended unduly to increase the power of the Church, was calculated to promote settled government. The coronation was followed by a new law of succession which, by asserting the principle of undivided monarchy and establishing the priority of legitimate offspring, promised a reform which went to the root of the trouble. It is true that the archbishop succeeded in inserting in the law provisions for election in doubtful cases which placed the ultimate decision in the hands of the Church; but even this made for certainty, and raised the matter of a King's succession out of the turmoil of partisan animosities. If too much power was surrendered to the Church, it must be remembered that Norway had so far had no experience of the dangers of entrusting that institution with political authority. It seemed a neutral body, whose judgment and decision would be based upon the highest of principles.

It is interesting to speculate what would have been the outcome if Magnus Erlingson's tenure of the throne had been finally established. At one time he seemed secure beyond the possibility of overthrow. The forces of opposition seemed to have degenerated into a flock of mere adventurers and banditti. When the rising of the pretender Eystein Möila was crushed at the battle of Ré, his followers were a mere tatterdemalion rabble, whose use of birch-bark to replace their worn-out footgear earned them the at first contemptuous name of Birchlegs (*Birkibeinar*). Yet, under their next leader, these Birchlegs were fated in a few years completely to revolutionise the situation, and to change the course of Norwegian history.

The leader referred to is undoubtedly the most interesting figure in his country's annals. In spite, however, of the admiration which must be accorded to his genius, it must be admitted that practically all the causes which operated to bring about the collapse of Norway at the time of the Union are directly traceable to the revolution which he effected. He was, to all seeming, the son of a combmaker from the Faroes named Unaas, and had been trained for the priesthood by his uncle, who from 1163 was bishop of those islands. He bore the Fareyan and plebeian name of Sverre.

The claim through which he was destined to rise to fame was that he was an illegitimate son of King Sigurd Mund, who was born in 1133 and killed in 1155. We must not be led away, however, to discuss the genuineness of Sverre's pretensions. Great as is the temptation to linger over everything connected with this unique figure, we must exercise self-restraint. Lucky, indeed, were the Birchlegs if they chose him as their leader simply upon his alleged lineage, and without experience of his strategic and tactical talents. It would be interesting to have some account other than his own of his movements from the time when he left the Faroes to the date when he appears as the Birchleg leader. If he was of royal birth, his character and tactics involved a complete breach with the traditions of the dynasty. If he had no share in the fortunes of Eystein Möila, or in the skirmishing which followed his defeat, the anxiety of the Birchlegs to secure his leadership is difficult to understand. If they simply chose a *soi-disant* member of the royal house of untried capacity, they stumbled by chance on a man who displayed the most entire lack of conventionally royal qualities, together with the most conspicuous gifts as a guerrilla commander. At the date when he lived, if he was to attain to power, it was necessary that some claim to royal descent should be set up, but in the qualities which he displayed and the policy he pursued he showed no trace of his pretended origin.

In March 1177, a year after his arrival in Norway and three years from his departure from the Faroes, Sverre appears as the leader of a small band of seventy men. Two years later Erling Skakke was killed in battle. In 1180 King Magnus was forced to flee to Denmark, and in 1184 his defeat and death at the battle of Norefjord put Sverre on the throne. His reign was, however, troubled by the rising of one pretender after another, and especially from 1196 by the activities of the *Baglar* or Croziermen, under the leadership of Bishop Nicholas of Oslo. The opposition of the Church naturally brought Sverre into the collision with the Papacy referred to in Chapter IX, but neither excommunication nor interdict succeeded in displacing him from his position, and on his death from illness in 1202 the opposing forces of the Church and the old aristocracy were fatally weakened. The age of pretenders, to which his success may have given a renewed stimulus, was not yet over, and civil disturbances lasted until 1240, in the reign of his grandson, Haakon Haakonson, the hero of Ibsen's well-known drama, *Kongs-emnerne* (" The Pretenders ").

At the outset of his career the country seemed almost unanimous in its support of the existing régime. Even when Sverre's cause had finally prospered, it was not to the nobility only that he was an object of detestation. As he said after his victory over Magnus Erlingson : " I think if the mind of all here could be perceived, and a horn stood from the forehead of everyone who thinks ill of me, that many a horn would appear here. The child who goes out with a rock in his hand and strikes it on the stones cries, ' Here should the head of Sverre be lying.' . . . The serving-maid who goes out with a washing-bat in her hand and beats it on the flagstones says the same." And earlier in the same speech : " Some say that I am the very devil come from hell, and that he has broken loose." There can be no doubt that Sverre was generally regarded as a wicked disturber of the peace which Magnus Erlingson's reign, to the satis- faction of all, had seemed about to establish.

Having all parties against him, or at all events none on whose loyal support in all circumstances he could rely, Sverre was forced to gather all the strings of power into his own hands. The dynasty which he founded became more and more autocratic. The authority, alike of nobles, Church, and people, was as far as possible supplanted by a centralised monarchy on which all depended. When that monarchy ceased to be national there was no alternative power left in Norway to main- tain her cause against alien oppression.

Instead of the old local aristocracy, whose interests were so closely connected with those of the *bönder*, and the nation generally, there arose a new nobility of courtiers and officials, to which the Crown could give what complexion it would. Even as Norwegians they copied the feudal knighthood and baronage of other lands in looking for wealth, not in the stimulation of national commerce, but in the accumulation of land and in the emoluments of office. If this tendency had to some extent shown signs of growth before Sverre's day, the rise of his dynasty enormously increased it. If already the nobles had largely abandoned direct participation in maritime trade, they had at least retained sufficient interest in it to create the nucleus of an urban commercial class. But from this class they now withdrew their financial support, with the result, remarked on in another chapter, that the burghers of Norway were unable to resist the com- petition of foreigners. King and nobles cared only to satisfy their requirements in the cheapest market. The rise of the Hansa was further facilitated by the definite discouragement of trade with England, which formed part of the policy of Haakon V. The con- stitutional developments in our country harmonised ill with that monarch's autocratic ideals. Even before his time, his brother and predecessor, Erik Magnusson, had contributed to the same result by his suppression of the native trade guilds. Everything combined to stifle the growth of a native commercial class, and to deliver the towns into the growing power of their German competitors.

The centralising policy of the Kings of Sverre's line had equally deleterious effects upon the *bonde* class. This section of the community was inevitably weakened by the accumulation of the freehold land in the hands of the Church and the new nobility. But, apart from this, the share which the *bönder* had formerly taken in the government of the country was reduced to nothing. The legislative power of the *things* fell into disuse, and even in judicial matters the real decision came to rest in the hands of royal officials. Thus deprived of their national responsibility, the *bönder* lost their national outlook : they could, and did, in the days to follow, repeatedly rise against the tyranny of some local official ; but under the Union they proved themselves altogether incapable of acting as a united nation, and their sporadic efforts were more or less easily crushed in detail.

Under Sverre's dynasty, too, the old popular basis of the national defence was suffered to decay and become obsolete, while the Crown relied more and more on an army of mounted knights and their followers, on European models, and on the construction of fortifications which, in the hands of the foreigners implanted there by the Union Kings, contributed only to the repression of such efforts as were made to cast off the yoke.

Between the Church and Sverre there had been a particularly bitter conflict, and the effect of his triumph was to crush all the hopes which had been raised by the concessions extracted from Magnus Erlingson. The party known as *Baglar*, or Croziermen, whose rising disturbed the latter years of Sverre's reign and continued into that of his grandson, Haakon Haakonson, was, as the name implies, the military expression of ecclesiastical antagonism to the dynasty. The cessation of this movement did not put an end to the struggle for power between Church and State ; in the reign of Magnus Lagaböter it led to the Tönsberg Concordat, the repudiation of which by the regency, during the minority of his son Eric, gave rise to a serious crisis, while Haakon V, by freeing the royal chapels from episcopal control, took steps to secure the independence of the Crown from ecclesiastical interference. It was therefore natural that during the early years of the Union the Norwegian bishops remained, on the whole, the most loyal supporters of a policy which kept their most formidable rival, the King, out of the country, and left them immeasurably the most important personages in Norway. In this attitude they persisted until threatened by the Reformation, when it was too late to interfere effectively.

Sverre and his successors had therefore brought about a state of affairs in which all depended on the King. The old nobility was practically extinct, the new Court aristocracy lacked the old national traditions, and was capable of dilution from foreign sources at the will of the sovereign. The people had lost their share in the functions of government, and with it their interest in the nation as a whole, the nascent burgher class had been systematically discouraged in favour of alien competitors, while the Church subordinated the interests of Norway to considerations of its own advancement. Such was the position when Haakon V died, and the kingdom passed to his grandson Magnus, who had been born and brought up in Sweden, and became heir simultaneously to the crowns of Sweden and Norway.

The colonial policy inaugurated by King Haakon Haakonson, and developed under his successors, was equally unwise. The empire resulting from viking enterprise was a source of strength to the mother-country so long as the only bond of union was that of a common race and language. The attempt to enforce

Norwegian sovereignty over the colonies, and thus to make them exclusively dependent on the support of the central Power, introduced the factor which affects all lands with poor natural resources, and which is usually known as "the waste of empire." In the case of the Hebrides, where Haakon, at the end of his reign, waged an exhausting and unsuccessful war, this was so evident as to lead to the cession of the islands to Scotland by his successor in 1266. But Iceland was also debilitated by the dependence on Norway which the assumption of sovereignty produced, while Greenland, after trade with that country was made a Crown monopoly in 1294, was rapidly starved into extinction. The natural source of supply for Greenland was obviously Iceland, rather than Norway. In fact, it is tempting to let the fancy play upon the notion of what might have happened if the colonies had been allowed to pursue their natural development. The connection between America (Markland) and Greenland can be traced in the Icelandic annals as late as 1347. Had the existence of Greenland not been stifled by the Norwegian monopoly, a knowledge of the lands discovered farther west might have passed through Iceland to Norway, and there been preserved at a time when the interest taken in the New World during the sixteenth and seventeenth centuries introduced an important fresh factor into the commerce of the world. And thus the first discovery, instead of being forgotten, might have been turned to the practical advantage of Norway.

Sverre has been praised, even in modern times, as the inspired deliverer who put an end to an age of anarchy in Norway by the introduction of strong and centralised monarchical government. It may be doubted whether this praise is deserved. Once the reform, proposed in the reign of Magnus Erlingson, the abolition of joint sovereignty, was adopted, the essential mischief would have been remedied. By his intervention, Sverre merely revived for some sixty years a state of civil war which was on the point of coming to an end. A constitution in which King, Church, lendermaend, and *bönder* all played a part was more in conformity with the spirit of the age than an uncontrolled autocracy, and would in all probability have worked well, since the undue influence of each would have been held in check by the opposition of the others. It can hardly be supposed that the nobles would have succeeded in oppressing the people, in view of the power of resistance displayed by the *bönder* against the aristocracy of Denmark, who were accustomed in their own country to tyrannise as they wished over a helpless and enslaved peasantry, and who were actuated by no higher motives than those of self-interest. Attempts at self-aggrandisement by the Church would have encountered the opposition not only of the Crown but of the nobles and people ; it was not an individual King, but a regency commission, which in the minority of Eric Magnusson threw over the Tönsberg Concordat. The *bönder* would have felt and acted more nationally, and by their united effort the Union would probably have been broken as it was in Sweden. In all respects it seems a matter for regret that Magnus Erlingson was overthrown.

The union between the Crowns of Norway and Sweden, which came about through the accession of Magnus, seems not to have been regarded in either country as anything more than a temporary arrangement, and it worked so badly in practice, both during the King's minority and afterwards, that it was ended in 1355 under the terms of an arrangement arrived at in 1343, soon after the birth of Magnus' two sons, Eric and Haakon. In accordance with this agreement, Haakon acceded to the throne of Norway on attaining his majority, while Magnus remained King of Sweden, and his elder son Eric was to succeed him. As we are not here concerned with affairs in Sweden, it is sufficient to say that Eric died in 1360, that in 1363 Haakon, the King of Norway, was married to Margrete,

the daughter of the Danish king Valdemar "Atterdag"; while shortly afterwards Magnus was deposed
by the Swedes in favour of his nephew, Albrecht of
Mecklenburg. Olaf, the infant son of Haakon and
Margrete, had thus an indisputable claim to the
Norwegian succession through his father, a powerful
claim to succeed Valdemar in Denmark through his
mother, and a plausible claim to Sweden through his
grandfather Magnus. In the two latter cases the
House of Mecklenburg had rival pretensions. Albrecht
of Mecklenburg was *de facto* King of Sweden, and his
nephew, also Albrecht—which is rather confusing—
was the son of Ingeborg, the elder daughter of the
Danish King. Denmark, however, was an elective
rather than a hereditary monarchy; while the Mecklenburg claim to Sweden had consistently been opposed
by Haakon of Norway and his Queen Margrete. This,
then, was the foundation on which Margrete's brilliant
diplomatic intrigues for a Scandinavian union were
built.

Valdemar "Atterdag" died in 1375, and in the following year the Danish *rigsraad* were successfully per-
suaded to elect the infant Olaf to the vacant throne.
In 1380 King Haakon Magnusson also died, leaving
the talented Margrete in the position of regent for her
son both in Norway and Denmark. In 1385 Olaf
was declared of age, but his mother still continued to
hold the reins of government; indeed, her position was
the stronger, from the fact that she was now free from
the restraint exercised by the councils of State in the
two kingdoms. Meanwhile, the Mecklenburg rule had
become so unpopular in Sweden that the nobles of that
country had started negotiating with Margrete, when
in 1387 all the Queen's deeply laid schemes appeared
to be wrecked by the sudden death of her son Olaf.

It is a striking tribute to Margrete's wonderful
statecraft that this apparently fatal blow had no influence on the course of events. The Queen's position
was no doubt strengthened by the fact that her re-

moval would only have paved the way for a Mecklenburg in each of the Scandinavian kingdoms. Denmark and Norway at once appointed her to the regency
till such time as she and they should be able to agree
upon a successor, while the Swedish nobles were by
this time too fatally committed to withdraw. Universally supported, Margrete invaded Sweden, and in
February 1389 she won a decisive victory at Falköping,
in the course of which the King of Sweden was captured. From this point the union of the three Scandinavian kingdoms was accomplished *de facto*, though
Stockholm, which was mainly in the hands of Albrecht's
Germans, held out for some time longer.

In order, however, to regularise the position, it was
necessary for Margrete to appoint a King. Her choice
fell upon her great-nephew, Eric of Pomerania, who
was then a child about seven years old. It was always
Margrete's policy to develop her schemes patiently
and slowly, and she was now in no hurry to have
her successor formally recognised. In Norway he was
proclaimed as early as 1389, but nothing was done in
Denmark or Sweden until 1396, and the final step was
not taken till the following year, when the young
King was solemnly invested with the sovereignty over
all three kingdoms at a meeting at Kalmar, at which
conditions for the permanent establishment of the
Union were agreed and drafted.

The Act of Union, however, never got beyond a
draft. What was agreed upon was no more than a
personal union under a single king. Each country
retained its own laws and customs ; obligations in
case of war went hardly further than a defensive
alliance ; above all, the monarchy was to be elective,
not hereditary. What Margrete wanted was the complete fusion of the three kingdoms in a hereditary
monarchy, governed as far as possible from Denmark.
Having failed in this, she simply laid the unsatisfactory draft aside, and attempted to secure the union
she desired by different methods. The chief of these,

which formed an integral part of the policy of all her earlier successors, was the appointment of Danish nobles to the important posts in all three kingdoms, in order to provide the cement for a structure which was otherwise threatened with speedy dissolution.

It was inevitable, in any case, that in a Scandinavian union Denmark should occupy the leading position. The population was as large as that of the two other kingdoms combined, and the geographical situation of the country rendered it more central, both from the point of view of domestic and foreign policy. The aristocracy of Denmark was more powerful than that of either Norway or Sweden : it was accustomed to an elective monarchy, and able to exact its own price for the privilege of election. Norway, being comparatively helpless, and unused to bargaining with her hereditary sovereigns, was at their mercy. It was natural, apart from deeper political considerations, that the Union Kings should seek to gratify, at her expense, the Danish nobles on whose suffrages they depended. Denmark, in fact, was the one of the three nations which stood to gain by the Union, while Norway had most to lose by the arrangement.

But apart from this, the introduction of Danish nobles into Norway was the deliberate policy of Margrete and the Kings who succeeded her. From their point of view, permanent union was impossible without a more intimate fusion of the elements of the three nations than the conditions drafted at Kalmar could provide. Since, moreover, the Kings were of Danish or German origin, and felt no ties of birth or sentiment with Norway, it was naturally from their own compatriots that the aristocracy was recruited. This, in fact, was one of the dangers to which the change from a local to a court nobility, brought about by Sverre and his successors, had given rise. When the King ceased to be national, it was inevitable that his entourage should change its character in the same way. Personal preference, the desire for a uniform and

homogeneous realm, and the necessity of satisfying
the nobility which exercised a preponderant voice in
the election of a sovereign, all worked in the same
direction, and overshadowed every consideration for
the national well-being and independence of Norway,
with the result that that independence was rapidly
and systematically diminished. And the reduction in
the numbers and importance of the native aristocracy
of Norway, which had already taken place, provided
an excuse for such a policy, which was lacking in the
case of Sweden.

Other circumstances are often said to have contributed to the weakness of Norway at this juncture.
The Black Death, though it may have taken a proportionate toll of the populations of the rest of Scandinavia, had more serious economic effects in this thinly
peopled country. Large tracts of land lay uncultivated,
and the native nobles and leading landowners were
ruined for lack of tenants. It is also suggested by some
that the climate at this time underwent a change for
the worse, which would naturally be more severely felt
in the north than in the south. Recent investigations
in Greenland lend some colour to this theory, though
it seems possible that the change in that country was
merely a local phenomenon, dependent upon a new
movement of the drift-ice. But the main reason for
Norway's subjection was undoubtedly her lack of
natural leaders. In Sweden the Union was always
insecure : it kept on breaking, and in little more than a
century the tie was finally severed. But Norway had
no candidate whom she could set up as a national ruler.
Her choice was limited to taking sides in such matters
with one extraneous candidate or another, while she
was in any case unused to the idea of an elective
monarchy, and perhaps too instinctively loyal to those
who were appointed to rule over her. The hereditary
principle had always been her sheet-anchor, and
deprived of this, she drifted helplessly at the mercy of
wind and tide.

The disadvantages of this were clearly seen when the fall of Christian II in Sweden and Denmark gave rise to a new crisis. Up to this time some shadow of independence had been maintained in Norway. The *riksraad*, however apt to fall into line with the views which obtained elsewhere, and however little attention was usually paid to its demands, had continued to function, in some respects not ineffectively. But from the time of Christian's deposition both council and people were afflicted with a disastrous cleavage of opinion. The council at first adopted Frederic I, but the new King's growing sympathy with Lutheranism soon alienated the ecclesiastical party, of which the archbishop, Olaf Engelbriktsson, was the able and distinguished leader. On the other hand, men such as Vincents Lunge, son-in-law of the celebrated Lady Inger of Östraat, who was far from being the disinterested patriot depicted by Ibsen, began to see the chances which the Reformation would offer them through the confiscation of Church property. Already the sequestration of the monasteries had begun, not without profit to Lunge and his no less self-seeking mother-in-law. The imprisonment of Christian II put an end for the moment to the archbishop's resistance, but with the death of Frederic I in 1533 the disputed succession offered a fresh opportunity. Even in Denmark the success of Christian III, an avowed and fanatical Lutheran, hung for some time in the balance, owing to dissensions in the Danish *rigsraad*, and the outbreak of what was known as the Count's War (*Grevens Feide*), so called from Count Christopher of Oldenburg, who at the instigation of the Hanseatic League ostensibly championed the cause of the deposed Christian II. Having regard to the new candidate's religious convictions, the issue, so far as the Church was concerned, was clear, and unanimity with promptitude in the Norwegian *riksraad* might have saved the situation. But this body was hopelessly divided, the party of Vincents Lunge being whole-

heartedly in favour of Christian III, while apart from
the captive Christian II there was for the moment
no obvious alternative.

Eventually, the archbishop and his party, realising
that the accession of Christian III meant the inevitable
downfall of the Catholic Church in Norway, clutched at
the hope of setting up a rival candidate in Pfalsgraf
Friedrich, son-in-law of Christian' II, with the support
of the Emperor. To secure the unanimity of the
Norwegian *riksraad* the archbishop had recourse to a
coup d'état, in which Vincents Lunge lost his life and
the remainder of his party were arrested. This forlorn
hope was, however, destined to failure ; the Emperor's
help did not materialise, and with the triumph of
Christian III the Church, the *riksraad*, and the very
pretence of Norwegian independence fell together.
The Reformation was introduced at once, while in the
charter or *haandfestning*, granted according to custom
by the new King of Denmark on his election, he
promised that on securing possession of Norway he
would reduce that country to the status of a mere
province or dependency, which should no longer rank
as a separate kingdom. In substance this pledge was
only too well redeemed. Though public documents
continued to speak of " the kingdom of Norway," the
reason suggested by Fredrik Scheel (*Lagmann og
Skriver*, p. 3) is probably the real one. " It was for a
long time part of the Byzantinism of official language
to count up a whole series of kingdoms and territories
which this or that prince was lord over. They were like
so many jewels in his crown." In other respects the
incorporation of Norway in Denmark was very nearly
complete.

So it continued until the nineteenth century. After
the fall of the effete Danish nobility and the introduction of autocracy in 1660, Norway secured some
amelioration of her lot and some improvement in her
status. A country where the right of a King was by
tradition hereditary was more to the taste of its new

despotic rulers than one where it had hitherto been constitutionally elective, as Denmark. All power being now in the hands of the Crown, Norway enjoyed, from this time forth, a constitution which placed her on a level with Denmark. The gallant conduct of Norwegians both by sea and land in the Swedish wars also aroused a new respect for this hitherto despised and downtrodden people. The oppression of the *bönder* mostly ceased with the fall from power of the Danish nobles, and for some time before the final separation Norway seems to have been contented, loyal, and prosperous. Towards the end of the period such events as the founding of the *Norske Selskab* in 1772 give proof of a recovery of national pride. Even at an earlier stage there had been good reason for this. The losses sustained during the Swedish wars were all due to the weakness of Denmark ; Norway had always successfully defended her soil from invasion, and the recovery of territory at the peace of Copenhagen was the result of national effort. Molesworth, indeed, tells us in 1692 that " the inhabitants . . . esteem themselves much superior to the Danes, whom they call upbraidingly Jutes," though the accuracy of this observation is challenged by a contemporary critic (*Animadversions on a Pretended Account of Denmark*, p. 49).

Yet, whatever the inhabitants may have thought of themselves, to the outside world Norway was still merely a Danish province ; and Sir Walter Scott, in *Marmion*, could go so far in his confusion of Norwegians with Danes as to introduce Denmark into the battle of Largs, between Haakon Haakonson of Norway and the Scots, in 1263.

> " Of Largs he saw the glorious plain,
> Where still gigantic bones remain,
> Memorials of the *Danish* war :
>
> .   .   .   .
>
> While all around the shadowy kings
> *Denmark's* grim ravens cower'd their wings."

A similar confusion helped Denmark to retain the Norwegian colonies—Iceland, Greenland, and the Faroes —at the time of the Treaty of Kiel, and accounts to some extent for the attitude of the European Powers to the Norwegian struggle for freedom which preceded the union with Sweden.

The period of eclipse was long and full of gloom, yet perhaps these centuries of subordination to a foreign government worked in the end to the advantage of Norway. External pressure gave the necessary compactness and solidity to a population prone, in times of prosperity, to disintegration, and forced into a sympathetic equality those who under different circumstances might have formed antagonistic classes in the nation. It thus prepared for the coming democratic era a race peculiarly qualified to take advantage of it. Though the country was enslaved the masses of the people remained free, more free perhaps than they would have been under a ruling class of their own nationality. The Danish *bonde* sank into serfdom ; the Norwegian was always independent and impossible to crush or intimidate. Hardship and adversity trained the spirit of the nation as its individuals were schooled by their constant strife with a stubborn and a stony nature, and as the long nights of the northern winter were passed in dreams of high adventure or thoughts of things divine, so the darkness which had fallen on the people of Norway gave time and leisure for the development of a more purposeful and united effort, when the destined hour should dawn.

CHAPTER IV

THE REVIVAL

AFTER a long period of almost complete subordination to Denmark, Norway emerges in the early years of the nineteenth century. It is true that about a century longer was to elapse before the nation could claim full independence; but the separation from Denmark was marked by an immediate resurrection of the national spirit, which asserted itself so continuously during the whole history of the union with Sweden that the predominant interest of the period lies in Norway's effort to establish her right to self-determination. The constitution which she enjoys to-day dates in substance from 1814; and while Norwegian historians and politicians rightly protest against the idea that their nation was but a product of the nineteenth century, that century does, in fact, mark her resurrection.

The starting-point in the chain of events leading up to the unlucky experiment of the union between the crowns of Norway and Sweden is to be found in Canning's annexation of the Danish fleet in 1807. This action has been the subject of unending criticism at home and abroad, both on moral and political grounds, the verdict abroad—especially in Scandinavia—being almost uniformly adverse, while English historians have, as a rule, found much to palliate and even justify Canning in the policy which he pursued.

To understand the question, some knowledge of the general European situation is essential. After the battle of Trafalgar in 1805, it was clear to Napoleon that the one formidable obstacle to his complete success was the maritime supremacy of Great Britain. Immediately after his defeat of the Prussian forces at the battle of Jena, he issued his famous Berlin decree, by which he inaugurated the " continental system," directed against the commerce and, therefore, the economic life of our country. After the victory of Friedland, in the following year, had brought the Czar of Russia to negotiate at Tilsit, Napoleon was in a

75

position to bar practically the whole continent of Europe to British commerce, with the exception of Sweden, which was hostile to him, and Denmark and Portugal, which remained neutral. In view of the Emperor's determination to bring these countries into line, it was clear that a state of neutrality, which had for some time been difficult, would shortly be impossible to maintain. On 19th July 1807 Napoleon wrote to Talleyrand, " the day after your arrival in Paris you will apprise the Portuguese minister that on the 1st of September the ports of Portugal must be closed to England ; in default of which I declare war on Portugal." A letter of 31st July gives similar directions in regard to Denmark, and even suggests that an understanding of some kind with that country was already supposed to have been reached. For in this letter Napoleon expresses " mon mécontentement de ce que *les promesses qu'a faites le Danemark* n'ont point d'effets et que la correspondance continue avec l'Angleterre." And, as is well known, the secret articles of the Treaty of Tilsit provided for the compulsion of Denmark, Portugal, and Sweden to fall into line with the continental system. Denmark was consequently placed in a serious dilemma, between forces which Canning aptly described as " a balance of opposite dangers." Had Denmark and Norway been subject to separate rulers, it seems most likely that they would have adopted opposite decisions. Denmark was bound to see in hostility to Napoleon the almost certain loss of her mainland possessions. On the other hand, Norway, if she sided with France, was faced with ruin and starvation. Sweden on the land side, and Great Britain by sea, were in a position to cut off all supplies, to say nothing of the fatal blow to the Norwegian export trade which would be struck by the severance of commercial relations with our country, at all times by far the best customer which Norway possessed for her most valuable products.

Torn between such conflicting interests, it is no

wonder that Frederic, the Prince Royal, on whom as
Regent the responsibility of decision rested, clung to an
obviously untenable neutrality. As is usually the case,
the vacillations which this policy involved only aroused
the suspicion of both the belligerent parties. As we
have seen, words construed as " promises " by France
seem to have been uttered only to be disregarded. On
the other hand, the British Minister at Copenhagen,
Mr. Garlike, had given his Government good reasons
for believing that resistance to French demands could
not be relied upon. No preparations had been made
for defence, violations of Danish neutrality had elicited
but half-hearted protests, troops had been withdrawn
from Holstein on the approach of the French forces,
and many influential Danes were known to have
strongly Napoleonic sympathies. In any case it was
obvious that Denmark, with the best will in the world,
was not in a position to resist the Emperor's demands.
It is true that Dr. Worm Müller, in his brilliant and
exhaustive work, *Norge gjennem nödsaarene*, maintains
that Prince Frederic's repeated assurances, that if
called upon to accept the continental system he would
make common cause with England, were " no figure of
speech, but his serious, honourable intention." It
is hard, however, to reconcile this view with the
statement of Pierrepont, the British representative at
the court of Sweden, contained in his dispatch of 20th
July 1807. " His Royal Highness (Prince Frederic)
appears to have conversed with considerable frankness
with Baron Decken (Pierrepont's informant) upon the
subject of the measures that might follow the cessation
of hostilities between Prussia and France, and re-
gretting, at the same time, the necessity which might
be imposed upon him, of acting in opposition to his
wishes, he said enough to justify an apprehension of
his closing the Danish ports against His Majesty's
flag, if called upon to do so ; and proved, I think,
clearly by his conversation, as it was stated to me,
that, after balancing the advantages and disadvantages

of siding with either party, the result (if pushed to the question) had been to abide by the wishes of France."

In these circumstances, while the morality of Canning's *coup* remains, perhaps, open to question, there can be little doubt as to its political wisdom. A Denmark under the control of Napoleon meant the complete severance of connection between Great Britain and her Swedish ally, and a probable accession to the naval strength of France which might prove exceedingly formidable. Canning therefore took time by the forelock, and dispatching an overwhelming naval force to Danish waters, delivered, through a regrettably tactless intermediary, an ultimatum demanding the delivery of the Danish fleet to British safe-custody until the termination of the war, in return for a subsidy and a promise of assistance against France. These proposals having been declined, Copenhagen was bombarded, and after a few days' fighting the Danish fleet and naval stores were transferred to England.

The result was to bring the Danish Prince, who shortly afterwards succeeded to the throne as Frederic VI, decisively down on the French side of the fence. He abandoned neutrality, allied himself with Napoleon, and adopted the continental system with considerably more loyalty to its principles than most of the other countries concerned. As an immediate consequence, Norway was blockaded by the British fleet, cut off from all regular communication with Denmark and the Danish Government, deprived of her trade, both export and import, and involved in a war with Sweden which, by calling up her men, seriously hampered her home production.

It is only fair to Canning to say that the chief blame for this catastrophe must be divided between the tactless British emissary, Jackson, and the Danish autocrat. The display of force which Canning had thought advisable was primarily intended to preclude hostilities and save the face of Denmark in the eyes of Napoleon. War with Denmark he bitterly regretted, and did his best to stop. What he had anticipated was something in the nature of a Danish alliance, founded indeed on duress, but capable, in view of the friendly relations subsisting at any rate with Norway, of developing into a voluntary association against the Power which threatened to dominate Europe. Probably he had under-estimated the historical and traditional antagonism of Norway and Sweden, and thought, like many of his countrymen at the present day, in terms of " Scandinavia." Sweden was already his ally, and he pictured Norway and Denmark as fighting, once their neutrality was abandoned, on the same side. As a matter of fact, the bond between England and Norway had always been closer than that with Sweden, and Canning had good *prima facie* grounds for imagining that all would be well.

But he had to reckon, not with the sentiments of a nation, but with the will of an autocrat, in whose eyes a personal insult outweighed all the true interests of the races over which he ruled. The result was war. The consequent difficulty of maintaining communication between Norway and Denmark led to the immediate appointment of a regency commission to manage the affairs of the northern country. At its head was Prince Christian August of Augustenborg, who was also in supreme command of the military forces of Norway. Having regard to the difficulty of receiving speedy or frequent instructions, it may be said that the commission was allowed too limited a degree of independent control to enable it to deal adequately with its tremendous responsibilities. In the financial and economic situation in which Norway found herself, the difficulties were great enough in any case, but they were enormously increased by the attitude of Frederic VI, whose despotic instincts led him to interfere with the handling of every problem, and to demand that no step of importance should be taken without reference to Denmark. Considering how it was handicapped, the work of the regency commission merits the highest praise ; in procuring supplies and investigating the possibilities of satisfactory food-substitutes, it performed a great work, but the country, face to face with starvation, must have seen increasing cause to regret the hampering fact of the union.

Meantime the position of Sweden seemed equally desperate. There has been a tendency among the most recent historians to some extent to rehabilitate the character of King Gustav IV. He used to be represented as a raving lunatic, but there is reason to believe that this verdict is prejudiced and exaggerated. Still, when all is said, he was hardly a ruler competent to govern and defend a country faced with such difficulties and dangers as Sweden.

On the one side, the Russian Czar, true to his pledges at Tilsit, was threatening the Swedish province of Finland, which he invaded in February 1808. All along the western frontier lay Norway, in allegiance to a king who, at Napoleon's dictation, was now equally hostile. The very existence of the country was threatened. At the meeting at Erfurt, in September 1808, between Alexander of Russia and Napoleon, a dazzling prospect was held out to Frederic VI, of retaining any portions of Sweden which he might manage to occupy in the course of hostilities ; and there seems to have been some suggestion of a partition of the country between Russia and Denmark-Norway, by which the districts south of the Motala river were to pass into the possession of the latter Power.

Threatened thus on all sides, with Finland already in Russian hands and the mainland of Sweden on the point of being invaded, the army turned in revolution against their incompetent King. On 7th March 1809 the chief conspirator, Lieutenant-Colonel Adlersparre, marched his troops from Karlstad towards Stockholm. To secure the now defenceless frontier he took the extraordinary step of sending Major Anckarsvärd to Christian August at Kongsvinger, to request a promise that the Norwegians, in view of the project which he had to disclose, would refrain from invasion at this critical juncture. It is now clear, in spite of Swedish statements to the contrary, that this remarkable attempt to suborn the Norwegian commander was unsuccessful. It is true that the prospect of a Swedish revolution was necessarily most welcome to Christian August. Invasion by Norway was, moreover, at best a rash and hazardous policy, which he was naturally unwilling to undertake. But Christian August was, throughout his career, a supremely loyal and honourable subject of the sovereign whom he served. He would give no definite pledge. He was manifestly suspicious as to the trustworthiness of the information supplied to him, and took all possible steps to satisfy himself that the revolution was an actual fact. If it were so, he professed himself willing to refrain from taking advantage of the situation, in the absence of definite orders for an offensive from Denmark, and provided further that no Russian or Danish advance in the meantime rendered it advisable. In addition, the division which had left Karlstad for Stockholm was not to be used against the Russians. In fact, Christian August secured himself in every way, and in abstaining, as he actually did, from invasion in the circumstances, he acted in the best interests of Norway.

At the same time, there can be no doubt that the Norwegian commander put himself both now and later in a compromising situation by entering, even to this limited extent, into these negotiations with the enemy. It was possible, with but a slight departure from the truth, to give the proceedings an ugly look, and his actions were in fact misrepresented by the Swedes at a later stage with the object of bringing about a rupture between Christian and the King of Denmark. For the plans of the conspirators went beyond the mere deposition of Gustav IV. Though no suggestion of the kind came to the ears of Christian August at the time, Adlersparre's emissary did actually mention to a General Staffelt, while waiting for the Prince's reply, a possibility that the ultimate succession to the Swedish throne would be offered to the Norwegian commander. The plot in fact, in its fulness, seems to have been this : the deposition of Gustav IV and the exclusion of his line, the appointment to the throne of the old and childless Carl, Duke of Södermannland, and the choice as his successor of Christian August, followed by the revolt of Norway from the Danish domination, and the ultimate union of the two kingdoms of the Scandinavian peninsula. Perhaps the whole project was not at first as clear-cut and definite as this. For the moment, the progress of the plot went no further than the accession of the Duke of Södermannland to the vacant throne as Carl XIII, and the definite exclusion of the Gustavian line—a step as necessary for the future protection of the conspirators as for the development of the larger scheme above indicated. But though it was some time before the offer of succession to the Swedish throne was definitely made to Christian August, as a rumour and a clear possibility it must have reached him almost from the first.

Union between Norway and Sweden was, on the other hand, clearly an object from the outset ; in fact it was the one point on which Norway, Sweden, and Denmark were at this time disposed to agree. As to the exact nature of the policy to be pursued with this end in view there was, on the other hand, the widest difference of opinion, and the cross-purposes which arise from this fact give the inner history of this time its special interest. The plan for which Christian August worked loyally, from the first moment when he recognised that a union with Norway would be welcomed by the Swedes, was to make Frederic VI the king of a united Scandinavia, which should adopt Denmark's policy of loyalty to Napoleon and his continental system. With the general lines of this scheme the King of Denmark, on being informed of the situation by the Norwegian commander, was in complete agreement. But between him and Christian there was a fundamental disagreement as to the means whereby this desirable result was to be obtained. Christian August favoured a suspension of hostilities, and the promise of a constitution for Sweden more liberal than the autocracy which Frederic represented in Denmark. Anything of this kind the King was slow and reluctant to concede, and he preferred the fatal plan of exercising military pressure and thus forcing the hapless Swedes to come to terms.

The leader of a very different policy was the young Count Wedel Jarlsberg, the most brilliant member of the regency commission. At first he had shown signs, indeed, of working for Frederic; but he soon felt the impossibility of this project, and adopted a policy which involved the grossest treason to his sovereign. In a letter to the Home Government marked "most secret," and dated 5th May 1809, the English Chargé d'Affaires at Stockholm, Foster, reveals the plot as it was detailed to him by the Swedish conspirator Armfeldt. Norway was to revolt from Danish control and enter into a union with Sweden and an alliance with England. This last proviso was Wedel's own special contribution to the problem. Having just dethroned the fanatically anti-Napoleonic Gustav, the Swedes might naturally have been expected to have reversed his policy and sided with France, more especially as this was an obvious step towards reconciliation with a country which, however unwillingly, was ranged upon that side already, and a policy which would have removed, at this stage, the *raison d'être* of the Russian offensive. To some extent, at all events outwardly, Sweden seems to have had leanings in this direction, for she consulted Napoleon on the question of the succession; but it seems clear that the ringleaders of the conspiracy were quite willing to adopt Wedel's opposite plan in all its implications.

It was in the development of this plot that the nomination of Christian August to the vacant succession assumed its real importance. Whether regarded as a bribe, as a forcing of the hand of the Norwegian commander, or as a means of embroiling and discrediting him with the Danish Government, it was a trump card to play. The Swedish misrepresentation of Christian's actions at the time of the Kongsvinger negotiations was calculated to further the two latter aspects of the policy ; the first, owing to Christian August's transparent honesty, was soon shown to be of little efficacy. It was to force the Prince's hand that Wedel, though with a fatal misreading of his character, urged upon the Swedish intermediary, Baron Platen, that he should strain every nerve to secure the nomination of Christian August. The Prince's fine sense of honour, which his opponents could never appreciate, eventually wrecked the scheme. Christian, who for a long time was kept in the dark as to what was afoot, would never hear a hint of a union behind the back or against the will of the Danish King ; to the last he worked for Frederic's now hopeless cause, and would never go further than a strictly conditional promise to accept the proffered succession, as a *pis aller*, with his royal master's consent and after peace had been arranged. At the same time, his unremitting efforts to secure the way of peace and conciliation combined with other circumstances to throw the shadow of suspicion over his motives and actions, and to strain his relations with the Danish King. Possibly, indeed, the glamour of the prospect held out to him rendered him still more unwilling to disturb his popularity and prospects by untimely hostilities ; but, as has been said, Christian regarded such a policy as equally fatal to the chances of Frederic of Denmark.

In the middle of July the Swedish estates formally elected Christian August as heir to the throne. He was stated, *à propos* of the Kongsvinger negotiations, to have "done Sweden the greatest service which she had ever received from a foreigner"—a misrepresentation doubtless calculated and intended to embroil him

hopelessly with the Danish King. The offer was duly
conveyed to the Prince, but he would go no further
than the strictly conditional acceptance which he had
adumbrated before. At the end of the month, however, news from Russia reached Frederic, which convinced him that the game was up so far as he was
concerned. The Czar would not hear of the dis-
memberment of Sweden on which the Danish King
had hitherto pinned his hopes, and there was nothing
for it but to make peace. Negotiations were therefore opened immediately, and in December peace in
the north was finally concluded at Jönköping. The
new Crown Prince left Norway, where he was universally
popular, for the country which had adopted him.
The Swedish conspirators were foiled in their main
object—the union with Norway ; they were merely
saddled with an heir to the Crown from whom no
political advantage, whether by way of the recovery
of Finland or other territorial compensation, was to be
hoped. Their deep-laid scheme had foundered on the
rock of the Prince's loyalty and incorruptible honour.

In May of the following year he suddenly died. It
was natural in the circumstances that there should
have been a general suspicion of foul play, since the
continued existence of Christian August obstructed the
plans alike of the Gustavians, on whom the popular
suspicion fell, and of their opponents. The inexplicable
failure of the authorities to protect the Gustavian
Count Fersen from the vengeance of the mob might
easily lead one to entertain suspicions against the
opposite party. But it is fair to say that it seems
satisfactorily proved that the Prince's death, however
opportune, was due to natural causes.[1]

---

[1] The suspicions which naturally gathered round the death of the
Crown Prince and the murder of the Gustavian Count Fersen took
also a third form. The *Annual Register* for 1810 suggests a notion
that both events were part of a Napoleonic plot to clear the way for
Bernadotte. This is of course absurd, but is mentioned to illustrate
the prevailing atmosphere.

The event was productive of the most startling and unforeseen results. Competition for the vacant position of heir to the Swedish throne was once more thrown open. The candidates originally envisaged by the various parties interested were four, but of these only two were ever seriously in the running, and, as will be shown, all were finally defeated by the darkest of dark horses, entered at the last moment owing to the undisciplined and freakish action of a young Swedish subaltern. There was first of all King Frederic of Denmark, whose claims were originally favoured by Napoleon, but whose uncompromising adherence to autocracy and efforts to force the issue with a high hand had fatally ruined his chances. Next there was a Prince of Oldenburg, who had the support of Russia, but whose claims were, on that very account, unwelcome both to Sweden and to Napoleon, who was by no means anxious to strengthen the hand of so temporary and untrustworthy an ally as the Czar. The son of the deposed King Gustav was supported in certain quarters, and would probably have been the successor whom Charles XIII would privately have preferred ; his election would, however, have entailed a long minority, and his candidature was, on other obvious political grounds, unlikely to win anything like an adequate number of adherents. Finally, and for a long time in the position of a hot favourite, there was the Duke of Augustenborg, brother-in-law of the Danish King, and elder brother of the dead Prince Royal, Christian August.

Meantime a party, at first small and insignificant, had other views. Sweden seemed, as one official observer had described her, to be " in the agony of death," and the appointment of any mere figure-head was only likely to hasten her collapse. But the loss of Finland was still so recent that optimists continued to regard the recovery of it as possible, if only the opportunity now open were utilised to secure a Crown Prince of the necessary military distinction. The eyes of this party turned therefore towards the Napoleonic army, and lighted upon the Marshal who, as Governor of the Hanseatic Towns, had been brought most prominently to Swedish notice. This man was Bernadotte, son of an obscure legal official in the South of France, who, after many years spent in the ranks of the Royalist army, had risen, with the dramatic suddenness possible to military talent under the Napoleonic régime, to be a Marshal of France and Prince of Ponte Corvo. He was a man of great personal charm and tact, which had won the Swedish prisoners of war formerly under his care, and, though not always in the highest favour with his Imperial master, he was a soldier of undeniably brilliant qualifications.

In spite of these attractive characteristics, his candidature originated almost by chance, through the irresponsible action of a wholly unofficial intermediary. The young Baron Otto Mörner, an infantry lieutenant, happened to be entrusted, as King's Messenger, with the conveyance of a letter from Charles XIII to Napoleon in Paris, apprising the Emperor of the death of Christian August, and desiring his advice in the matter of a successor. The candidate suggested in the letter was the Duke of Augustenborg. With consummate impudence, Mörner, after the conclusion of his official business, approached Bernadotte, and suggested his candidature for the vacant position of Swedish Crown Prince. His action was first of all received with consternation by the Swedish authorities, and the young king-maker was, on his return home, placed under arrest; but the seed thus sown took root with remarkable rapidity, and the French Marshal was soon in a position to undertake an energetic canvass.

During the sittings of the Diet at Örebro, which was charged with the election of Christian August's successor, Bernadotte had, indeed, an advantage over the official candidates, since his agent, Fournier, was enabled to remain on the spot from which diplomatic representatives were excluded. Bernadotte's candidature was represented as having the support of Napoleon, and in fact this to some extent was the case, though the Emperor was prevented, by a desire to keep on good terms with Russia, from coming forward openly in support of his officer's claims. The result is well known. On the 21st August Bernadotte was unanimously elected, and the old King, Charles XIII, though with some misgivings, acquiesced in this strange choice of a successor. Stranger still, of all the dynasties to which the Napoleonic era gave rise, this one, so fortuitously founded, has alone struck permanent roots in the soil.

The situation which followed is by no means lacking in irony. In choosing Carl Johan—to give the new Crown Prince the names by which he became known in his adopted country—the Swedes had been actuated by the hope of three results. They expected, in the first place, if not an alliance, at least a friendly understanding with Napoleon ; secondly, as a result of this, they hoped that the commercial intercourse between their country and Great Britain would be excepted from the general application of the Continental system ; lastly, or rather primarily, they looked forward to the recovery of Finland. Yet the immediate sequel to Bernadotte's appointment was a declaration of war upon Great Britain, and within a short time Sweden was fighting in alliance with Russia against Napoleon. The situation in which Carl Johan found himself was, indeed, one of considerable embarrassment. So long as the Czar and the Emperor were allies it was hopeless to think of the recovery of Finland, and once the alliance was broken it was doubtful if the power of Napoleon would remain sufficient to enable him to assist in any such project. Bernadotte therefore turned his thoughts from the first to the acquisition of Norway as an equivalent. But this put an end to the notion of a voluntary union which had had its adherents in both countries, since, in order truly to balance the loss of Finland, Norway must be annexed to Sweden as an integral part of that kingdom, with the complete loss of that independent status which was a *sine qua non* of voluntary union. And here again no hope of assistance from Napoleon could fairly be entertained. The King of Denmark was his faithful ally, and the Emperor could not possibly lend official sanction to the annexation of a part of his dominions. Moreover, to strike at the commercial interests of Great Britain was a cardinal point of Napoleon's policy; any country, therefore, which desired to stand well with him was bound to break off all trade relations with our country. In the economic situation in which Sweden now found herself, it was absolutely essential to open the door to British merchandise. The formal declaration of war, therefore, which was notified to England on 17th November, was accompanied by explanations which turned it into the merest farce; Napoleon himself remarking, with a dry laugh, " Que c'était à lui, et non aux Anglais, que la Suède déclarait la guerre " (*Correspondence of Napoleon*, No. 17,229, 22nd December 1810). Bernadotte, in fact, was quicker to realise than were those who had elected him that the prosperity of Sweden involved an understanding with Russia, and continuous friendly intercourse with the British Isles. When, therefore, in the following year, the Czar began to show clearly a desire to back out of the alliance formed at Tilsit, it was plain that all the interests of Sweden would shortly lie in the anti-Napoleonic camp. If Bernadotte was a traitor to his country and false to his old commander, he might at least plead the dilemma that he was bound to betray the interests either of his native or of his adopted country.

For some little time, indeed, he seems to have clung rather desperately to his old allegiance. In March 1811 we find Bernadotte making a definite proposal to the French Minister, Alquier, that Napoleon, in exchange for active assistance on the part of the Swedish troops, should secure him the concession of

Norway. To this attitude he adhered for some time, but the Emperor's response was invariably cold, and almost hostile. Meanwhile he was being sedulously courted by Russia, whose coming breach with Napoleon was growing increasingly evident, and also by Great Britain. In 1812, therefore, he ranged himself definitely with Russia on the side of Napoleon's enemies in exchange for the definite promise of the coveted Norway. On the 3rd of March, in the following year, a Treaty was signed between Sweden and Great Britain to the same effect, slightly qualified by the provisos that force should only be employed in the last resort, and that the union should " take place with every possible regard and consideration for the happiness and liberty of the people of Norway." In April a similar agreement was concluded with Prussia. To carry out his own side of the bargain thus concluded, Carl Johan landed the Swedish forces at Rügen on the 17th of May.

It had once more become impossible to govern Norway from Denmark. Accordingly, Frederic VI appointed to the position of viceroy or statholder for Norway, his cousin, Prince Christian Frederic, who crossed the Skager Rak disguised as a common sailor on the 21st of May. The outlook was threatening, but there was to be some respite, while the Swedish Crown Prince and his forces, which included Prussian and Russian contingents, were involved in operations against Napoleon. Bernadotte's participation in these operations, up to and including the battle of Leipzic, was the subject of much criticism on the part of the Allies, who formed the opinion that he was inclined to spare his Swedish troops, and also to deal more gently than the occasion demanded with his own former countrymen, the French. Sensitive to the atmosphere of suspicion which surrounded him, Carl Johan seems to have begun to entertain some doubt as to whether, if he waited till the end of the war, the pledges of assistance and support in his project with regard to

Norway would be redeemed. Accordingly, in the autumn, he took matters into his own hand, and diverting the forces under his command towards the north, proceeded to attack Denmark. As the troops entrusted with this manœuvre comprised Prussians and Russians as well as Swedes, the result was a foregone conclusion. The Danes resisted bravely, but were completely outnumbered, and by the end of the year the negotiations were in progress which terminated in the Treaty of Kiel.

By thus attending to his own interests Bernadotte had still further endangered his chances of European support. In a letter of 8th February 1814 Castlereagh expresses feelings of dissatisfaction which were doubtless shared by the other Allies (*Correspondence of Castlereagh,* vol. ix, p. 245). This circumstance has to be borne in mind in estimating the policy pursued by the Prince to whose care Norway had been entrusted by the King of Denmark. It could no longer be regarded as certain that the Powers to whom Bernadotte had accorded so unsatisfactory an adherence would be inclined to help him when it came to the point.

By the Treaty of Kiel, 14th January 1814, the King of Denmark renounced, on behalf of himself and his successors, in favour of the King of Sweden, his rights and title to Norway, reserving, however, the colonial possessions of Greenland, Iceland, and the Faroes, in which the Swedes were not interested, and of Norway's historical claims to which the Swedish negotiator was ignorant. From the point of view of Sweden this treaty thenceforth constituted her clear and indisputable title to Norway. The attitude, however, taken up in Norway itself was very different ; for the Norwegian people declared that while the King of Denmark might, if he chose, abdicate a part of his sovereignty, the title thus renounced could not be transferred to another Power, but devolved upon the people, with whom the ultimate decision as to their future constitution thenceforth rested. This view, which seems to anticipate doctrines as to self-determination not then generally recognised, was, in fact, in strict agreement with the principles laid down by every authoritative writer on International Law (see *Grotius*, Lib. II, 6, lv ; *Vattel*, Lib. I, chaps. 16, 17). The parliamentary debates of the time show clearly that the justice of the Norwegian claims, though officially ignored, was perfectly recognised in this country, and even Canning, though he considered himself bound by our treaty obligations, subjected the pact with Carl Johan to severe criticism during a debate which took place on 18th June 1813.

The viceroy, Christian Frederic, from the first repudiated the provisions of the Treaty of Kiel, both in so far as it purported to transfer Norway to a new and unwelcome sovereignty, and in respect of the words by which King Frederic had ostensibly bound his successor (*i.e.* Christian Frederic himself) to concur in the transfer. His first impulse was to claim the vacant throne of Norway by right of inheritance. In his private opinion this was manifestly the ground upon which his title rested. But at an informal meeting of advisers, called together at Eidsvold on the 16th of February, he was prevailed upon to assume for the moment no higher title than Regent, and to await election to the Crown at the hands of the Norwegian people, whose choice was, in the circumstances, a foregone conclusion. He continued, indeed, in public utterances, to describe himself as " *odelsbaaren til Norges trone* " (entitled by right of birth to succeed to the throne of Norway), but he abandoned, in conformity with the advice tendered to him, any claim to immediate sovereignty based upon such grounds.

The policy with which Christian Frederic was thenceforth identified has been the subject of much criticism, and he has been blamed for encouraging, in the interests of his personal ambitions, an obviously futile resistance to the inevitable. Before passing judgment upon the Prince Regent, it is necessary, however, clearly to grasp all the surrounding circumstances.

To begin with, it is indisputable that in the desire and intention to resist to the utmost any annexation to Sweden, the Norwegian people was nearly unanimous. Whatever had been the Regent's attitude, they would have opposed the claims of Bernadotte ; they needed, however, a leader, and this position Christian Frederic had certainly the best right of anyone to assume. A conflict being inevitable, the prospects of complete success, as they appeared at the time, were by no means hopeless. As Carl Johan had shown by his independent action against Denmark, the extent to which he could rely on the support of his allies in his project was doubtful. Nor was that support more likely to be accorded him after he had presumed to take matters into his own hand. As far as Great Britain was concerned, it was arguable, and was, in fact, argued in both Houses of Parliament, that after the Treaty of Kiel no obligation to intervene remained. The arrangement between this country and Bernadotte was that force should not be employed " unless His Majesty the King of Denmark shall have previously refused to join the Alliance of the North." By Clause 6 of the Treaty signed at Kiel between Great Britain and Denmark, Frederic VI acceded to this Alliance, and, by Clause 10, the cession of Norway by Denmark was treated as fulfilling the engagements contracted with Sweden by Great Britain. Or there was this dilemma. We were now at peace with Denmark. If Norway had not been ceded, we were therefore at peace with her, and, if she had been ceded, we had no *casus belli*. This view of our obligations was considerably fortified by Castlereagh's explicit statement that our engagement with Sweden did not amount to a guarantee of the possession of Norway (*Hansard*, 18th June 1813, p. 779). Canning, as already stated, had, on the same occasion, expressed his disapproval of the bargain with Sweden, and the cause of Norwegian independence had manifestly a number of influential supporters in this country. Now if, in endeavouring to enforce his claims to Norway, the Prince Royal of Sweden was to be restricted to the use of Swedish troops, the odds would then be sufficiently equal to be faced with equanimity, particularly in a country so favourable to guerrilla tactics as Norway. In view of the idea of their own superiority which the Swedes soon after developed, it is interesting to study the anxiety and misgiving with which their military experts faced the problem of an offensive at the time. In any case, Sweden stood no chance of achieving a military success so long as their Crown Prince and a large part of the army were engaged elsewhere, which was the case when Christian Frederic had to form his decision upon the nation's future policy.

The Norwegian Regent was, however, no soldier, and never seems really to have relied upon the ordeal of battle. He hoped, by demonstrating to the world the unalterable determination of the nation to resist annexation, to deprive Carl Johan of much of his promised support, a policy which, in that age of shifting alliances and kaleidoscopic changes, was in fact anything but chimerical. In particular, he placed reliance on the ancient friendship of Great Britain, dispatching thither his friend and supporter, Carsten Anker, to sound the Government and carry on the necessary propaganda. As we have seen, there was considerable ground for hope in this direction, judging from the public utterances of responsible statesmen. The bargain struck with Bernadotte had been made with obvious reluctance, and to have wriggled out of it on plausible grounds would not have been a difficult diplomatic feat, though the event proved that even Canning, much as he disliked the arrangement, felt in honour bound to adhere to it.

> " His honour, rooted in dishonour, stood,
> And faith unfaithful kept him falsely true."

But there was yet another possible turn of Fortune's wheel on which the Regent placed some reliance.

If Napoleon were defeated, the question of his successor still remained, and it was an open secret that Bernadotte was a candidate for the position who was believed to have the support of Russia. This promised a way out for all concerned. The Frenchman would disappear from the Swedish arena, leaving the field clear for a Scandinavian union to which none of the parties were likely to raise any serious objection. Christian Frederic himself would be elected successor to the Swedish throne, bringing with him a loyal and contented Norway; while the process might ultimately be completed by the addition of the third Scandinavian throne, to which he was heir, and to which, indeed, he ultimately succeeded.

The stakes were therefore high enough to warrant a bold plunge, and in any case the nation stood to gain rather than lose. Tamely and immediately to capitulate meant complete subordination to Sweden ; by a determined resistance, carried on as long as it was justified by circumstances, a large degree of independence might be, as in fact it was, retained.

It was in these circumstances that Christian Frederic started his great game of bluff. The first step was to secure the election, throughout the country, of representatives of the nation in whose hands the lapsed sovereignty now rested. Considering the limited time at the Regent's disposal, and the absence of any constituted electorate to which to appeal, the arrangements were satisfactory. A questionable feature, perhaps, was the large measure of representation allowed to the army as such ; but this, when the conclusions to be arrived at were likely to be put to the arbitrament of war, was a not indefensible arrangement. The task before the representative Assembly thus created was to draft the future constitution of the country, agree upon the form of government, and elect their ruler.

The place of meeting selected was the Iron Works belonging to Carsten Anker at Eidsvold, where the pre-

liminary discussions, held on 16th February, had taken
place. Eidsvold had many practical disadvantages;
there was no proper accommodation for so large an
Assembly, and access to it, in the thaws of spring, was
unpleasant and difficult. But as the site of the ancient
Eidsiviating it had inspiring historical associations, and
it was perhaps fitting that the working out of Norway's
independence should continue where it had begun.
The comparative difficulty of access secured the deliberations of the Assembly from unwelcome interruption, and it is, at any rate, due to the Regent's choice
that Eidsvold to-day stands for one great event in
Norwegian history. The associations of Christiania or
any other important town would doubtless have
tended to obscure to some extent the pre-eminence of
this unique occasion.

The Assembly met on 10th April, and on the
following day the proceedings began. Rapid progress
was made, facilitated by a decision arrived at by the
narrow margin of a casting vote on the 19th, to the
effect that an inquiry as to the attitude of Foreign
Powers was unnecessary. This decision has been
vigorously criticised ; but, after all, to have paid
attention to such matters could only have delayed and
hampered the work in hand. If the Foreign Powers
were favourable, no harm was done ; if, on the contrary, they disapproved, they could interfere less
effectively with a *fait accompli* than with the initial
stages of the proceedings. " Shall we," a speaker
forcibly observed, " before we think of the Constitution,
first request the permission of Foreign Powers ? And
of whom, but just those who, on account of our present
position and their political situation and relation to
the neighbour kingdom, cannot give it, however much
they secretly favour our cause, and would even secretly
assist to further it ? " There was, in fact, no sound
reason for any more careful investigation of outside
opinion, and the strongest possible reasons against
any such course. Possibly the condition of blindness

under which the Assembly decided to act affected most
seriously the deliberations of the Finance Committee.
On the data before them, they arrived undoubtedly at
too favourable a conclusion.   But here again there
was truth in the cry which rose, " Who wills the end
must will the means ; " if Norway was bent on independence, what use was it to consider too minutely
the sacrifices involved in that courageous decision ?
So the Eidsvold Assembly carried through its task
unfaltering to the end, and on 17th May, a date
to remain for ever dear to the Norwegian heart, the
Constitution was completed and Christian Frederic
elected King.

Meanwhile, however, developments in the European
situation had falsified all the hopes which the Regent
had entertained.   Encompassed as we are to-day with
machinery by which time is absolutely annihilated in
the transmission of news, we are perhaps inclined to
forget how slowly intelligence filtered from one country
to another little more than a century ago.   The Allies
had entered Paris, and had decided on the restoration
of the Bourbons at the end of March ; but Christian
Frederic was not in possession of these vital facts till
the 21st of April.   This put an end to all hopes based
on Bernadotte's pretensions to the sovereignty of
France, though as recently as the middle of March the
Russian Emperor had undoubtedly favoured his candidature.   It was, indeed, possible to take an optimistic
view of the news, as it showed that Carl Johan, probably
on account of private correspondence with a French
general, had begun to forfeit the confidence and
support of the Allied Powers.   To this aspect of the
situation Christian Frederic, as his diary shows,
immediately transferred his hopes, not without some
justification, if contemporary expressions of Allied
opinion are any guide.   One is left with the impression
that a hair would have turned the scale against Bernadotte's chances of support, when one reads such
remarks as the following in a letter of Castlereagh's :

" Charles Jean has no great claim to favour ; but
as none of the Powers could well justify a breach of
treaty to Sweden upon the grievances and, I must say,
strong suspicions we are justified in entertaining of
their General, and as Russia perseveres in execution
of her Treaty, I think we must, in good faith as well
as policy, use our best endeavours to finish the business,
without suffering the people of Norway to embark in
a contest, in which we must at least navally fight
against them, under the stipulations of our Treaty "
(*Castlereagh's Correspondence*, vol. ix, p. 512).

But on the very day following the consummation of
the labours of the Eidsvold meeting, messages reached
the new King from Russia and Prussia which dissipated
all these hopes. These Powers were determined, if
necessary, to intervene by force on behalf of Sweden.
The same determination had been asserted by the
responsible Ministers of Great Britain in debates which
took place in the two Houses on 10th and 12th May
respectively. The game was evidently lost. Christian
Frederic clung, however, to a last desperate hope—
that the Powers would be content with bringing about
the union of Norway and Sweden, after removing Carl
Johan from the position of Prince Royal, and, by means
of a new election, substituting himself. This was a
fantastic dream, but the Norwegian King was now in
the position of the drowning man who clutches at
any straw.

In view, however, of the evident sympathy which the
bold action of the Norwegian people had won for them
in foreign countries, it was nevertheless wise to push
the matter to the point of war, in order to show the
reality of the national feeling and supply a further
lever for bargaining. As soon, however, as hostilities
began, towards the end of July, Christian Frederic
realised that his bluff was called, and negotiations between Norway and Sweden began almost immediately.
It is sometimes urged by Norwegians that a more pro-

longed resistance should have been maintained. There is some force in the criticism. The conquest of Norway would have been a slow and difficult, if not impossible task, and the speedy cessation of hostilities gave the Swedes an altogether false idea of their own superiority, which led to much of the friction of later years. But the fact is that the proposals which formed the basis of negotiation came not from the Norwegian side but from Carl Johan himself, who, substantially accepting what he had immediately before rejected, offered terms which gave the Norwegian people the benefit of their new Constitution and of independence subject to a merely personal union under the Swedish King, which involved, of course, the abdication of Christian Frederic. In these circumstances practically nothing remained to fight about except the Norwegian King's personal interests, and he rightly hesitated to shed the blood of his subjects in furtherance of his own ambitions. Certainly he did not shine as a soldier, but he cannot fairly be blamed for accepting at once a chance of settlement so favourable to the nation. On 14th August a convention embodying the terms proposed was signed at Moss.

The King's only remaining task was to summon an extraordinary meeting of the Storting, and place his resignation in their hands. On the 26th of October he left Norway, after the Storting had duly passed a few days before, with but five dissentients, the proposal for union with Sweden. On the 4th of November, the Eidsvold Constitution having received the few modifications necessitated by the circumstances, Charles XIII of Sweden was formally elected King of Norway, and the experiment of union began.

CHAPTER V

THE SWEDISH UNION

OWING to the circumstances under which the union of Norway and Sweden had come about, it was, from the first, visualised by the two countries in wholly different ways. Carl Johan had uniformly represented the acquisition of Norway to the people which had adopted him as a definite extension of Swedish territory which could be regarded as a compensation for the loss of Finland, and the treaties concluded with Great Britain and her Allies in furtherance of the project spoke in similar language of the "annexation . . . of the Kingdom of Norway as an integral part to the Kingdom of Sweden." In the original draft of the Treaty of Kiel it was laid down that Norway should belong to Sweden and be incorporated in that kingdom, and though, in anticipation of difficulties which might arise, this phraseology had been altered to make the transfer a personal one to the Swedish King, and Norway was to have the status of a kingdom rather than a province, yet this modification was no doubt regarded as a matter of form rather than of substance. The annexation of Norway, in fact if not in name, was of the essence of the Swedish programme. There could be no compensation for the loss of Finland, in the eyes of the people of Sweden, in the fact that their sovereign was also the King of another country, which was otherwise wholly independent.

For a time it was generally believed in Sweden that Carl Johan had achieved his promised objective. On his return from his brief campaign he was hailed as a conqueror, and there was loose talk in the Swedish press of "the former frontier." But even when the effect of what had occurred began to make itself dimly perceived, there was still a tendency to regard the Treaty of Kiel, rather than the Convention of Moss, as the document governing the situation, and the acts of Christian Frederic and the Eidsvold Assembly as a lawless and irrelevant interlude. There were, of course, many who were better informed, but even these refused to regard the Convention of Moss as a final settlement of the relations between the two countries, and looked forward to the speedy realisation of a union more in conformity with what had originally been contemplated.

This was especially the attitude of Carl Johan himself, and there was superficially much to encourage such hopes. In the financial stringency which prevailed, there seemed at first small prospect of the economic independence of Norway. The crisis after the Napoleonic wars practically annihilated the old commercial aristocracy of the country. The burdens laid upon the people in the process of establishing a national bank were so heavy that it was said that the Storting was doing its utmost to make the people " tired of their so-called liberty." An attempt to raise the necessary capital from an issue of shares to be taken up voluntarily having failed, it was found necessary to resort to the expedient of compulsory cash deposits. Besides this, the calling in of the old notes involved further taxation. Discontent was only too likely to be prevalent, and this Carl Johan, who succeeded to the throne in 1818, and had in fact ruled the two kingdoms previously to that date, set himself deliberately to encourage. In 1816 a Swede named Röslein appeared in Norway, and toured round encouraging the populace in the belief that their heavy financial burdens were due to the existence and mismanagement of the Storting. He represented himself as an emissary from the Crown Prince, and as the statholder who ordered him to leave the country fell into disfavour, and was soon afterwards removed from his post, it seems probable that in this respect he told the truth, especially as it is difficult to imagine an adequate motive to induce a private individual of Swedish nationality thus to interfere in the internal affairs of Norway. The result of the agitation was a rising of the *bönder* in 1818 under the leadership of Halvor Hoel. This was nipped

in the bud without difficulty, and the ringleader tried
and convicted. The fact that much of his sentence was
remitted, and that he was awarded a pension from Carl
Johan's private resources, gave, and still gives, serious
ground for the suspicion that the King was interested
in these activities.

Feeling in Norway was naturally much embittered
by such incidents as these, while the soreness was perpetually aggravated by tactless utterances on the part
of the Swedes, who persisted in regarding the Norwegians as deficient in civilisation, and in harping upon
the poverty which, they thought, must soon put an
end to this farce of independence. More trivial matters,
such as the placing of the name of Sweden first in all
public documents, whether Norwegian or Swedish, also
helped to promote the irritation.

Another episode which caused Norwegians to feel
that their interests were not seriously regarded under
the union was the so-called Bodö affair.

Into the details of this interesting and complicated
case it is not possible to enter here. A member of an
English trading firm, named Everth, came into conflict
with the Norwegian law in respect of two matters—
armed resistance to an eviction from some buildings
belonging to the Norwegian Government, of which the
firm was in occupation as tenants at will, and smuggling
on a considerable scale. In respect of the former offence
he was imprisoned without trial from 24th September
to 22nd November under conditions which, if we make
due allowance for exaggeration, seem to have been at
least as rigorous as those which might be applied to a
convicted criminal. Everth was about to be arrested
once more in relation to his offences against the customs
laws when he escaped to England, after overpowering
the guard of the warehouses where some of the confiscated property was stored, and removing a quantity
of goods. Before the date of his flight the matter of
Everth's imprisonment had been brought to the notice
of the British representative at Stockholm, Lord

Strangford, who immediately took energetic steps to obtain his release. The matter had, therefore, at an early stage been transferred from the judicial arena to the diplomatic. A man named Denovan, who acted for Everth, with colossal impudence now concocted a baseless and fraudulent claim for compensation, which again, instead of being asserted by action in the Norwegian courts, was pressed through diplomatic channels. After long delay and much acrimonious correspondence, the matter was settled on terms which gave to the English traders a wholly unmerited triumph. A severe judgment is often passed by Norwegian historians upon the action of the British Government in this affair, and it would certainly have been better if the pecuniary claims of the parties had been left to the decision of a judicial tribunal. At the same time, the long and rigorous imprisonment of a British subject without trial was a matter calling for diplomatic inquiry, and it was in respect of this branch of the affair that our representative first obtained cognisance of it. And with regard to the matter of the claim, which was mainly pressed in the name of a Mr. Stead as owner of some of the confiscated property, there was at the time every reason to regard this gentleman as an innocent sufferer, though in fact it is now quite clear that he was a party to Everth's traffic in contraband. The real fault lay, as the Norwegians at the time seem to have perceived, in the encouragement which the British demands received from the King and the Swedish Ministers. Carl Johan, at an early stage, gave a definite pledge that Stead's property should be restored, while highly placed Swedes went beyond the British authorities in their condemnation of the Norwegian attitude, representing the country, in fact, as a place where no justice was to be expected. Count d'Engeström, for example, the Foreign Minister, admitting the King's promise and " the monstrous and unprecedented outrages which marked the whole of both cases," stated his opinion " that the King ought to and must,

for the vindication of his own authority, punish those
who had disobeyed him; but he urged in extenuation
the difficulty of communication with Norway, the in-
tractability of the Norwegians, and the laxity of the
laws in those latitudes; such events could not have
taken place in Christiana (*sic*), he said, 'because there
the King had troops.' . . . He promised to urge the
King again on the subject, lamenting that they had
been involved in all these difficulties by the absurd
obstinacy (and he alluded to the bad faith also) of
Count Wedel Jarlsberg and of other persons in Norway.
Indeed of them, and of the motives of individuals
connected with these transactions, he spoke without
reserve" (Letter from Vesey Fitzgerald, Lord Strangford's successor, F.O. 73, 113).

No better example, in fact, than the Bodö affair
could well be given of the disadvantages of the Union
in relation to foreign affairs. From the point of view
of Norway, arbitrarily deprived of seizin of a matter
within their domestic jurisdiction, and unjustly compelled to pay compensation to a gang of smugglers,
this is too obvious for further comment. But Sweden,
too, might rightly complain of the diplomatic pressure
to which she was subjected in respect of matters with
which she had nothing to do, and over which, constitutionally, she had no control. It was perhaps
natural in the circumstances that her statesmen sought
to rid themselves of a troublesome affair, in which their
country was in no way interested, by conceding all
demands without resistance.

It may also be urged, in extenuation of the attitude
of Sweden towards Great Britain in this matter, that
Carl Johan was at the same time being subjected to
pressure in regard to a more important matter—the
Norwegian share of the Danish debt. By Clause 6 of
the Treaty of Kiel the King of Sweden was pledged
to discharge a share, proportionate to the population
and resources of Norway, of the public debt of Denmark-
Norway existing before 1st January 1814. The Great

Powers were insisting that this liability should be discharged. But here a difficulty arose. The sanction for the arrangement was the Treaty of Kiel, and with this it was likely to be contended by the Norwegians that they had nothing to do. On the other hand, considering the disappointingly small advantages which the King had conferred on Sweden through the Union as in fact concluded, he could not well call upon that country to discharge the liability. In these circumstances he became naturally nervous of foreign intervention, though he carried his feelings of anxiety to absurd lengths when he suggested that external Powers were likely to find a *casus belli* in the abolition by the Norwegian legislature of the insignificant last remains of their hereditary nobility—a perhaps rather crude expression of democratic sentiment which was, besides being a purely domestic matter, profoundly unimportant. This proposal had been twice passed by the Storting, and vetoed on each occasion by the King, and in 1821, when it was under consideration for the third time, and would, under the terms of the Constitution, become law automatically if carried yet again, Carl Johan left no stone unturned to prevent this result. His threats and manœuvres were, however, unavailing, and on this point the Norwegian people carried the day.

More satisfactory to the King was the eventual settlement of the question of the Danish debt. There was, indeed, some talk of repudiating the liability so far as Norway was concerned ; but the matter had really been concluded by a decision of the extraordinary Storting of 1814, and when it came to the point calmer counsels prevailed. It was felt that to make Sweden take over the debt—and that someone must pay it was evident—would have struck a blow at Norwegian independence, and that those who paid the piper might, with some show of justice, insist upon calling the tune. On 29th May 1821, therefore, a considerable majority decided in favour of Norway's acceptance of the liability.

This satisfactory termination of the question was immediately followed by another sinister and suspicious incident, which, had the Norwegian vote gone differently, might have developed in a very serious fashion. In spite of the serious financial stringency in Norway, which had been rendered even more severe by the acceptance of the share in the Danish debt, the King, in July of the same year, ordered some expensive and elaborate military manœuvres, in which 3000 Swedish troops were to participate, to take place in the neighbourhood of Christiania. On the eve of the display the uncomfortable discovery was made that the Swedish soldiers, but not the Norwegian, had been supplied with ball-cartridge. At the same time, a Swedish naval squadron entered the harbour. That a *coup d'état* was contemplated is a matter which hardly admits of doubt. At the last moment, however, the volatile King seems to have changed his mind, and the manœuvres, though wholly superfluous and criminally extravagant, passed off quietly.

For some time after these events Carl Johan concerned himself with ineffectual efforts to modify the Norwegian Constitution, and with undignified and short-sighted attempts to prohibit the celebration of May 17, the anniversary of its completion by the Eidsvold Assembly. The latter culminated in the so-called *Torveslag*, or Battle of the Market Place, 1829, where a perfectly inoffensive crowd of both sexes was charged by the military, under the orders of the tactless Swedish statholder, von Platen. This policy only served to give a permanence which it otherwise would have speedily lost to the celebration of the anniversary. The *Torveslag* came at a critical moment, just as the generation which had grown up under the Union was coming to man's estate, and consequently had, in all probability, an effect on the future political history of Norway out of all proportion to its intrinsic importance.

In spite of his many attacks upon Norwegian independence, the King, in the concluding years of his reign, contrived to gain a very considerable popularity in Norway. It is perhaps remarkable that he should have been idolised by so thoroughgoing a patriot and nationalist as the poet Wergeland ; but this great Norwegian was decidedly erratic and unaccountable in thought as in action, and his nationalism was always characterised by antipathy to Denmark rather than to Sweden. Wergeland was profoundly influenced by the French Revolution, and looked upon the self-made Bernadotte as a product of that event. Hero-worship for a great soldier also entered into the question : probably the thing which had least influence was the pension which the poet, to the disgust of his friends and associates, consented to receive from the royal purse. As regards the feelings of the Norwegian people generally, other causes for their affection can be adduced. The King was growing old, and, with age, the vigour of his assaults on the Constitution diminished. The attacks to which he was subjected from the pen of Crusenstolpe in Sweden, and the popularity these writings enjoyed in that country, led Carl Johan to think more kindly of the sister kingdom. Again, though questions relating to the Union, which subsequently were to assume great importance, were continually arising, principally under the influence of the Norwegian politician J. A. Hielm, and the King, as late as 1836, arbitrarily dissolved the Storting, yet new men and new currents of thought were beginning to enter the political arena, and attention was to some extent diverted from the central problem of relations under the Union.

For all its democratic Constitution, Norway in the early years of the Union remained a bureaucracy, of the same type which had actually managed its affairs under the nominal autocracy of Denmark. Now, however, the character of the Constitution was beginning to be generally realised, and the nucleus of a *bonde*-party, opposed to the old officialdom, was appearing in the Storting, with the result that that body began to consider narrower issues of immediate interest to a comparatively bucolic and uneducated class of members, and to neglect the remoter themes of the Constitution and the Union. Many of the questions discussed were of great importance : it was in these years that the first steps were taken towards popular local government ; but the age and consequent inertia of the King, and the preoccupation of a large section of Norwegian politicians with other matters, served to produce a lull in the central controversy.

The calm was accentuated after Carl Johan's death in 1844, and the accession of his son, Oscar I. One of the first acts of the new King was to remove many of the minor causes of irritation which had embittered the relations of his two kingdoms. The Norwegian arms were no longer to be used on the Swedish coinage ; the name of Norway should stand first in official documents relating to that country ; above all, Norway was to have her own naval flag, in addition to the commercial ensign which, since 1821, her merchantmen had been entitled to fly. This last concession was, indeed, to some extent counterbalanced by the stipulation that the mark of Union should be borne on both these flags, whereas previously the commercial flag had been free from it ; but this, for the moment, did not modify the general gratification.

The domestic strife occasioned by the growth of a popular opposition to the bureaucracy served, moreover, to promote reactionary tendencies. Threatened from a new quarter, the governing class turned from their conflicts with the Crown to face a fresh and growing danger. This change of front had its concomitants. The merits of a strong king who could veto immature legislation began to be recognised. To be narrowly and exclusively Norwegian became bad form—the hall-mark of the now feared and hated provincial ; while the opposition possessed as yet neither the power nor the breadth of view to concern themselves greatly with constitutional problems. In terms of literature, as is pointed out elsewhere, Wergeland underwent temporary eclipse, and the taste of Welhaven became the fashion.

The first mutterings of the storm connected with the Slesvig-Holstein controversy in Denmark tended to foster Pan-Scandinavian sentiment. The Labour agitation of Marcus Thrane (1848–51), while it gained little for the working class beyond a slight improvement in the condition of the *husmaend*, served to scare the Conservatives into a still more anti-democratic attitude, which naturally involved a more friendly relation with the Crown. In fact, the reign of Oscar I gave rise to opportunities, never again to recur, when tactful handling might have rendered the Union a permanency, and even modified the Norwegian Constitution into closer conformity with Swedish ideals.

It was not to be. With the death of Oscar I in 1859, and the accession of his son Carl XV, who, owing to the state of his father's health, had been for some time the actual ruler of the two kingdoms, the storm broke loose again. Carl was, indeed, a convinced " Scandinavian," but for what now occurred no blame attaches to him. The Constitution of 1814 had given power to the King to nominate a statholder or viceroy for Norway, who might be, and for some time actually was, a Swede. The provision had now lost its original importance, and in any case there had been for many years no question of filling the post with anyone who was not a Norwegian. There had been a number of proposals from time to time to abolish a post, the existence of which was naturally calculated to irritate Norwegian sensibilities. On his accession, in imitation of his predecessor, Carl contemplated making some popular concession, and he gave the Norwegian legislature to understand that if a proposal for the abolition of the office of statholder were passed, it would receive the royal sanction. But he had reckoned without the Swedish politicians, who, when the Storting duly passed the suggested proposal, set up a tremendous outcry, contending that this, as a matter directly concerning the Union, could not be left to the decision of the Norwegians alone. At the same time they indulged in language particularly wounding to Norwegian feelings, and started an agitation for a general revision of the conditions of the Union to bring it more into line with the Swedish conception. Carl XV was therefore constrained to withhold his sanction from the measure, and the old state of friction was once more introduced. There was a unanimous protest against the Swedish attitude, which was calmly ignored by the politicians of that country.

It is a striking illustration how far Scandinavianism had now progressed, that within a very few years a new Norwegian Ministry, under Fredrik Stang, actually agreed to the institution of a committee of both nations for the purpose of revising the Act of Union. There was, however, a great difference between the Norwegian Government (*statsraad*) and the Norwegian Storting. Proposals that the *statsraad* should be given the power of participating in parliamentary discussions had hitherto not appealed to the more democratic party, which feared that the innovation would give too much power to the Government. But, as Björnson pointed out in a speech of 24th June 1881 (*Artikler og taler*, vol. i, p. 525), "the negotiations over the Union committee led to the thought of introducing parliamentary government." The "lawyer party," as it was called, led by Johan Sverdrup, and the *bonde* party under Sören Jaabaek, came round to the view that the participation of the Ministers in the discussions of the Storting would further democratic control and consistency of policy; the question of the Union came once more to the front, and the two parties coalesced to form the great Liberal or *Venstre* (Left) party, which in 1870 won a crushing victory at the polls, after having in the previous year carried another important point in their programme—the introduction of annual meetings of the Storting. The first result was that a proposal for a new Act of Union was defeated by an enormous majority; the next that the proposal for the participation by the *statsraad* in the discussions of the Storting was carried by 80 votes to 29. On the advice of the Ministry, however, the Royal Assent was refused to the measure, and when this was followed by a vote of want of confidence in the Ministry, the King in 1872 declared his intention of keeping them. On September 18 of the same year Carl XV died, and his brother Oscar II therefore came to the throne at a critical juncture.

Like his predecessors, the new King began his reign with a conciliatory step. In 1873 the proposal for the abolition of the post of Statholder, and the substitution of a Norwegian Prime Minister, was passed and sanctioned, the new post falling, in the first instance, to the Conservative Fredrik Stang.

But seeing that the post of Viceroy, and the power to appoint a Swede to it, had for years been without any practical importance, there was little substance in this long-delayed concession. And in regard to other matters in controversy the King was to display anything but a conciliatory spirit. The proposal to bring the Ministry in touch with the Storting was four times passed and four times vetoed. Technically it was only carried thrice, as the creation of the post of Prime Minister had occasioned a slight change in the wording, though not the substance, of the motion. But on the fourth occasion it seemed to have fulfilled all the conditions which, under paragraph 79 of the Constitution, entitled it to legal validity, notwithstanding the royal veto. Meantime the Liberals had gone from strength to strength at the elections, but the Conservative Ministry continued to enjoy the confidence of the King. Sverdrup, the Liberal leader, now proposed (9th June 1880) that the Storting's resolution should be declared valid law, and that the Ministry should be directed to promulgate it. This proposal was carried by a large majority, but the Government still refused to recognise

the alteration of the law, contending that in matters
concerning the modification of the Constitution the
royal veto was not merely suspensive but absolute.
The matter therefore attained a constitutional importance beyond its actual scope, though the change, from
the point of view of parliamentary control, was in any
case considerable. At this stage Stang, the Prime
Minister, retired for reasons connected with his increasing age, and was replaced by Selmer; but the new
Ministry was in other respects of the same character
as the old, and persisted in the same obstructive
attitude. Indeed, as though to fill up the cup, it proceeded to raise two fresh constitutional questions, by
recommending the King to veto a financial resolution
connected with the newly constituted *skytter-lager* or
rifle-clubs, and to exercise a " divided veto " in another
case, with the result that a proposal of the Storting was
sanctioned in part and in part rejected. The effect
was to give to the elections of 1882 a particularly
excited character : the poll was unprecedentedly
large, and many persons secured "faggot votes" to
give them a right to the suffrage. The Liberals won
a decisive victory, and at once proceeded to take
the drastic step of impeaching the Ministry. Before a
court constituted on such party lines as the *riksret*
which was to undertake the trial, the verdict was a
foregone conclusion ; but, while the proceedings were
subjected to some criticism on that account, there is
force in Björnson's contention that it was a judgment
of the nation. Selmer and seven other Ministers were
sentenced to loss of office ; the remainder were fined.

The King protested, but submitted. After two
abortive attempts to create a fresh Conservative
Ministry, he sent for Sverdrup, in June 1884, and the
Liberal victory was complete. The first stage in the
constitutional struggle had ended in the triumph of
parliamentary principles.

It may be thought that this struggle with the
monarchy had little to do with the question of the

Union. Superficially, of course, this was the case, but in reality the two matters had the closest possible connection. As already pointed out, the desire for parliamentary control was induced originally by the attitude of a Ministry out of touch with Norwegian feeling on the question of Union reform. But, apart from this, there is truth in Björnson's contention (*Artikler og Taler*, vol. i, p. 483) that the King of the two countries was, in reality, always a Swedish King. Not only was he known in Norway, as in Sweden, by a title strictly applicable only to the latter country (*e.g.* Karl XV), but he was Swedish in birth, upbringing, and entourage. " In almost eighty years that the dynasty has existed," said Björnson in 1892, " it has altogether not passed three years here in our country." In Court circles, the representatives of Norway, in the earlier days at least, made but a poor show. The men who could bear the expense of Court society were, owing to the financial crisis from which Norway suffered after the Napoleonic wars and the Union, for the most part self-made men of little polish, whereas Sweden retained her courtly aristocracy. It was, therefore, little to be wondered at that Swedish opinion and Swedish prejudice carried a disproportionate weight with the sovereign of the two countries. Finally, the link between Norway and Sweden being personal, the King was in fact the Union, and an attempt to gain freedom from the sovereign's control could not be anything else but an attempt to loosen the bonds of union.

As such there can be little doubt that the Liberal victory of 1884 was regarded by the Swedish people. In the very next year legislation was passed by the Swedish Rigsdag, bringing foreign affairs, which had been hitherto technically under the unfettered discretion of the King, more directly under parliamentary control, in the hands of the Foreign Minister. This was legitimate enough, but seeing that, of two alternative proposals put forward, that which would have given Norway the more effective voice in these matters was rejected, it is tolerably certain that a desire to assert Sweden's pre-eminence in the Union played its part. However this may be, the change, however salutary and justifiable in itself, was bound to lead to friction. In the striking language of the Norwegian historian, J. E. Sars, although the *de facto* control of foreign affairs had hitherto been actually in the hands of a Swedish Minister, yet, since it was technically a matter for the common King, "the indignity for Norway had had a fig-leaf behind which it was hidden ; now . . . the fig-leaf was to be taken away."

This was partly perceived by the King and the Swedish authorities, and negotiations were set on foot to give Norway an increased representation in the council before which foreign affairs were discussed, but since the Swedes insisted upon words emphasising the Swedish nationality of the Foreign Minister, the attempts at settling the matter proved abortive. Norway was now united in opinion that something must be done to obtain for the nation some voice in foreign and diplomatic questions, but on the method to be adopted there was a clear line of party cleavage.

The Conservatives, and the moderate Liberals, of whom the old party leader Johan Sverdrup was the controlling spirit, favoured the modification of the conditions of union by the creation of a common Foreign Minister, who might be either Norwegian or Swedish, equally responsible to both kingdoms ; this, as Sars points out, was a policy calculated to lead ultimately to closer amalgamation and a common parliament ; the extreme or " pure " Liberals (*rene venstre*), on the other hand, agitated for a separate Foreign Minister for Norway, a treatment of the problem tending in the direction of what actually occurred in the end, the complete termination of the Union. Had the Conservative proposal been acceptable to Sweden, it seems possible that the desire of that country to reduce Norway to the status of a province might ultimately have been attained, since the closer the amalgamation the more certain was the predominance of Sweden, which possessed a far larger population ; and in 1888 a Conservative Government, owing to the split in the Liberal ranks, came into power.   In Sweden, however, at this time, largely owing to the adoption of a protectionist policy which attracted the agricultural electorate to the Conservatives, the aristocratic or *stor-svensk* party was in office, and would abate nothing of its haughty assertion of Swedish supremacy.   Tactless expressions with regard to Norway, appearing constantly in public speeches and in the Press, contributed further to the embitterment of Norwegian opinion.   When, therefore, the *rene venstre* made the appointment of a separate Norwegian Foreign Minister the leading plank in their platform during the elections of 1891, they were returned by a large majority.

It was one thing, however, to make speeches advocating a Norwegian Minister for Foreign Affairs, and quite another to think of any means for bringing the project within the ambit of practical politics.   Once in office, therefore, Steen, the leader of the successful party, moderated his ambitions, and, instead of raising the main question of Norway's control of external affairs, contented himself with tackling the more modest problem connected with a separate consular service. To this there can be no doubt that Norway was entitled, and it could have been set up without in any way modifying the existing constitution.   As a Power in possession of a great maritime trade, Norway was really more in need of consuls than was Sweden :   there were places where the commercial interests of the two kingdoms came into competition, and other places, especially outside the confines of Europe, where Norway was really the only country concerned.   A telling example of the evils of the existing system was given by Björnson in a speech in Gausdal in 1892.   In Shanghai there had been a Swedish consul, though scarcely a single Swedish ship came there.   In his days the Norwegian trade in the port amounted to 50,000 kroner annually.

Later, a Norwegian was appointed to the post, and the volume of trade quickly rose to 200,000 kroner. In many important regions there was no consul, because the Swedes were not interested ; in others, where Norway was not concerned, consuls were maintained and paid for. In these circumstances, in ventilating the question, the Liberal Government was on solid ground.

A committee was appointed to go into the question, which reported unanimously in favour of the change. In June 1892 the Storting voted 50,000 kroner towards the furtherance of the plan for a separate consular service, and directed the Ministry to take steps to negotiate the matter with Sweden.

The Liberal attitude in the matter was that, though such a negotiation was desirable and even a practical necessity, yet the question was one which involved no constitutional change, and with which, accordingly, Norway was entitled to take an independent line. As consuls are specifically mentioned in paragraph 22 of the Norwegian Constitution, there can be little doubt that this attitude was juridically sound, though the way in which it was emphasised may be open to a charge of intransigeance. In Sweden, on the other hand, it was contended that this was a matter in which both kingdoms were concerned, and which, accordingly, under paragraph 5 of the Rigsakt, should be dealt with in a joint meeting of the Councils of State of both Norway and Sweden, and this view had also the support of the Conservative minority in Norway.

The King, under the influence of his Swedish advisers, gave it to be understood that he would not be prepared to sanction the proposals of the Storting ; and the Ministry, without waiting for the formal discussion of the matter by the King in Council, which might raise a difficult constitutional point as to their duty, under the constitution, to countersign a decision of the King of which they disapproved, tendered their resignations. A deadlock was thus created, which was terminated in 1892 by a compromise, under which the

Ministry resumed their offices, with a pledge not to resuscitate the consul question before the end of the current financial year. In 1893, however, there was a repetition of exactly the same procedure, with this difference, that on this occasion the King succeeded in prevailing upon the Conservative party to form an alternative government. The reign of a Ministry representing a parliamentary minority was, however, naturally beset with difficulties, especially as the Liberals felt that, had it not been for the Conservative betrayal, a repetition of the previous deadlock would have brought the King to capitulate. It was during the term of office of this Government, in fact, that a law deleting the symbol of union from the commercial flag was passed for the first time, though, naturally in the circumstances, it was refused the royal sanction.

In January 1895, in consequence of the unfavourable results of the elections of the previous autumn, the Conservative Ministry resigned their uneasy posts. The King was now for a time unable to form a government, as the Liberals would not accept his terms and no other party seemed possible. Only the serious danger of a military *coup d'état* on the part of Sweden, which was seriously contemplated and could not, in the existing state of defence of Norway, have been effectively resisted, brought about the formation, late in the autumn, of a Coalition Ministry under Professor Hagerup, which, in collaboration with the Swedish Council, appointed a joint committee to report upon the consular question. The report, which was issued in 1898, consisted of four divergent expressions of opinion, corresponding to the differences in the personnel of its members, and therefore contributed nothing to the satisfactory solution of the problem. After this abortive effort, the Hagerup Ministry gave place to Steen and his Liberals, who came in with an enormous majority as a result of the elections of 1897.

Except for the final passing of the law deleting the

sign of union from the commercial ensign, which was
again refused the royal sanction, but became valid
automatically under the constitution, little was done
for some time which was directly concerned with the
vexed question of the Union. But the ground was
thoroughly prepared for the final and decisive phase
of the struggle. A reform of the parliamentary
franchise was carried through, conferring the vote on
all male citizens over twenty-five years of age with a
five years' residence qualification. It was determined
that, when next the people spoke its mind, the expression should be fully representative. Besides this,
under the influence of humiliating memories of the
effect of Swedish threats in 1895, the defences of the
country were energetically handled, and put upon a
more satisfactory footing. These useful preliminaries
were the last work of Steen, who in 1902, being now an
old man, retired in favour of Otto Blehr, leaving his
party in a position of increased strength and importance.

Negotiations were now renewed at the instance of
Sweden, and in March 1903 a preliminary agreement
on general principles was reached. These negotiations were carried further by the Hagerup Ministry,
returned to power by the elections of 1903, and consisting of a combination of Conservative and Liberal
elements which favoured the settlement of the matter
by an amicable agreement with Sweden, while the true
Liberal programme talked of settling the matter in
the next session, whether by agreement or without it.
And the Hagerup Ministry carried its task to the very
brink of success, all seemed going well, when, in November 1904, the Swedish Prime Minister, Boström,
suddenly produced some new and quite unacceptable
demands. The most important point in these was that
the Norwegian consuls were to be under the control
of the Swedish Foreign Minister. Boström's intervention completely upset the proceedings, and in
February 1905 it was announced that negotiations
were broken off.

The arrogant attitude of the Swedish politicians had by this time brought about practically complete unanimity in Norway with regard to the consul question. There were some dissensions in the council with regard to the next step to be taken, and these resulted in a change of Ministers, Christian Michelsen becoming Premier. Under his talented leadership party cleavage ceased to exist. A proposal for a law setting up a Norwegian consular service was passed in May without a dissentient vote. But on the 27th of the same month King Oscar refused his sanction. In doing so, he clearly showed that he was in no true sense the King of Norway. Swedish interests and Swedish views were allowed to override the unanimous desire and the clear advantage of the whole Norwegian nation. The Union snapped at once. The Ministry resigned in a body. An alternative Government was out of the question, as the King himself recognised, refusing on that ground, so far as lay in his power, to accept the proffered resignations. The Ministry naturally persisted in its attitude, and on the circumstances being reported to the Storting, the following epoch-making resolution was carried unanimously and without debate : " Since all the members of the Ministry have resigned their offices, since His Majesty the King has declared that he is not in a position to provide the country with a new Government, and since the constitutional monarchy has thus ceased to operate, the Storting empowers the members of the Ministry which has this day resigned to execute until further notice the authority conferred upon the King in conformity with the Constitution and relevant laws of the kingdom of Norway, with such modifications as are necessitated by the fact that the Union with Sweden under one King is dissolved, as the result of the King's cessation to perform the functions of a Norwegian King."

The Union was thus at an end from the Norwegian point of view ; but it was still necessary to reckon with

Sweden, and with that object to gain the sympathy and approval of the outside world. The two kingdoms were in fact, in the autumn of 1905, on the brink of war : troops were everywhere mobilised, and only the quiet dignity and self-possession with which the Norwegians carried their point and presented it to the other nations of Europe enabled peace to be maintained. It is said in Norway that the good offices of England also contributed to this satisfactory result, and there is probably a considerable amount of truth in this universally held belief. But it was the necessity of appealing to outside opinion, rather than any idea of establishing upon a new sanction what was already a *fait accompli*, which led to the famous plebiscite of August 13, whereat, on a poll of 85 per cent. of the electorate, the decision of the Storting was confirmed by an overwhelming majority. In the late autumn the two kingdoms agreed to the terms of separation, the most critical point of which was the demolition of the Norwegian frontier fortresses, and on October 27 King Oscar formally abdicated as King of Norway. As he had refused the invitation of the Storting to allow a Prince of his House to become the new sovereign of the country, the present King, Haakon VII, was chosen, after another plebiscite, held in November, had decided in favour of continuing the monarchical form of government. The new King at once took up his residence in the country, and Norway was once more, as in the days of her early greatness, a completely independent kingdom.

CHAPTER VI

THE OLD LITERATURE

THE literature of a country may be approached in many ways and treated from various aspects. Such a study may take the form of a biographical catalogue of authors, with notes on their work; or it may be purely critical and technical, dealing with peculiarities of metre and diction in the poetry and style in the prose. Attempts may be made to trace the origin of characteristic forms, or to estimate the extent to which any and what external influences have affected literary development. To make such a study conform to the basic plan of this series, it would seem most profitable to subordinate most of these aspects of the subject to the consideration of the literature as a formative influence and as a revelation of national character. These two sides have really a close interconnection, since the types held up to admiration, and the national traits revealed in work good enough to survive, must almost inevitably exert no little influence upon the formation of the ideals of subsequent generations.

The extent to which such an effect can be produced must of course depend upon the degree to which an appreciative audience exists for literary work, whether ancient or modern. In this respect the conditions in Norway have at all times been unusually favourable. The products of Norse literary culture have been highly valued, even at times when Norway herself was deficient in literary talent. After the exodus to Iceland the arts of both prose and poetic composition were almost monopolised by the colonists. The most noted skalds, the best exponents of saga, whether spoken or written, were to a very great extent imported from Iceland. Yet they were held in the highest honour, were admitted to the closest intimacy with King and Court, and were not infrequently entrusted with important responsibilities, such as the diplomatic mission of St. Olaf's skald, Sigvat, to Sweden. As an instance of the distinguished position which they held, one may refer to the account of the battle of Stiklestad, where a little band of skalds was in close attendance upon the King, one of them, Thormod Kolbrunarskald, awakening the host to battle by the recitation of an old but most appropriate poem, the ancient *Bjarkamál* :

> " Dawns the day, to the cock's plumes shaken,
> Turns the thrall to his toil again ;
> Rise then, comrades, up ! and awaken !
> All the noblest of Adil's men.
> Hár of the hard grip, Rolf the bowman,
> High-born heroes whom naught can fray,
> Wake not to wine-cup or charms of woman,
> Rather I rouse ye to war's wild play."

Or again, we may remember how King Haakon Haakonson spent his last hours listening to the sagas of the kings.

Under the Union, Norwegian literature in the strict sense may almost be said to have disappeared. But that a taste for such things survived among the masses of the people is proved by the wealth of folk-tales and ballads, transmitted orally, which the industry of a later age has succeeded in preserving before it was too late. And when, with the re-establishment of Norwegian independence in the nineteenth century, there was a renaissance of authorship, the new writers found a receptive and appreciative audience already in existence.

The literature of Norway is sharply divided into two parts, the ancient and the modern, separated from one another by several centuries of practically unbroken silence.[1] There was, indeed, one brilliant interruption to this silence, the comedies and other works of Holberg; but this great writer, though a Norwegian by birth, lived in Denmark and addressed

[1] Of those who wrote in and for Norway, the highest level was reached in the seventeenth century by the son of a Scotsman, Petter Dass, whose *magnum opus* was a rhymed description of life in the extreme North, entitled *Nordlands Trompet*. But this would scarcely have made a sensation in a less barren age.

himself to the Danish people, so that in a sense he is a figure rather of Danish than Norwegian literature, whose appearance does not materially affect the truth of the generalisation. We do not think of Goldsmith and Sheridan as figures in Irish, but in English literature, and their position affords a fair parallel to that of Holberg. In respect of this long dormant period the literature of Norway resembles, indeed, that of Ireland, and one is tempted to trace a fanciful connection between independence and literary activity. The true explanation in each case, however, is not

> " Her songs were made for the pure and free,
> They never shall sound in slavery."

It is merely that the only possible patrons of literature became Danish or Danicised in the one case, English or Anglicised in the other, while the old cultural traditions were represented by inarticulate masses, out of touch with the pen and the printing press.

More difficult, perhaps, to explain is the interesting problem of Icelandic predominance in the field of Norse literature. For, after all, the Icelanders were Norwegians, and their supremacy coincided with a period of culture and independence in Norway. Many Icelanders, in fact, served Norwegian patrons, and were quite as much appreciated in the mother country as in their native colony. It is true that the great saga age fell at a time of much civil war and internal commotion in Norway ; but this does not in any way explain the phenomenon, for it was equally a period of strife and anarchy in Iceland. It may to some extent be true that the districts which contributed most to the settlement of the Icelandic colony were those parts of Norway where the highest degree of culture prevailed. The evidence of collectors of Norwegian ballads and folk-lore tends to some extent to support such a contention. But it is not an all-sufficing explanation. The real key to the riddle seems to be that neither the prose nor the poetry of the North was at the time of its composition strictly literature at all. It was not written, that is to say, but orally transmitted. What stood the best chance of being preserved was that which happened to be the fashion at the time of being reduced to writing. This was the prose saga, a form of composition no doubt originally common to both countries, but one in which the Icelanders, at the time in question, owing to causes to be mentioned later, had come to excel, till to all intents and purposes they monopolised the art. What has come down to us of the poetry of the skalds, or Court bards, is preserved for the most part in the form of extracts incorporated in the sagas, generally with the idea of giving the events described the confirmation to be derived from a more nearly contemporary source. The older mythological and heroic poetry had a very narrow escape from the fate of being altogether forgotten. Christianity and a change of taste well-nigh displaced it both in Norway, where it originated, and in Iceland, where it was in fact ultimately preserved. It owed its salvation to the fact that it provided the aspiring bard of the later school with mythological information, and an abundant supply of the necessary tags and synonyms. Snorre's *Edda* is, in intention and in fact, a *Gradus ad Parnassum* for the would-be Court poet of his day. What is known as the older *Edda*, a collection containing the greater number of the early poems known to us, was actually lost until 1643, and the verses included in it exist for the most part in one manuscript only. Its limited choice of subject points to the fact that it was preserved, not for literary reasons, but because heathen mythology and tales of mythical heroes interested some anonymous antiquary. The survival of the collection in these circumstances is a matter of sheer good fortune.

There is reason to believe, therefore, that much indigenous Norwegian literature has been lost. We know that many of the earlier skalds were Norwegians, though later, especially under Olaf the Holy, a demand for Icelandic bards seems to have come into fashion.

The case of the sagas, or prose narratives, is somewhat different. Family sagas, which form so large a proportion of Icelandic prose literature, no doubt existed in Norway originally. But the decline in importance of the local aristocracy, under the centralising government of the Kings, would largely account for the disappearance of these by the time such works were commonly reduced to writing. Iceland, on the other hand, had a large supply of Norse chieftains assembled in a restricted area, and periodically brought into touch with one another at the Althing. Under these circumstances the art of telling stories about such local magnates was specially fostered and developed. Hence the Icelander came so to excel in this *genre* as completely to supplant the Norwegian, and he thus became the Historiographer Royal of Norway when a connected prose history of her Kings was demanded. The *Historia Norvegiae*, and the work of Theodoricus Monachus, also suggest that in the mother country Latin composition had by this time superseded Norse to a far greater extent than was the case in Iceland.[1]

The almost accidental preservation of " the older *Edda*," alluded to above, is a piece of good luck which it is impossible to exaggerate. Not only does it contain poetry of an extraordinarily fine quality—in my opinion such a work as *Völospá* is among the masterpieces of the world's literature — but it possesses a special importance from the point of view of the present work, inasmuch as it is the source from which we derive nearly all our knowledge of the spiritual and ethical foundation on which the national character of Norway was built up. It is supplemented, no doubt, by the real *Edda*, Snorre Sturlason's treatise of that name, which bases its mythological information on

[1] The most important Norwegian work in the vernacular is the interesting didactic dialogue *Konungs Skuggsjá—The King's Mirror*— which throws an interesting light on the Court and commercial life of the time, and contains some interesting information with regard to the Greenland colony.

the poems of the older collection and others now un-happily lost. But the earlier work has the merit of giving us the poems themselves, unsophisticated by the commentaries of a later age.

The style of the older or poetic "*Edda*," as for con-venience it must still be called, is somewhat remarkable. Monologue, ostensibly in the mouth of a god or hero, or dialogues between two such characters, are far more frequent than descriptive narrative delivered by the poet in his own person. One is tempted to suppose that much of this class of poetry was originally a form of drama, but the advantages to a reciter of letting his characters speak for themselves, and subordinating explanations, may possibly be sufficient to account for this peculiarity, when it is remembered that the verses were intended to be sung or spoken rather than written. Verbal repetitions and echoed phrases suggest that improvisation originally played a large part in such compositions, and that it was desirable to give the poet time to think. But though the form is quasi-dramatic, the subject matter is usually quite the reverse. One of the most curious features of this heathen poetry is the extent to which it seems intended to serve a didactic purpose. *Grímnismál* is a typical in-stance. The story to which it belongs is full of possi-bilities : Odin's visit in disguise to the hall of King Geirrod, where he is bound and tortured between two fires. But all the exciting elements in the situation are deliberately dismissed to prose preface and post-script, and the audience is put off with a tedious dis-quisition by the captive Odin on the homes of the gods, the conditions in Valhalla, and other similar topics. *Alvissmál*, in the same way, starts with a promising situation, and immediately degenerates into a catalogue of synonyms. The different verses in *Hávamál* are all supposed to be uttered by Odin, but they are no more than a collection of proverbs and worldly wisdom. Even the splendid *Völospá* is marred by a long list of dwarfs. But the worst case of all is *Sigdrifumál*, where the newly awakened Brynhild interrupts the romance to treat Sigurd to a lecture on runic charms and a number of quite irrelevant proverbs. Many of these passages, indeed, have not unnaturally been dismissed as interpolations by modern editors, but much of the same sort remains, and in any case the poems must, at some time, before being reduced to writing, have assumed their present form. One is tempted to wonder whether many of the mythological poems did not originally form part of a religious ceremony, where they took the place of a sermon. At any rate, the didactic character of this literature makes it certain that its influence on life and character must have been considerable.

The study of the *Edda* provides a wide field for scholarship. To begin with, as already hinted, the title is a misnomer, and opinions differ as to what it means. The word *Edda* appears as a ἅπαξ λεγόμενον in the poem called *Rigsthula*. It is there the name of a person, and apparently means " great-grand-mother." It has hence been supposed that in giving this name to his mythological and poetic handbook, Snorre meant to confer some such title as *Old Wives' Tales*. Another theory is that Edda is the genitive of Oddi, and that the name *Eddabók* simply means the Book of Oddi, a place in Iceland, on the analogy of the *Flatey Book*, by which name another celebrated manuscript is known. In any case its application to the manuscript containing the older poems is due to a misunderstanding on the part of early commentators.

The date of the poems constitutes another problem. It used to be contended that none of them, in their present form, could be much earlier than the ninth century, when the form of old Norse in which they are composed was believed to have superseded the language used in the oldest runic inscriptions. The argument on which this theory was based has, however, been seriously shaken by the discovery, in 1917, of a stone belonging apparently to a seventh-century grave, covered with runic inscriptions in the language of the poems in question.[1] In any case, the subject matter might easily be of far earlier date than the verses in their present form, and there is much to induce the belief that it is so. As Professor Paasche puts it, " we may conclude from the sure style which the poetry of the *Edda* possesses, that its origin lies far back in time, farther back than any of the poems which are preserved " (*Norsk Litteraturhistorie*, i. 35). The belief of the editors of *Corpus Poeticum Boreale* that the religion with which the poems deal in such detail " was simply a wicking (viking) faith, lasting some three generations at most," is rather difficult to share. An elaborate mythology is not built up in so short a time, or anything like it. Of its essence are monsters like the Fenri wolf and the Midgard serpent, of too primitive a type to be readily associated with a belief originating when the rival force of Christianity was already in the field. In the poem called *Völospá*, and elsewhere, there are mythological allusions almost impossible now to explain with certainty : this tends to show that the original audience had a close familiarity with the myths treated in these verses, which could hardly have been postulated had they been a recent development.

Closely associated with the problem of date is the question of the possibility and extent of Christian influences. On this point there is considerable difference of opinion, ranging from the views of the late Professor Sophus Bugge, who saw traces of Christianity everywhere in the Eddic poems, to those of Professor Paasche, who is disinclined to admit that a clear case of Christian influence can be found anywhere. As the last-named authority points out, however, the more important question, for all except pure mythologists, is whether there are Christian ideas consciously introduced and

[1] Professor Magnus Olsen's description of the inscription on this Eggjum stone, and of the ingenious process of reasoning by which he arrived at its interpretation, is as thrilling as a detective story. The character of the inscription suggests that the earliest use of verse in Norway was in the composition of magic charms.

recognised as such. It may well be, indeed during the viking age with its enthralment of Christian captives it seems likely, that a few such notions crept in. But if at the outset of recorded history these accretions formed part of the accepted creed of heathendom, the question becomes of merely academic interest. Such, whatever its origin, was the religious outlook of the Norwegian when we first come in touch with him. These were the influences which moulded his thought and affected his subsequent development.

It seems safe to say that the religious thought of which these early poems are the expression was not wavering between a half-abandoned paganism and the rival attractions of Christianity. It gives the impression of an age when the old beliefs were sufficiently unchallenged for a jest at the expense of a deity to be free from danger. It is when an old creed is fighting for its life that profanity of this kind becomes a crime. In the year before the official acceptance of Christianity in Iceland, a man was outlawed for some coarse satirical verses at the expense of Freya. In the poem *Lokasenna*, insults quite as serious are heaped on nearly all the gods and goddesses in turn. This playfulness, which in some ways recalls the freedom of some of the miracle plays of mediæval Christianity, seems characteristic of an age which has not to defend its beliefs. A similar frivolity marks many of the tales of Thor : *Thrymskvida*, for example, where the god is dressed up as a bride, and astonishes the expectant bridegroom by his appetite, accounting at a single meal for an ox, eight salmon, three casks of mead, and other delicacies in proportion. *Hymiskvida* is conceived in a similarly comic spirit. *Hárbardsljód*, again, is a most undignified slanging match between Odin and Thor. Altogether, the seriousness of a faith in danger is conspicuously absent. We are in an atmosphere of comfortable, convinced, and careless heathenism.

Some of the supposed instances of Christian influence are undoubtedly heathen and primitive. Odin, for

instance, in *Hávamál,* who " hung on the gallows
tree nine nights long," has nothing whatever to do with
the crucifixion. Sir James Frazer's researches have
carried the idea of the " hanged god " to a very remote
past, and a connection between Odin and the gallows
may be traced as far back as the writings of Procopius.
The very fact that the allusion to Odin's execution is
confined to this one passage in the Eddic poetry indicates
that it was part of a primitive stage of belief which had
been to a great extent forgotten by the time these
poems were composed. But this is not the place to go
more deeply into a question of peculiar interest to the
student of comparative mythology.

Some of the apocalyptic of *Völospá,* on the other hand,
shows curious apparent affinities with Christian sources :

> " I see yet farther,
> And much can tell of
> The doom resistless
> That waits the Powers,
> The gods of triumph.
> Brother with brother
> Shall strive, and slay him,
> And kin with kindred
> In shame be sinning :
> Woe to the world, for
> Whoredom aboundeth,
> An age of axes,
> An age of swords, where
> The shields are shattered,
> A wind-age, wolf-age,
> Ere earth shall perish.
>
> .   .   .   .   .
>
> The sun grows dark, and
> The earth is sinking
> Beneath the ocean :
> Out of the heaven
> The bright stars vanish :
> Smoke rolls, flame rages :
> The high heat reaches
> The very heavens."

But even more probably attributable to Christian influences are the heaven and hell which are to follow :

"I know where a hall stands,
Fairer than sunlight,
Gold-roofed, at Gimle;
There shall the righteous
Dwell and inherit
Bliss everlasting.

. . . . .

I know where a hall stands
Far from the sunlight,
On the coast of corpses,
With door turned northwards:
In by the smoke-vent
Fall drops of venom;
That hall is wattled
Of coils of serpents.
Westward a stream falls
From vales of venom,
With swords and daggers
Its waves are laden;
Its name is 'horror.'
There shall be wading
Its grievous waters
The perjured liar,
And vile assassin,
And all seducers
Of wedded women."

This introduction of moral criteria seems entirely foreign to the ideas of northern paganism. But, indeed, the whole tone of *Völospá*, valuable as it is as a storehouse of heathen mythology in its most advanced stage, is somewhat alien, and unlike contemporary Norwegian thought. This wailing over an age of swords and axes compares rather incongruously with the words used by Egil Uldserk to King Haakon: "I was afraid for a time, while this long peace lasted, that I should die of old age in my bed." There may be something in Professor Paasche's fascinating and ingenious suggestion that *Völospá* may have been the work of a woman.

If, however, there is Christianity in *Völospá*, it is a Christianity so absorbed into orthodox heathen belief as to have become a part of it. The whole plan of the work is to give in poetic form the religious mythology

accepted at the time, from the Creation to Ragnarök.
Thus, like the other poems of the collection, it provides
much material for forming an estimate of the spiritual
and ethical value of the creed on which the founders
of Norwegian civilisation were nursed.   It was, in the
first place, a faith calculated to encourage that virtue
of self-reliance which Norwegians have always so
conspicuously exhibited.   The gods, though appeals
were made to them by prayer and sacrifice (*Hávamál*
tells us that these things are better undone than overdone), are represented as benefiting humanity less by
direct intervention in their affairs than by a ceaseless
and quite independent war against the evil forces of
nature, usually symbolised by the giants.   In this they
set a fine example : though there broods over them the
foreknowledge of final and inevitable defeat, they carry
on the warfare to the last.   As might be expected in a
warlike age, the lot of the brave and successful warrior
is preferable to that of the rest of humanity ;   he alone
is promised a future existence which involves any real
enjoyment, and is accorded an honoured reception in
Valhalla.   Yet the incentive to manliness and courage
is not the mere hope of future reward ;   the warrior's
final honour is to go down fighting desperately in a hopeless battle at the last, when the forces of evil triumph in
the day of Ragnarök—the Doom of the Powers.   The
real incentive is the hope of human renown, finely
expressed in *Hávamál* :

> " Cattle and kin die ;
> Thou diest also :
> One thing I know that
> Never shall perish—
> Fame that each dead man
> Leaveth behind him."

Stevenson in his *Fables* has grasped and effectively
applied the moral of this creed of Ragnarök.   " Odin
was to die, and evil triumph. . . .   ' I wonder if it is
too late to make it up with the devil ? ' said the virtuous
person.   ' Oh, I hope not,' said the priest.   ' And at

any rate we can but try. But what are you doing with your axe ? ' says he to the rover. ' I am off to die with Odin,' said the rover."

More remarkable, perhaps, in a primitive age is the pre-eminence accorded to learning and wisdom. Odin is not an attractive character. It is not surprising that we hear more of prayers addressed to the muscular and human, if occasionally ludicrous, Thor, than to the really inexorable chief of the gods. As the commonness of Thor-names proves, Thor was the god most usually chosen as a *full-trui* or patron, and when that rather unsatisfactory convert to Christianity, Helgi the Lean, was " much mixed in his faith," it was to Thor that we are told he appealed in an emergency. Yet Odin, though condemned by the gods themselves for unfair decision of the ordeal of battle, while a mere mortal, in the *Lay of Helgi Hundingsbane*, calls him " the author of all misfortune," holds an unquestioned pre-eminence. And this is on account of his wisdom. How highly this gift is to be prized is well brought out by the myth in which Odin pays with his eye for a single draught from the spring of knowledge at which the omniscient judge Mimi drinks eternally. The suggestion is that it is worth any sacrifice to win even an infinitesimal share of the inexhaustible fount of learning. The primitive Norseman would have taught that the Tree of Life was well forfeited in exchange for the knowledge of good and evil.

In the ethical wisdom of *Hávamál*, a kind of pagan Book of Proverbs, much the same qualities are held up to admiration. The conditions of life at the time render caution and prudence desirable :

> " Let every doorway,
> Ere a man enter,
> Be scanned and scouted :
> For no man knoweth
> If foes are filling
> The bench beyond it.
> .   .   .   .   .   ;

> Ne'er from his weapons
> Should a man wander,
> Out in the open :
> For no man knoweth
> When, on the highway,
> Spears are of service."

Yet courage and cheerfulness are the best qualities ; it
is no use worrying too much :

> " Best is the life of
> The brave and the bounteous,
> Scant are its sorrows :
> Cowards and cravens
> Tremble for trifles ;
> Aye frets the niggard.
>
> The child of a chief
> Should be sage and silent,
> But bold in battle :
> Gladly and gaily
> All men should bear them,
> Till fate shall find them.
>
> The craven counts that
> His life shall last him
> Who shuns the sword-play ;
> Yet eld shall never
> Accord him quarter,
> Though spears should spare him.
>
> Sleepless the fool frets
> All through the night-time,
> Troubled by trifles :
> Then in the morning
> Rises unrested,
> His cares unconquered."

But though the ethics of *Hávamál* would tend to produce a type of character in many ways attractive and
noble, its morality suits rather a stage of civilisation
where everyone has to fight for his own hand, than the
corporate feeling of a more organised society. It tends
to develop above all things the quality of self-reliance.
This is suggestive when we notice how powerful,

all through Norwegian history, has been the craving
for individual independence, and even for isolation.
Friendship, though valued, is represented as more or
less a matter of giving and receiving presents.

> " Vidrgefendr ok endrgefendr
> Erusk lengst vinir "

(gift and requital make the longest friends). In spite
of the severe condemnation of perjury contained in
Völospá, towards an enemy all methods are legitimate:

> " Hast thou another
> Whom ill thou trustest,
> Yet wouldst get gain of him,
> Fair shalt thou speak him,
> But ponder falsehood,
> Quit lies with lying."

It is not surprising that, though the best qualities
inculcated in this early poetry seem to have exerted
a permanent influence on the spirit of the nation, the
ethics as well as the mythology of the *Edda* passed
speedily out of fashion with the introduction of Christianity and a more centralised and socially organised
Government. The Court verse which replaced it has,
it must be admitted, little to commend it to the taste
of the present day. Almost its only merit in our eyes is
that of being the most nearly contemporary source available for the historical facts which it records. It seems
to have called, indeed, for a high degree of technical
dexterity, which in the best hands could be impressive,
but which soon degenerated into an artificiality to
which few other schools of poetry can show a parallel.
The whole art, as explained by Snorre, and illustrated
by the extant work of the Court poets, seems to consist
in finding the most complicated and roundabout way
of expressing a simple idea. Before speaking of a man,
the sea, wind, fire, gold, or a ship, the skald asked
himself how many intricate and obscure periphrases
(*kenningar*) there might be for each of these common
substantives. The result is, that to find a literary style

resembling that of Norse Court poetry, we must turn
to the reports of prize-fights in the early numbers of
Bell's Life. Probably the reason for the verbiage
employed is the same in both cases. " Smith blacked
Jones' eye, and made his nose bleed, until after some
rounds he succeeded in knocking him out," is felt to be
a bald description which has little to differentiate it
from the account of any other pugilistic encounter.
Equally " the King took his fleet to such and such a
fjord, where he met the enemy and defeated him with
heavy slaughter," could, but for the names of persons
and places, be regarded as common form. Like
Roxane in *Cyrano de Bergerac*, the poet's patron would
probably expect something more ornate. " C'est le
thême ; brodez." So in the one case the reporter tells
how " the Chelsea Chicken " or " Putney Pet," by
skilful use of his " bunch of fives," " tapped the claret "
or " rattled the knowledge-box " of his opponent,
exactly as in the other the King is called " the ring-
dispensing land-warder," his hand " the falcon's perch,"
his ships " leek-horses " (from the fancied resemblance
of the mast to a growing leek), gold " Frodi's meal " or
" Aegi's fire," the sea " Ymi's blood," etc. In the
worst cases, the art of poetry seems degraded to the
level of an acrostic or a rebus.

In other respects also the qualities sought for are
merely technical. To the rules of prosody and the
exigencies of alliteration and metre the skald constantly sacrifices the natural and intelligent order of his
words. Sense is subordinated to sound. The reason for
this decadence is possibly in part that the Court poet
was often called on to prove his skill on a given subject
at a moment's notice. For example, when King Olaf
Tryggvason presents the poet Hallfred Vandraedaskald
with a sword, he directs him to improvise a verse about
it with the word " sword " in every line.[1] In such a
case, genuine poetic inspiration or feeling was out of the

[1] Incidentally, this story seems to destroy the theory of Vigfusson
and York Powell as to the length of the line in Old Norse poetry.

question. A close acquaintance with the laws of verse, a brain well stocked with metaphors and synonyms, great readiness and ingenuity, were the equipment of the skald. He was a juggler with words, and his art was directed to displaying his own cleverness rather than to the expression of real poetic feeling.

There were, of course, exceptional cases where the Court skald produced work of remarkable quality. Especially is this true of memorial verses composed at leisure after the death of a patron, such as Eyvind Skaldaspiller's finely imaginative picture of the reception of the Christian king, Haakon the Good, into the heathen Valhalla. But for the most part the poems which have survived are valuable only as corroboration of historical facts, and have, judged by the taste of the present day, but little literary value.

Simultaneously, however, with the decline of poetry, the Icelanders were developing a most effective and original art of prose narrative. As has been already observed, saga-telling must have originated in Norway, but the special circumstances of the Icelandic colony encouraged and improved the art out of all recognition, till for its culminating excellence Norway can be allowed but little of the credit. The remoteness of the colony freed it from external contaminating influences ; no more original form of prose composition has, therefore, ever been evolved. The one source from which the saga-teller seems to have learnt something is the best of all models for the dramatic presentation of historic truth, the Books of Kings in the Bible. A saga, indeed, is not to every man's taste : treated as a story it frequently strikes a modern reader as lacking construction and continuity of plot. The art involved is far from obvious ; at the first glance, a saga seems often to be a photographic reproduction of the life described, without emphasis, selection, or arrangement. New figures cross the stage, interrupting the apparent thread of the story, with the irrelevance of real life. These characteristics are due to the fact that the earlier sagas aimed at substantial historic or biographical truth, and even the later ones, which were more confessedly fiction, based their style closely on the older models. As a matter of fact, however, abundance of art was needed to coerce the stubborn facts of real life into the mould of an effective story, with but little or no sacrifice of essential truth. There is a great deal of carefully camouflaged arrangement and composition in the best examples of this style.

Great movements are given dramatic emphasis by concentration on a limited number of typical cases. In the Saga of Egil Skallagrimson, for example, the widespread discontent aroused by the policy of Harald Fairhair is expressed by one or two leading characters. Similarly, in the Saga of Olaf the Holy, the conflict between the Crown and the local lendermaend of good family, brought about by the King's appointment of royal officials of mean birth to discharge functions formerly entrusted to the local magnates, affords the leading historical interest of the reign. But the drama is here played out mainly between three outstanding and representative characters. The local aristocracy, at its very best, is personified by Erling Skjalgson, whose enlightened administration of his estates and liberal treatment of his labourers is first described in a picturesque passage. The typical royal official is Thori the Seal, probably an extreme case, " thrall-born on both sides." An important feature of the question, the connection by marriage of many of the noble families, is made vivid and real by the introduction of Erling's nephew, Asbjörn. Many details of the drama in which the collision between the protagonists is brought to a head fall much too pat to be accepted as literal truth. That Asbjörn should arrive at Thori's house exactly at the moment when the low-born official is entertaining the King with a garbled and unfair account of the confiscation of the corn with which Erling had supplied his nephew is hardly credible. That he killed Thori in the royal presence in such a way as to make the King

say that he used the royal knees as a chopping-block
is equally unlikely. So, too, the tableau of Asbjörn's
rescue, where the King, returning from church, passes
through a double line of Erling's warriors to confront
the triumphant nobleman himself, shows evident signs
of artistic composition. Yet the whole story may be
said to be really truer than truth : it brings before the
reader, in an unforgettable form, the essential clash of
interests which characterised this reign. And so fairly
is the story told that it is impossible not to sympathise
almost equally with both protagonists, for each of whom
there was, in fact, much to be said. Only a pedant
will deny that this is genuine and unimpeachable
history, for the modifications of detail do not affect
the accuracy of any of the facts which a modern scientific historian would mention ; but it is history under
the inspiration of a muse. Whether Asbjörn really
used the King's knees as a chopping-block, or whether
Olaf actually found that hedge of steel outside the
church door, is quite irrelevant to the political history
of the period ; but these touches are of the very essence
of dramatic story-telling.

In the greatest of the family sagas there is the same
use of consummate art in the presentation of essential
truth. Njal's saga, for instance, is so dispassionately
told that one can sympathise both with Njal and with
the burners, or some of them. But with all this
apparent absence of partisanship the characters are
delineated in a masterly manner, and the individuality
of each clearly brought out. The fact is, as it seems to
me, that it is a mistake to classify saga as fiction. When,
eventually, foreign romanticism contaminated it, the
style evolved for a different purpose was, indeed,
pressed into the service of fiction, and it has most
clearly influenced, not always for the best, nearly all
modern Norwegian novelists. But it was a style
created for the presentation of historical and biographical narrative, and loses much when we know that
the substance is as consciously invented as the details.

We call, then, for more emphasis, a more connected plot
with a definitely worked-up crisis and *dénouement*.   On
the other hand, if historians would study the sagas and
the historical books of the Bible, and learn from such
models how to breathe the breath of life into the dry
bones of their subject, a real art would revive with no
detriment to education.   It may be true that all these
exciting things did not happen exactly as stated, but
it is equally true that the events on which the scientific
historian concentrates were brought about by living
individuals in action, and it is a method at least as
false and misleading as the older one to eliminate all
life and all excitement merely because the details are
not susceptible of logical proof.   Olaf the Holy was
brought to his death by the action of men such as Kalf
Arneson and Haarek of Tjotta, not by a vague abstrac-
tion called " lendermands opposition."   If history will
only bring this home to us, we can forgive a certain
amount of manipulation of unverifiable details.

With the passing of the saga age the first period
of Norse literature, that composed in the old Norse
language, comes to an end.   Continuity with the most
ancient literary tradition is, however, preserved to a
striking extent in the folk-tales and ballads which the
industry of collectors from the middle of the nineteenth century has succeeded in rescuing before it
was too late.   The literature falling under this category
is in some ways the most interesting and characteristic example of purely national culture which exists.
Here, again, a resemblance to the conditions prevailing
in Ireland and the Highlands of Scotland may be
observed.   During the silent centuries of Danish rule
the peasantry succeeded in maintaining, through oral
tradition, an unbroken connection with the most
ancient types of national literature, while the very fact
that the custodians of this treasure were deficient in
education gave to the songs they sang and the fireside
stories which beguiled the long winter evenings a rich
and uncontaminated racial quality, which renders these

simple compositions of peculiar value to those who would understand the distinctive characteristics of the nation.

The study of folk-culture was, indeed, begun by men who but imperfectly appreciated its real value, with the ulterior object of providing themes through which modern writers could satisfy the taste for romanticism which marked the second quarter of the nineteenth century. Collectors such as Faye, therefore, were at no pains to preserve more than the general lines of the plot, and their sophisticated versions of peasant tales sacrificed, to a deplorable extent, the substance for the shadow. The real pioneers in this *genre* were Jorgen Moe and P. C. Asbjörnsen, who, triumphing over the great difficulty of preserving the essential characteristics of a story told in dialect when translated into a language acceptable to the educated public of their day, revealed for the first time how rich a mine for the student of Norwegian culture had remained unexploited. Since the publication of the collections of these authors the vein has been worked by a number of extremely learned and industrious specialists, but they would be the first to admit that the results of their labours have been the merest gleanings compared with the wealth which Asbjörnsen and Moe gave to a delighted world.

The verse is, on the whole, less interesting than the prose. It shows, for the most part, marked affinities with the ballad literature of other countries, though the subjects treated have in some cases great historic and antiquarian value. The ballads of Heming, for example, carry us back to the days of King Harald Haardraade, and the *Draumkvae* to those of Olaf the Holy, while the latter also shows an evident connection with the *Sólarljód* of the *Edda*. In certain cases, too, the subject-matter of the prose tales is drawn from the storehouse of the remotest past. " The Mill which stands grinding at the bottom of the sea " is the subject of the *Grottasöngr* preserved in Snorre's *Edda*. Similarly, " The Boy who ate in

competition with the Troll" contains reminiscences of
the eating and drinking matches which figure in the
Eddic story of Thor in Utgard. In the very typical
Norse story of "The Smith whom they durst not let
into Hell," the incident of the shoeing of the horse
has much in common with a story told centuries earlier,
in which the part taken by "Our Lord" in the modern
version belonged originally to Odin. But it is rather
in the attitude to life and religion displayed by the
characters that the closest resemblance to ancient
thought is to be seen. Free and frivolous criticism
of the gods is a feature of the Eddic poems to which
attention has already been drawn. In this respect
the similarity of some of the folk-tales is striking. The
nonchalant way in which the smith, in the story above
referred to, addresses both Christ and the devil is one
instance. "Who are you?" says Our Lord to the
smith, who has set up over his forge a placard adver-
tising his supremacy in his art. "Read above the
door," answers the smith. "But perhaps you can't
read writing; if so, you must wait till someone comes
who can help you." But for comparison with such
utterances as "Odin alone is the author of all misfortune" (Helgi Hundingsbane), or Lokasenna's indictment of Odin for unfair decision in battle, the best
example is a passage from "The Lad with the Beer-
keg." "I am Our Lord, and I come from Heaven,"
said the man. "I will not drink with you," said the
lad, "for you make so much difference between people
here on earth, and apportion their rights so unevenly,
so that some grow very rich and some very poor ;
no, with you I will not drink." It seems, then, as if
the viking type which "believed in his own might
and main," and feared neither God nor devil, descended
unmodified through centuries of obscure peasant life
to reappear in the nineteenth century transmitters of
these tales, in which the spirit of the *Edda* still lives
and moves.

Again, as in the old poems, it is the quality of self-

reliant resourcefulness which is emphasised and ex-
tolled. The Norwegian peasant seems to have inherited
unimpaired from his ancestors a reserve of the qualities
making for success in great emergencies, and to have
been subconsciously aware of the fact. It is true that
the successful younger son in the Norse Tales has
superficial elements in common with the folk-lore of
many other countries. But Askelad or Tyrihans has
a native self-confidence based on hidden capacity
which is lacking to his equivalent elsewhere. And it
is noteworthy that his ultimate success owes far more
to his own ingenuity than to the wonder-working
accessories with which he is sometimes provided.
" The Boy who went to the North Wind " is an exception to the general truth of this statement. More
typical is the Askelad who silences the scolding princess
with no better weapons than a dead magpie, a worn-out
boot-sole, and a similar collection of miscellaneous
rubbish. In " The Charcoal Burner " there is a
mixture of astuteness and luck ; in " The Priest and the
Sexton," a Norwegian version of " King John and the
Abbot of Canterbury," the element of luck is absent,
and the sexton triumphs through his own native wit.
Though the accessories used by " The Smith whom
they durst not let into Hell " are three wishes granted
him by " Our Lord," the choice of these wishes is so
independent as to meet with the reproof of St. Peter.
And in the final episode, when he hurls his sledge-
hammer into a chink in the door of Heaven, he is
relying on himself exclusively. In the " Hare-herd-
ing " story there is again a magic accessory which
owes much of its effectiveness to the clever use to
which it is put, and the expedient by which Askelad
escapes in the end is helped by nothing but the boy's
own resourcefulness. " The Small Boys who met the
Trolls in the Hedal Woods " is a further instance of
success achieved without supernatural assistance.
Altogether, the moral of most of these tales seems to
be, " Bide your time, and you will rise to the occasion."

Self-reliance, indeed, seems to be a virtue to which the folk-tales of Norway sacrifice all other morality. The success assigned to deliberate fraud, in such stories as *Peik*, is set down with the moral detachment of the sagas, and seems more closely related to the ethics of *Hávamál* than to the surprising honesty which characterises the Norwegian peasant of modern times. The bad side of the old teaching appears to have been discarded, while the good has been retained. Self-reliance seems to me in fact to be an outstanding characteristic of the race. One of the most striking things about a Norwegian peasant is his ability to turn his hand to anything, and to find a way out of every difficulty. It is this which makes the Norwegian emigrant so uniformly successful. Ibsen, indeed, as is well known, saw the Askelad in his countrymen differently. His Peer Gynt, nurtured on such tales, is always dreaming of unlimited achievement, and invariably failing when tried. But I can only say that neither my experiences of individuals nor the facts of Norwegian history seem to confirm this indictment. The teaching of the traditional folk-lore, and the old literature generally, might doubtless produce either a good or a bad effect. It might lead to vain dreams of bygone glory and an idle self-satisfaction which accomplishes nothing. Or it might, by giving confidence and dwelling on illustrious examples, be an encouragement and a stimulus, and, judged by its results, it seems most frequently, when put to the proof, to have had the latter and better effect.

CHAPTER VII

THE MODERN LITERATURE

In the report of the Departmental Committee on the teaching of English in England (1921) there is a melancholy insistence upon the " divorce between literature and modern life." " We are bound," says the report, " to acknowledge the essential truth . . . that, whatever be the cause, modern literature . . . (1) no longer springs from the life of the people, and (2) is not generally recognised as having any direct bearing upon their life." " We were told that the working classes, especially those belonging to organised labour movements, were antagonistic to, and contemptuous of, literature." Again, " we find . . . an indifference among middle-class persons to the claims of literature even more disheartening than the open hostility which we are told exists among certain circles of working-class opinion."

Nothing of this kind could have been written about Norway at any time during the nineteenth century, and even at the present day it is evident that a demand for good literature is far more widely spread in Norway than in England. When a historical novel of the length and complexity of Sigrid Undset's *Kristin Lavransdatter* not only achieves a *succés d'estime* but commands a sale of thousands of copies, it is clear that there is not much amiss with the taste of the Norwegian public. Where the population is as small, and the language as little known outside the national frontiers as is the case in Norway, we may be sure that the capacity for æsthetic appreciation of which such sales are evidence cannot be restricted to any one class or narrow section of the nation. It is, in fact, noteworthy that the Norwegian author is apparently able to steer almost completely clear of " pot-boiling." " Shockers " and detective stories to be seen on Norwegian bookstalls, or running as *feuilletons* in the daily papers, are practically all imported wares, mainly translations from English. The author with literary

pretensions seems to leave what we should call
"popular" writing severely alone. This, of course,
is not due to independence of financial considerations.
In fact, a brilliantly written criticism of American
literary standards which recently appeared in *Samtiden*
suggests the thought that true literature flourishes best
where it cannot be heavily bribed to prostitute its
ideals. The career of even the most successful Norwegian writers has usually entailed a hard struggle.
The fact noticed is rather evidence of the existence of
an exceptionally cultivated taste among the reading
public. In a democracy like Norway, the fact that a
grant of public money has frequently been voted for
the support of authors shows, in spite of the disparaging remarks of disappointed applicants and their
supporters, the high value set upon literature by
the nation as a whole.

The excellence of the national taste is also shown
by the state of the Norwegian daily press. A newspaper depends so much on its circulation that it may
be assumed that the public gets the press which it
desires—and deserves. Many, if not all, of the newspapers of Norway provide a most refreshing contrast
to those of most other countries, including some of our
own. Instead of staring headlines and a chaotic mass
of sensational tit-bits, they provide deep and thoughtful
articles on literary, historic, and scientific subjects,
as well as political, written by eminent professors and
other distinguished authorities. In fact, the principal
Norwegian dailies are models of all that a discriminating
public would demand. There are, in fact, few peoples
among whom there has been a closer interplay between
popular thought and literary production, and, this being
so, the literature of modern Norway calls emphatically for consideration among the forces which have
affected, and are still affecting, national development.

It has probably been to the advantage of literary
Norway that the population of the country is so small,
and the language and subject-matter of its writers so

little understood in other lands. There has been no temptation to seek the limited admiration of a clique ; the Norwegian author is almost compelled by circumstances to be " aut Cæsar aut nullus," a force in the development of his nation, or altogether ignored. For there are two more or less conflicting conceptions of the province of literature, and especially poetry, which may be roughly classified as the artistic and the prophetic. We have on the one hand the writer whose aim is admittedly limited to the production of works of intrinsic beauty, calculated to appeal merely to a restricted circle of æsthetically qualified readers, who neither achieves nor appears to desire a wider popularity, nor attempts to exert any effective influence upon the thought and ideals of his age. This æsthetic or artistic view of their function seems to be that which is most widely held by authors with literary pretensions in England at the present day ; to be " popular " is regarded as a reproach, and consequently our writers frequently approximate to the type satirised by Father Knox in his amusing symposium *Sanctions* : "All were literary men, but all wrote the kind of literature you did not read unless you yourself were literary."

In sharp contrast with this theory is another which regards literary talent as something which, like other human faculties, is best employed in the service of humanity as a whole, or at least of the particular race to which the author belongs. The primary purpose of the highest literature, according to this view, is to influence the mind and actions of the reader ; fine prose or melodious verse is, like rhetoric, a way of uttering in a peculiarly impressive or attractive form some message which requires to be delivered. The poet speaks in poetry because only so can he stir the heart as deeply as he wishes ; but the message is the important matter, the form is only secondary.

This second conception of the author's function is that which would have found general acceptance all down the ages ; the author of the present day who deliberately addresses himself to a limited coterie is doubtless influenced by considerations which are entirely modern, a revulsion against commercialism, and a confusion of thought which leads him to feel that because some popularity is attained by a prostitution of art therefore all popularity is to be shunned as an evil in itself. In Norway, at any rate down to a very recent period, a healthier tradition seems to have been established and maintained. In this respect the old models set a good example : in prose, the saga, a tale told in plain language to a mixed audience round an Icelandic or Norwegian fireside ; in poetry, the Eddic verses, celebrating the deeds of gods and heroes, or expounding the national religion of their day, followed by the court verse of the skalds, who served, indeed, an individual patron, but who would have failed in their primary object of adding to his renown unless their work had been capable of being appreciated by the populace as a whole.

However this may be, there can be no doubt that what I have called the prophetic theory of literature has prevailed to a remarkable extent in Norway, at any rate throughout the nineteenth century. Two major prophets, Henrik Wergeland and Björnstjerne Björnson, divided the century between them : the activity and industry of each was boundless, and their influence deep and enduring. But, though outstanding examples, they were not isolated instances.

The rest of literary Norway was also among the prophets. " In the whole Norwegian literary fleet," writes Björnson in a celebrated essay, " not a single pleasure-boat ; even yonder madcap has his appointed mission. There is always something which he will free us from, or which he wishes us to attain. He, too, feels himself enlisted in the service of the fatherland, more strictly every day. Norwegian literature professes in its works that it will take its share, the greatest share, of the common responsibility."

That this characteristic of Norwegian literature has

been to the advantage of the community can hardly be disputed. We have often spoken of the independence of the Norwegian character, but the national patriotism of which this quality is a cause is not its only, or even its most natural expression. In every democracy there is, at any rate in its early stages of development, a tendency to parochialism, an inability on the part of the masses to grasp big ideas, or to interest themselves in matters outside the ambit of their immediate daily experience. Here is a serious danger, and one with which schoolmaster, journalist, priest, and politician are to some extent impotent to deal. The schoolmaster's influence ceases before those whom he educates are personally confronted with these large issues ; the priest can do something, but his voice is confined within the building in which his pulpit stands, and we cannot expect an inspiring or enlightened handling of great themes in every country parish. The politician, if he is to secure election, must to some extent conform, if he does not pander, to the views and prejudices of his constituents ; the press, too, must give its public what that public wants. The literary genius alone, in a country where a taste for good literature is widely developed and forms, as in Norway, an element in the life of the people, can hope to impress upon a large circle of readers thoughts and ideals in advance of those which they already possess. For a good author, in such a country, will be read for his intrinsic merits even where he is disagreed with : the unpalatable truths he has to offer are covered by his art as a pill with jam, and will be swallowed with beneficent results. It is for this reason, one may remark in passing, that the " divorce between literature and modern life " in England, alluded to at the beginning of this chapter, must be regarded with the most serious misgivings.

For the first few decades after the national self-realisation which followed the work of the Eidsvold Assembly, Norwegian writers expended their energies on natural and unanimous expressions of the popular enthusiasm. There was, in fact, no distinct Norwegian literature ; there were writers who were Norwegians, but their spiritual home was still in Denmark. As early as 1772, indeed, when the *Norske Selskab* was founded, there had been rivalry between Norse and Danish authors, but they sat cheek by jowl, writing the same language and applying similar literary standards, in the coffee-houses of Copenhagen. These standards were hardly calculated to develop any very striking results. The heroic drama, as developed in France by Corneille and Racine, had penetrated to Denmark through Germany, especially during the vogue of Klopstock, and had fallen in this process of migration to a wretched blend of artificiality and bombastic sentiment. A prize offered for an original Danish tragedy was won, in 1772, by a Norwegian, Johan Nordahl Brun, with *Zarine*, a piece which, though it was enthusiastically received, exhibited these defects in an unusually marked degree. It was immediately followed by the well-known burlesque, *Kjaerlighed uden Strömper* ("Love without Stockings"), by another Norwegian, Johan Herman Wessel. This brilliant bit of fooling, which recalls in some respects "The Rovers" in the *Anti-Jacobin*, though the school against which it was directed is long since extinct, has sufficient intrinsic humour to delight audiences even at the present day. The tragic conflict between the claims of love and honour is here brought about by the tailor-hero's lack of a pair of stockings suited for the wedding, which his sweetheart, under the influence of an ominous dream, insists must take place that very day. In these circumstances the hero is driven to steal from his rival, and on the discovery of the lapse the whole cast commit suicide. Every character strives, under ludicrous circumstances, to conform to the conventions of heroic behaviour, and to express himself in sonorous Alexandrines. Every lapse on the part of the hero is ascribed to Fate, thus :

MADS. The Devil tempted him.
GRETE.   How dare you, sir, traduce
  Heroic natures thus ?   Learn, then, for future use,
  It is the hand of Fate, when heroes turn to evil,
  Only the vulgar herd goes wrong and blames the Devil.

But this merry travesty is one bright spot in a rather
dreary mediocrity. Even after the separation from Denmark in 1814, little was produced in the earlier years of
a higher level than spirited patriotic songs of the type
of Nordahl Brun's *For Norge, Kjaempers Födeland*,[1] and
Bjerregaard's melodious and stirring *Sönner af Norge*.
It was, in fact, necessary to wait for the renaissance until
the first generation of students at Christiania University
had come to man's estate. But the change was not long
delayed, and appropriately enough the protagonist in the
cause of Norwegian literary independence was nurtured
at Eidsvold.

Among the more prominent defenders of Norwegian
liberty and independence at the Congress of 1814 was a
priest named Nicolai Wergeland. From a date shortly
after the union with Sweden he had come to live in the
neighbourhood of his political exploits as rector or
vicar of Eidsvold. His son, Henrik Arnold, developed
at an unusually early age a promising literary talent,
in fact, he had appeared in print before his fourteenth
year. In his student days he established himself in a
position of leadership among his contemporaries, and
it was perhaps not without influence upon his nascent
political views that he was himself subjected to the
violence of the military at the notorious *Torveslag*, or
Battle of the Market-Place (see p. 106), of 1829. His
generous instincts expanded as he grew up into a deep
sympathy for humanity, coupled with an engaging love
of nature and animals, and a passionate love of liberty
which naturally found its chief expression in enthusiasm
for the lately won emancipation of his country. In one
of his finest poems, *Följ Kaldet* (" Follow the Call "),
Wergeland's philosophy is developed in a clear train of

---

[1] This particular song was in fact written much earlier.

thought. With his conception of the poet's vocation, he is at first deeply depressed by the limitations imposed upon him by race and language. How few will hear his message to humanity!

> " Royal eagle, captive made,
> Broken-winged, with fettered limb,
> He that twenty years and more—
> Since the shot that crippled him—
> Plies the humble watch-dog's trade
> By a lonely cottage door,
> Cannot know
> All the wretched poet's woe,
> Of a little nation born,
> In a spot remote, forlorn,
> With a speech
> Which can never further reach
> Than the uttered breath may go.
> He is like a bell men hush,
> Muffled close in clammy folds,
> Like the rose's radiant bush
> Which a covering basket holds." . . .

But, after all, the world, like his nation, is still in its infancy, and the modifying processes of nature, though slow, and exercised through apparently insignificant agencies, are very sure :

> " Young as yet the world must be ;
> All our tedious history
> Still is but its cradle-song,
> And its childhood's fairy-tale.
> Creatures of the prime prevail ;
> Megasaurs in forests sleep,
> Jonah's monster haunts the deep,
> Giant serpents, vast and strong,
> Wastes, a thousand miles along,
> Thousands o'er,
> Thundering with the lion's roar,
> Mock our busy human ways :
> Mountains, as in Noah's days,
> Undecayed,
> Still their splintered peaks parade ;
> Not a sign is yet revealed
> That to earth at last that shoulder
> Down shall moulder,

To create a fruitful field.
Nay, but mark yon mountain rude
Glittering like a crystal clear
Where the precipice falls sheer,
Heavenly blue or violet-hued :
What that Alpine horn has ploughed,
Smoothed its flank and polished bright,
Piece by piece and grain by grain ?
Drops of rain :
Just the gentle touch of white
Atom-woven cloaks of cloud,
Plumes upon the helm of mist.
What has ground the rock to sand,
Washed away the ruddy schyst,
Till the heaps beneath expand,
Purer, whiter, at the base ?
Yonder lake's soft liquid round,
Yonder ocean's measured pace,
Lapping billows, blithely curled,
Ever in a stir profound,
Like the breathing of a world.
While in summer time the moss,
Through millenniums long to tell,
Tiny silver cups will toss
On the crag's grey, barren shell,
Till in scattered bloom at last
Lofty pines are rooted fast."

Above all, none of the formative energy of nature seems
to be wasted :

" There is nothing, great or small,
Nothing fruitless, no decay,
There is purpose in its fall,
Howso vaguely cast away ;
Fallen dews,
Steaming up in sunny heat,
In the cloud's wide bosom meet,
Like a veil that flutters gay,
Woven but of blossom-hues ;
And the slender downy flakes
Spun by ancient willow trees,
Busy as the wife who makes
Wraps against a winter's day,
Drift not lost adown the breeze ;
For the ant, where'er they come,
Draws them thence to make his home."

And in all this there is encouragement for the poet, even though he appears to be but a voice crying in the wilderness :

" Must the poet's word, the pure
    Dew of light's own sparks, that start
Warm as blood from out his heart,
Here, where all things else endure,
Unremembered and untraced
Disappear and run to waste ?
Up !   If God's own voice invest
With a storm thy heaving breast :
Cry aloud in desert ways,
And the dawn of better days
From the dark thy word shall raise.
Up !   If hands that sweep the string
To the sound of noble lays
Radiant light in darkness fling.
From that little rugged crowd,
Inarticulate and cowed,
Some shall yet—like Lapps who dwell
On a wild and stony fell,
Called by sight of flames afar
From the hovel where they are—
Hasten where the bard afire
Tunes the sinews of his lyre,
And when next he lifts his gaze
There his scanty audience stays,
Serves his ends,
He will crave no longer now
Thronging millions ranged below,
Just a little band of friends."

Wergeland's poetic gifts, rendered original by a frequently too unrestrained imagination, degenerating sometimes into extravagance, soon endeared him to the more independent patriots of his country.   His singular originality of style and fancy marked him in their eyes as the personification of Norse as opposed to Danish literary expression.   So far as the feelings they entertained were confined to admiration for his prolific muse, this was right and proper.   Unfortunately, his appearance was made the occasion for an outburst of narrow nationalism, which scouted everything external or imported, and repudiated in doing so all established canons of literary criticism. Contrasted with his adherents, the poet himself had wide and even inconsistent sympathies, which were by no means confined within the limits of the national frontier. Though he inherited from his father a hatred of Denmark, he warmly approved of the union with Sweden. With democratic convictions which put him out of court with the official class, he contrived to reconcile an admiration for Carl Johan amounting almost to worship. Probably he overlooked the monarch in the self-made product of the French Revolution. By the Revolution, indeed, he was fundamentally inspired, but this did not prevent him from feeling the deepest affection for England. In this he went so far as to execute a metrical translation of that most insular of all national songs, "Rule, Britannia!" Of eccentricity he could well be accused, but hardly of narrow-mindedness. Indeed, what are probably his finest poems were written to champion the cause of the excluded Jews against his own countrymen. At the same time, his genius distinctly bade defiance to the critical standards of those who would fit all artistic work into existing categories, and Wergeland was therefore identified with the revolt against Danish taste by friends and opponents alike. The poet, therefore, soon became the bone of contention between the exponents of two distinct literary creeds.

The leader of the opposition, himself an unusually gifted poet and distinguished critic, was Johan Sebastian Welhaven. At the present day we are in a position to sympathise impartially with both antagonists, and to feel that there was plenty of room for both. Welhaven, in his way, was just as enthusiastic a patriot as Wergeland ; he merely objected to his countrymen making fools of themselves in the eyes of the outside world. He was perfectly right to insist, as he did, that Norway should not cut herself off from contact with the older culture of other lands. Honey, he urged, was no less sweet, and no less the product of a particular hive, because the bees had gathered their material outside the narrow limits of their owner's garden. Had Wergeland not been identified, by the undiscriminating enthusiasm of his supporters, with the school of thought which his opponent abhorred, it is probable that the latter would have been less blind to his merits. As it was, he looked upon him as a conceited, overrated, provincial charlatan, and the result was a literary war in which the whole of the educated community joined in a state of wild excitement. The first shot took the form of a satirical poem, published anonymously by Welhaven, in which he thus addressed his popular antagonist :

> "How long will you indulge in senseless raving,
> In crazy brandishing of Quixote's spear ?
> See how, for all your airy wings a-waving,
> Straight for a bottomless morass you steer.
> The sun you seek is wildfire of the bog ;
> A crawling eft the Pegasus you flog." . . .

The " marsh " metaphor of this stanza was later made by Wergeland the subject of a graceful defence in the well-known *Address to Collett* from the Radical paper, *Statsborgeren,* which the poet edited :

> "I send you greeting ; but to-day
> ' A marsh ' they call me, as before,
> The folk who jostling edge their way
> Within your foeman's door.
>
> There was a toad, the clumsy brute,
> Hopped from us once to trouble you ; [1]
> ' Marsh ' is a name that seems to suit ;
> Well, I suppose it's true.
>
> Yes, ' marsh ' ; yet wholesome herbs are found,
> If somewhat bitter, by its rim ;
> Like Venus when she bathes, around
> The water-lilies swim.

---

[1] An allusion to a personal attack on Collett which appeared in the paper under an earlier editorship.

> There stalks the heron proud, and holds
>   A speckled serpent in his bill ;
> While unimagined peace enfolds
>   That wildness hushed and still.
>
> And round, in glittering reeds and high,
>   Their magic harps the fairies tune ;
> And there full many a song must die,
>   Too fair to die so soon." . . .

Welhaven returned to the charge with a stinging but amusing essay, wherein Wergeland's claims as a poet were challenged in detail. The victim certainly was not invulnerable ; the floods of his fancy entirely refused to be confined in recognised channels ; the versification, though remarkably melodious at its best, was often loose and careless, the imagery crude with a frequent tendency to bathos. His most ambitious work especially, *Creation, Humanity, and Messiah,* an epic drama of portentous length, written at a feverish pace, teems with extravagances and lapses from taste of which the hostile critic could not fail to make effective use, though his attack is marred by unfair selection, and is distinctly one-sided. The poet's father replied with a tamer but well-reasoned rejoinder, in which he protested against the Procrustean standards which rejected everything which could not be fitted into the accepted classification. In 1834 Welhaven enlarged the scope of his attack. In *Norges Daemring* (" The Dawn of Norway ") he turned from Wergeland himself to criticise the national literary ideals which he represented. The poem takes the form of a sonnet sequence, though the style is more reminiscent of Byron's *Don Juan* than of the kind of versification which we ordinarily associate with a sonnet. In particular he inveighs against the prevalent literary exclusiveness which looked upon external influences as contamination :

> " Mid this world's realms you set your country high—
>   But ah, what glory or what might is there,
>   When all the time it needs a nurse's care,
>   Like a sick baby or a schoolgirl shy ?

That vaunted independence that you prize,
What is it built on if, to your despair,
You find the land's digestion cannot bear
The food the culture of the world supplies ?

Why, you are frightened lest a foreign taste
May stamp our people with an alien mark,
Effacing all that's special to the nation :

But surely this anxiety is based
On nothing worse than nightmares of the dark :
Some parables, by way of illustration." . . .

This is followed by the metaphor of the bees, seeking
the material for their honey far and wide, of which
mention has already been made.

The poem was received with execration, and some
copies were actually burnt on the 17th of May, at the
instigation of Wergeland's father. But the reading
public was by this time divided into two keenly
opposed camps. At the production of Wergeland's
play, *Campbellerne*, in 1837, the Welhaven party made
an ill-advised attempt at organised disturbance, which
resulted in a free fight in which the dramatist's supporters were victorious.

This was the hour of Wergeland's triumph. For the
moment it was short-lived. In 1839, having accepted
a pension from the King, he was regarded by many as
a renegade, and lost much of his popularity. Hard
times were now in store for him, but he continued with
the utmost courage to produce poems, some of which
are now regarded as among his finest efforts. In 1840,
having obtained a position in the Public Record Office,
he produced his *Constitutional History of Norway*,
which, *pace* the *Encyclopædia Britannica*, is by no
means "forgotten." *The English Pilot* is a poem from
this period of special interest to this country. Much of
it is very beautiful, though it is marred here and there
by the introduction of supposedly English phrases which
cannot but strike us as ludicrous.

In 1844 Wergeland fell ill, and in the following year
he died. His output remained wonderful to the last,

and many judges regard his death-bed poems as his best work. One of these, *Til min Gyldenlak* ("To my Wallflower"), has been repeatedly translated into English, the best version being that by Sir Edmund Gosse. The finest of all, which is actually entitled *Paa Sygeleiet* ("On the Bed of Sickness"), is but ineffectively represented in a translation, but I am tempted to try an inadequate version of one or two stanzas, which may at least call attention to the undefeated courage of the dying and forsaken poet :

> "That stab of flame, this icy thrill
> That shudders through my breast,
> Are these death's triumph ? Nay, they bring
> Wafts of the variable spring
> That opes in heaven, now hot, now chill,
> The April of my rest.
>
> .   .   .   .   .   .   ;
> Yes, to this barren loneliness
> Driven by my country's ban,
> By raging fools, who little guess
> How glorious here the woods are grown,
> Where I have dwelt, like cage-bird flown,
> Or ranging Indian.
>
> Brazil's inviolate forest, where
> Majestic palm-trees tower,
> Whose stems the gay camellias twine,
> Mingled with azure passion-flower,
> Has naught to show so proud, so fair,
> As this lone haunt of mine."

Wergeland's reputation has not merely survived him : he is now to Norwegians what Burns is to the Scotsman —an object of perhaps almost too undiscriminating worship. He, rather than Ibsen, who criticised and misrepresented his compatriots, or Björnson, who is too recently dead for political antipathies to have become quite extinguished, is now *the* national poet of Norway. At his best he is fully worthy of his position ; his faults were a too unbridled fancy and a fatal fluency which effectually precluded him from maintaining his highest level. His output was prodigious ; besides poetry of all kinds, it includes history, tracts, speeches, tragedies, and farces, and no man could possibly maintain a worthy standard in all these branches of literature. But as a dominant figure whose influence is great and growing, and a representation of one side of the Nationalist movement in literature, he deserves attention, more especially since his merits have in this country been unrecognised or undervalued.

His rival, Welhaven, survived him by many years; indeed, he did not die until 1873. But from 1868 he was prevented by illness from working, and his best verse belongs to the romantic movement which affected literature in Norway during the second quarter of the nineteenth century. An element of romance attached to his earlier feuds as well, since Wergeland's sister Camilla, best known as Camilla Collett, herself an authoress of distinction and a pioneer of the feminist movement, fell in love with him, playing the part of Juliet to the Wergeland-Welhaven Montagu and Capulet, though, alas! her Romeo was unresponsive. When at last the poet had to cease his labour, the students of Christiania honoured him with a torch-light procession, and Björnson complimented him in some of his most graceful verses:

> " Smilest thou not at the end ?
> Thou who through winter didst nurse
> Spring's coming verse.
> Light that thy courage did lend,
> Tears that bedewed it in gloom
> Brought it to bloom :
> Till to thy shoulder it came,
> Filling thine arm,
> Wreathing with roses thy name,
> Crowning thy poesy's magic and charm."

So far as poetry is concerned, the interval between these earlier masters and the arrival of Björnson and Ibsen in the second half of the century was occupied by the vogue of Andreas Munch, whose gentle fluency calls for no special observations at the present day.

This middle period of the nineteenth century marks also the date when the language-reform movement (see Chapter VIII) was started by Ivar Aasen, and when the folk-tales of Asbjörnsen and Moe were first published. It was the time of the passing of the old officialdom and the coming into power of the democracy, so that the hitherto neglected *bonde* now came into his own, and began to be recognised as the real representative of the country as a whole. The taste for romanticism which characterised the period assisted the movement, but had not, I think, quite so much to do with it as is sometimes asserted.

The wave of romanticism, which about this time overran many parts of Europe, was never, as it seems to me, completely acclimatised in Norway. Its appearance there was rather a temporary symptom of the triumph of the tastes of Welhaven and his school. It hardly lasted long enough to form a phase in the literary development of the nation. The influence of Grundtvig, the Danish preacher, poet, and educationalist, is more clearly to be traced in the revival of the second half of the century than that of a mere literary fashion. But Grundtvig's dream of a great popular renaissance, inspired by the historical traditions of the past, which he regarded as the guiding spirit of the North, had a wide appeal mainly because of the special circumstances of the political situation. It was a stimulating time. The attitude of Sweden, combined with the Scandinavianism of Conservatives in Norway, made the cause of the country one with that of her growing democracy. The inspiration of national patriotism reinforced and hallowed that of political Liberalism. All who had powers of expression found great themes to their hands and a growing band of eager and enthusiastic listeners. The problems of the day afforded opportunities to poetry, the drama, and the prose of fiction, and with characteristic versatility most of the Norwegian authors of the period availed themselves of all these modes of expression in turn.

Versatility, as has been elsewhere pointed out, seems of the very essence of the national character. It is true, in a different and better sense than that in which Ibsen meant it, that his countrymen are " a little bit of everything." This characteristic seems doomed to pass away in other departments of life with the progress of industrialism, and at the present day there seems to be slightly more specialisation, even in literature, than was formerly common. Throughout the nineteenth century, however, the Norwegian author, in the majority of cases, made all literature his province, besides exerting a considerable influence upon the political and social life of his age. This is a very distinctive trait in Norwegian writing. With us, with few exceptions, a novelist is a novelist, a playwright a playwright, and a poet a poet. To find any of these taken seriously as a politician, without losing his reputation as an author, would surprise us extremely. In Norway it is all the other way. Of examples we have almost an *embarras de richesses*. Wergeland's fluency in a vast variety of modes of expression has already been mentioned. Jorgen Moe was a fine lyric poet as well as a collector of folk-tales. Ivar Aasen supported the claims of his *landsmaal* not merely by direct advocacy and the compilation of his grammar and dictionary, but by writing both poetry and plays, and though the best of the latter, *Ervingen*, shows few traces of dramatic talent, much of his verse is of high quality. The novelists Lie and Kielland both made excursions into drama. Vinje, the *maalstrever*, was lecturer, journalist, and poet. Garborg, another great representative of the *landsmaal*, combined with the art of fiction much political and polemical writing, at least one successful play, and a most impressive sequence of eerie poems—*Haugtussa*. Ibsen, of course, was at home both in prose and verse. But the most striking instance of the quality to which I have referred is the Wergeland of the second half of the century, Björnstjerne Björnson.

There can be no doubt that to those who are considering the literature of Norway mainly in relation to the life and thought of the people the work of Björnson is of greater importance than that of his great rival and contemporary, Ibsen. It would be difficult to find a more fundamental contrast than is presented by these two outstanding figures of modern Norwegian literature. Ibsen was a disillusioned and incurable pessimist ; Björnson an irrepressible optimist. The difficulties and obstacles in the path of national progress which daunted the one, had a merely stimulating effect on the other. While Björnson was never so happy as when he was in the thick of things, Ibsen was temperamentally a recluse. While Ibsen's constitutional despondency spread from despair over his countrymen to torturing misgivings as to his own call, Björnson was never troubled by any lack of confidence either in himself or the national destiny. Ibsen therefore plied the rod with the joyless conscientiousness of a schoolmaster ; Björnson whirled the shillelagh and looked everywhere for heads to crack with the light-hearted combativeness of an Irishman at a fair. The fact that he found a far greater variety of objects of attack than his rival never dimmed his unwavering faith in his country's future.

The difference between the two men is well illustrated by their attitude to the history of Norway. To Björnson the past was a perpetual source of hope and encouragement. His message to his generation is continually reinforced with historical allusion. The nation was to him a living organism to which the past belonged equally with the present. In his earliest period, and to some extent later also, he deliberately emphasised this continuity of new and old by producing alternately, and, indeed, almost simultaneously, his sketches of contemporary peasant life, written in a style admittedly modelled upon that of the sagas, and dramas in which the characters of history were made to render up to a later generation the eternal ideas for which they stood. This conception of history is revealed in Björnson's partiality for Sverre, revolutionary, reformer, and king, whom he called his spiritual ancestor, and to whom also he compared the *bonde* leader, Ueland. It is also clearly stated in the creed he professed in his poem, *En Sangers Kall* :

> "A poet's calling is the seer's,
>   And most in times of birth and need,
> When over men who fight and bleed
>   His faith the bright ideal rears :
> *Now ancient champions round him stand*
> *Now from the new his host is manned.*"

To Ibsen, on the other hand, the past was a dead thing, the continued preservation of which was a sign of insane self-deception and a danger to the community. Even in so early and melodramatic a work as *Fru Inger* this note is struck in the opening words, and in the epic draft which eventually developed into the poetic drama, *Brand*, it is stated explicitly :

> "The sickness has begun.   A corpse I see,
>   Monstrous, as where an Ymi's carcase lying
> Wafts its infection over shore and lea,
>   A plague whereof both high and low are dying.
>   .   .   .   .
> Madman, bring out your dead, no more conceal it,
>   As Harald did his Snefrid's corpse bestow ;
> The heart is stilled, think not, like him, to feel it
>   Beat 'neath the shroud, or see the cheeks aglow.
>
> That which is dead, no lying may restore it,
>   That which is dead must down to darkness go :
> One task alone the dead can have before it,
>   To enrich a soil from which new seed may grow."

There is, in addition, in these two men, something suggestive of the conflicting ecclesiastical ideals of the preaching friar and the solitary hermit. That all-pervading national trait, the passion for independence exhibited by Norwegians all through their history, affected Björnson and Ibsen in curiously different ways. In the former, the ideal it fostered was that of freedom for Norwegian democracy achieved by solidarity. The *samlings-tanke*, the idea of union, permeated all his thought. He was, indeed, pronouncedly patriotic and nationalist, from his first public appearance, when he led an organised disturbance in the theatre to protest against the importation of Danish performers, to the dissolution of the union with Sweden, but all the same he could contemplate larger combinations—a Scandinavia of independent parts, but united in the face of Europe, and ultimately a Pan-Teutonic League, including, oddly enough in the light of later events, both Germany and England.

In Ibsen, on the other hand, the instinct for independence shrivelled to a narrow individualism. His ideal was *Athanasius contra mundum*, or Doctor Stockmann, in *En Folkefiende*, finding freedom and strength at last in complete isolation from his fellows. While his rival was binding the masses of Norway together with the spell of his matchless eloquence, Ibsen, in Rome, a shy and embittered recluse, was working out his own salvation in fear and trembling. In this metaphor of the anchorite, indeed, the truth goes deeper than at first sight appears. Ibsen had about him a good deal of the temperament of a flagellant. Sometimes unconsciously, but not infrequently, I think, consciously, he rains his blows upon a form easily recognisable as his own. In *Kongs-emnerne*, the protagonists, the confident and triumphant King Haakon and the hesitating, doubt-tortured Duke Skule, are admittedly symbols for Björnson and himself. Again, " it is certain," he writes in 1870, " that by self-analysis I brought to light many of both Peer Gynt's and Stensgaard's qualities." The home surroundings which are responsible for the development of Peer Gynt are confessedly autobiographical, while Brand, whom the author claimed as himself in his best moments, is merely Peer Gynt reversed in the artist's

mirror. But other cases are nearly as clear. We see
him in Fru Inger, shrinking at the magnitude of her
single-handed task of rallying the country ; and later
in Solness, the architect, his heaven-reaching spires
and pinnacles abandoned for the task of " making
homes for human beings," just as the author relin-
quished his ambitions of national regeneration for his
later social dramas, sighing in final disillusionment,
" this building homes for human beings is not worth a
halfpenny." We meet him again in the lonely Borkman,
deserted and shunned, brooding over all he might have
accomplished :

BORKMAN. It was a dreamland, we looked out over then.
ELLA. Our life's dreamland, yes. And now that land is covered
with snow. And the old tree is dead.

He reappears in Rubek, the sculptor of *Naar vi döde
vaagner*, whose portrait busts have behind the " striking
likeness " the beast faces with which his fancy endows
them, the man who has promised his Maja the kingdoms
of the world and the glory of them, as Solness promised
Hilde a kingdom and a palace. A desire to preclude
misunderstanding alone prevents one from indicating
many other characters in which the model, intentionally and cruelly distorted it may be, yet remains recognisable through all attempts at disguise.

It was, indeed, inevitable in one who thus shut himself away from the society of his fellow-men that he
should become introspective and self-analytic, and in
the failings of which he thus became conscious see
national characteristics. Like an artist who is out of
touch with models, he drew from his own reflection,
and it was inevitable, however much he differentiated
his characters, that a family likeness should remain.
Ibsenites, indeed, protest with great plausibility that
the characters of his plays are strongly individualised,
but no one who reads them without prejudice can, I
think, help feeling a kind of composite portrait or
common type emerging. The worst of it is, and it is

this delusion which I specially wish to dispel, that many persons here in England identify this morbid, inhuman apparition with the typical Norwegian. Now I have never found in any native of that country anyone who was not almost the antithesis of the type presented by Ibsen's plays, and having inquired diligently and impartially from both Norwegians and Englishmen who have had opportunities of judging, I am glad to find my impression universally confirmed. The fact is that the grim ghost which haunts these plays is the spirit of the author.

When that is said and grasped, there remains an enormous amount to which we can yield unqualified admiration. In effectiveness of construction and realism of dialogue Ibsen is unrivalled. Even in the early and melodramatic *Fru Inger* all the old tricks of the trade have been mastered, though the new and original have not so far been evolved. In the *Doll's House* the essential difference between male and female mentality is so searchingly observed, and the plot so dramatically developed, that the impossible *naïveté* of the heroine, after many years of married life, however her husband may have treated her, passes almost unnoticed. So, too, it must be conceded that both *Peer Gynt* and *Brand* are masterpieces of poetic drama, however unjust the application intended by the author. Brand, indeed, though his relentlessly consistent application of the maxim, " Nothing or everything," would be even more disastrous in real life than it proves in the play, is a really noble and sublime figure, of the stuff of which martyrs are made. In the field of historical drama too, *Kongs-emnerne* stands extraordinarily high. With regard to the later social dramas, I confess to a feeling that the technical excellence of the dialogue and construction produces an effect as incongruous as the introduction of a troop of goblins into a suburban parlour. The setting is unapproachably realistic ; the action belongs to a world of dream or nightmare. A commonplace fellow like Ekdal, the photographer, destroys the atmosphere in which we are prepared to accept symbolic rabbit-shooting in the attic. Set to music of a De Bussy type, even *Naar vi döde vaagner* might be impressive, but these resurrections seem out of place in the Norse equivalent for a hydro. The upshot of it all is that Ibsen must be admired as a unique and cosmopolitan genius, who may not be measured by the standard of ordinary mortals, but that he is by no means a national type, and that in considering Norwegian literature as an expression of the life of the people, and an influence upon it, we are justified in turning our attention rather to his great contemporary, Björnson.

Björnson best expressed himself as an orator and as a poet. He was primarily a great personality, charged with big ideas, and the effect of such a personality is best felt when its possessor addresses his public directly. The dramatist or the story-writer must, to a great extent, sink his own individuality ; he must let his characters convey his message, and if, as in many of the works of Mr. Bernard Shaw, they speak as replicas of the author, they become mere puppets, while if, on the other hand, they are realistically portrayed and differentiated, the message loses in directness and often in clarity. The gifted orator and inspired poet forgoes his most telling advantage when he lets others speak for him. Again, while every great idea can be stated in a speech or a poem, not by any means all can be adequately developed in a drama or a narrative. To do Björnson justice, his stories do not attempt so much. They are, to English notions, like the sagas on which they are modelled, distinctly lacking in plot, and their chief charm is the descriptive style, and the songs and lyrics with which they are enriched. In the technique of the stage, Björnson is a long way behind not only Ibsen but many a lesser dramatist. *En Fallit* ("A Bankruptcy"), which is perhaps his best acting play, is really complete in the first three acts, but a wholly superfluous fourth one is added, merely because the author feels he has more to tell us about his principal character. In the two plays of his later period in which he tried to expose what he felt to be the dangers of the creed he had abandoned, *Over Aevne* ("Beyond our Powers"), parts 1 and 2, there is far too much talk and too little action. The principal act in each is taken up with a set debate, and in the second of the two plays the author has eventually to blow the meeting up with dynamite in order to bring the scene to an end. In both there are fine ideas, but one feels that the right vehicle has not been chosen for their expression.

On the other hand, Björnson's poems and songs are prominent among the great forces which carried his country to victory in the long struggle for independence. Where Ibsen could only criticise and despair, Björnson, with his quenchless faith that—as he put it —there is a surplus balance of good in life, could supply that encouragement which is the secret of leadership. It is idle to inquire, as some have done, whether by abstention from politics he could have risen even higher as a poet. The political circumstances of his age were his inspiration, and poet and politician are one and indivisible. He was, in fact, the human embodiment of the spirit of his nation, and it is as skald and prophet that he must be judged.

None of Björnson's contemporaries will bear comparison with him as a national force. From a purely technical point of view the vivid descriptive novels of Jonas Lie and the delicate satire of Alexander Kielland rank extremely high. But Lie dealt less in problems and propaganda than any of his important contemporaries ; his *métier* was to supply accurate and graceful pictures of Norwegian life, especially that of the disappearing bureaucratic society in which he had been brought up, in the remote and little-known districts of the extreme North, and of the seafaring life for which he was originally destined. As for Kielland, the subtle irony and polished satire which he employed are weapons

effective only against antagonists sufficiently sensitive
to appreciate them, and these are generally a small
minority. Few writers are better worth reading, but
Kielland may be compared to a boxer who wins on
points, leaving his opponent quite unconscious that
any serious damage has been done to him.

The most definitely propagandist writer among
Björnson's later contemporaries was Arne Garborg, the
most formidable champion and exponent of the
maalstrev. He was the first writer satisfactorily to
accomplish the *tour de force* of applying the *landsmaal*
to an urban environment in which it had no kinship
with the natural speech of the characters represented.
Garborg was the apostle of freedom and independence
in every department of life. Himself a freethinker in
matters of religion, he championed the cause of those
who rejected dogmatic Christianity while they were
still unpopular, but when their teaching in turn became
dogmatic, and constituted—as he said—" the very
latest seminarism," he turned his weapons, with perfect
consistency, against his former allies and supporters.
This apparent change of front gave rise to much misunderstanding, but Garborg never returned to the
orthodox fold, though religious thought occupied his
attention increasingly as he grew older. With equal
courage he challenged conventional morality, and incurred not only opprobrium but pecuniary loss through
his outspoken statement of his convictions.

In many respects, though in fact they seldom agreed,
Björnson and Garborg show points of resemblance in
respect of the guiding principles of their lives. But
there was more realism and less poetry in Garborg's
composition ; and in one of his best works, *Bonde-
studentar* ("Peasant Students "), he lets loose a flow of
most effective satire on fanciful Grundtvigian methods
of popular education. As a vivid and amusing picture
of a certain stage in the progress of Norwegian democracy, this book is of special importance. The mistake which Garborg makes here and elsewhere seems

to me to be that he accentuates the cleavage between town and country, treating these two elements in the national life as absolutely irreconcilable, a dangerous theory unhappily evolved through his advocacy of the *landsmaal*. Those who used the alternative form of the Norwegian language he thought and spoke of almost as foreigners.

After a great period of progress achieved by confident idealists there is usually a reaction. We have seen this in England in the temporary vogue of Mr. Lytton Strachey's irreverent presentment of the great Victorians. It seems as though humanity could not live for long in such exalted regions. In Norway the ebb and flow of national effort is peculiarly noticeable, since it needs a great cause and exceptional leadership to counteract the centrifugal and parochial tendencies of the national passion for independence. Contemporary literature seems to be going through such a period of reaction. The old enthusiasms have achieved their objects, and no great uniting inspiration has for the moment arisen to take their place. The most obvious theme for literary treatment, the conflicting ideals of the old agricultural life, and the new industrialism, has indeed inspired Norway's greatest living novelist, Hamsun, whose earlier work seemed strongly influenced by the Russian realists, but who has returned to a truly national style and subject in his great saga of the old way of life, *Markens Gröde* (" The Growth of the Soil "), in which the successful struggle of a peasant farmer with new ground is magnificently depicted. In his books dealing with the rising industrial town (imaginary) of Segelfoss, the author seems to adopt the same standpoint, his sympathies being altogether enlisted on the side of the old and threatened régime. The other side of the question has been effectively voiced by Hjalmar Christensen in *Den gamle bygd og den nye*. But literature, as a rule, finds no inspiration in Conservative ideals; and since the materialism of industry is equally unattractive, Nor-

wegian authors of the present day, in so far as they
represent a national standpoint, have tended either to
substitute the past for the present or a particular
district for the country as a whole.

The most successful example under the first of these
categories is Sigrid Undset's historical novel, *Kristin
Lavransdatter*. The treatment of her subject by this
authoress shows remarkable originality and exceptional
learning. Most writers in this *genre* are content to
turn to history for their plot and characters, while
surrounding the latter either with a conventional
" Wardour Street " atmosphere or with that of their
own day. But in *Kristin Lavransdatter* the atmosphere
is the thing which is really borrowed from the past.
Few historical events, except the Black Death, are
introduced : the effect is as though a modern realistic
writer of fiction had been transported back into the
fourteenth century, and had there sat down to produce
a novel of everyday life. The book, though too long
for the circulating-library tastes of our country to-day,
is a really amazing *tour de force*, and must be included
in even the most superficial summary of contemporary
Norwegian literature.

A sketch of a bygone generation which also deserves
mention, though hardly in the same breath, is Hjalmar
Christensen's *Fogedgaarden*. As a sympathetic study of
the period of transition from officialdom to democracy
it provides a most illuminating background to nineteenth-century Norwegian history.

A tendency to stake out a claim in a particular
locality has been evinced by quite a large school of
Norwegian authors, of whom Olav Duun is probably
the most distinguished. This movement is perhaps a
symptom of the centrifugal tendencies before alluded
to. Norwegians rally periodically round a great cause,
but in the absence of any such connecting bond are apt
to disintegrate into town and country, east and west,
county against county, as they were in the distant days
of Harald Fairhair. This is no doubt partly due to

geographical and linguistic causes, but it is also, I think, an effect of the instinct for independence to which I have so often had to allude. The same instinct which makes the Norwegian nationalist reject the culture of other lands easily degenerates into a parochialism which regards the inhabitants of an adjacent valley or neighbouring town as strangers, and makes of its own district its world.

This necessity for a common rallying-point, and the existence of a regrettable amount of mutual suspicion and dislike, seem to be the main themes of Hans Kinck's poetical drama, *Driftekaren* (" The Cattle Dealer "), which many competent critics compare with Ibsen's *Peer Gynt*. Kinck is undoubtedly a genius, though by writing in an intermediate language of his own, freely interspersed with the broadest dialect, he contrives to hide much of his light under a bushel, even from his own countrymen, while the foreigner who can read him " with his feet on the fender " must be rather remarkable as a linguist. Kinck's work as a whole represents another phase of the modern reaction to realism. His *bönder* have not only ceased to be the discrowned kings of nineteenth-century romanticism, but have been deprived of all the good qualities which they in fact possess, and are earth-bound, suspicious, and brutal. Such so-called realism is, of course, no more true to life than the work of the school against which it is a protest. But when geese have been called swans *ad nauseam* there always arise men who refuse to allow that they are anything more than ugly ducklings. This is what is called realism, and it usually represents a distinct ebb in the literary tides of a nation. There can be no doubt, however, that Kinck is a remarkable artist, with much partially suppressed poetry in his composition, who deserves a far wider public than his peculiar vocabulary is likely to secure him.

In contrast to the untranslatable work of Kinck stands that of Johan Bojer, which is probably more appreciated in England and elsewhere in Europe than it is in his own country. There is no very special feature about his stories which calls for comment, except possibly a certain sentimentality which is characteristic neither of Norwegians nor of their literary traditions. His novels, like those of most of his countrymen, show the influence of the saga style.

Verse still holds its position with the Norwegian public, but its nature has been much affected by the modern reaction. A comparatively short time ago nearly every Norwegian poem clearly betrayed its origin. It was coloured throughout by the patriotic ideals of the nation. The present vogue of the rather trivial verses of Herman Wildenvey is symptomatic of the modern craving for novelty. For this kind of light verse is a new thing in Norway, though common enough here in England and in other countries, where it may be doubted whether this poet would have been regarded as in any way an outstanding figure, in spite of a certain metrical dexterity and felicity of phrase. He is a literary butterfly whose vogue is probably ephemeral, and he has certainly produced nothing entitling him to compare the adverse criticism of Theodor Caspari to "the braying of Balaam's ass." Caspari, the author of such lovely lyrics as *Jeg elsker dig naar svalens röst dig vaekker* ("I love thee wakened by the swallow's singing"), is clearly qualified to discuss this branch of literature.

The greatest living poet in Norway, one who might justly be called great in any country and any age, is a survival from the previous generation, Nils Collett Vogt. Almost everything which he has written is imbued with a rare poetic quality which it is difficult to praise too highly. His range is remarkably wide, for while much of his best work is serious and even tragic, in a lighter vein he can produce such a little gem as *Maaneskin*—out of a telephone conversation between two separated lovers on a moonlight night—which recalls Mr. Austin Dobson at his best. Vogt comes of an old Conservative family, but his impressionable artistic temperament was not proof against the emotional influence of the great national democratic movement into which he was born. This led, as he has told us, to disturbance and misunderstanding in the home circle, yet there was never anything of the practical politician about him. Like an Æolian harp, moved by the wind to melody, he felt the stir of a great time, and reacted to the stimulus instinctively, because there was poetry, and nothing but poetry, in his composition. To vary the metaphor, he neither knows nor cares very much whither the tide is leading, so long as he can feel the excitement of being tossed about and borne along. Like the sailor in the psalm, " he is carried up to the heaven and down again to the deep," and the alternating moods of exaltation and depression which characterise his verse reflect, in a singularly beautiful manner, the storm and stress of a great national movement. Like the sailor, he is out of sight of the destination, and not much concerned as to where or what it may be. But the life, with all its ups and downs, its dangers and disappointments, he feels intensely, and, as he tells us repeatedly, would not change for anything. His message is therefore full of hope and encouragement; but it is really not the message which counts. His verse, unlike that of Björnson, is not a means but an end; not a trumpet-call to action, but an exquisite orchestral accompaniment to the national drama in which others are playing their parts. In Vogt, the thought and ideals surrounding and inspiring him are not so much expressed as distilled into the pure essence of poetry.

Another Norwegian poet of the present day in whom the true fire seems to burn is one of the youngest, Arnulf Överland. He combines with really poetic ideas a remarkable power of emphasising them through the media of rhythm and language. To anyone who can read Norwegian, for instance, the mere sound of

the following lines must convey an extraordinarily
vivid picture of the age described :

> " Jerntidens runetavler melder i mörke kvad
> Om vinternaetter, da baalet blaffet om blodige guder.
> Seiden kokte i mörke og koktes av brunst og had :
> Og maendene möttes paa holmen i jern og i dyrehuder."

Such lines defy the translator.

> "Carved in the age of iron, the mystic runes relate
> How flames would flicker on blood-stained gods in the winter
> feasts.
> Spells were brewed in the dark, and the brew was of lust and
> hate ;
> And men would meet in the holm-gang, in steel and the skins of
> beasts."

The meaning is fairly close, but how much is lost of
the mysterious gloom and metallic resonance of the
original. I pay my tribute to Mr. Överland and his
haunting verses, and, in doing so, take my leave of this
necessarily incomplete and superficial survey of the
modern literature of Norway. Looking back, one cannot
help being impressed by the richness of the production
in a country with so small a population. In spite of the
handicap of a language not widely known or studied,
European, or even world-wide reputations have in
some cases been established. There must be something, one feels, in the country and the composition of
its inhabitants which has thus produced outstanding
literature in its earliest and in its latest days. And,
even if at times the springs of inspiration seem to flow
but slowly, in the light of the past, both ancient and
recent, there seems no reason to be anxious about the
future of Norwegian literature.

CHAPTER VIII

THE LANGUAGE QUESTION

THE language-reform or *maal-strev* movement, a cause of bitter dispute and burning controversy in Norway, which has from time to time assumed the importance of a crucial political question at election times, has not hitherto aroused much sympathetic attention in this country. The well-known passage in *Peer Gynt*, in which Ibsen satirises the language reformer in the person of Hu-hu, a lunatic desirous of preserving and cultivating the speech of aboriginal apes in Malabar, is taken by most Englishmen as the final word on the question.[1] " It is difficult," says Sir Edmund Gosse in the *Encyclopædia Britannica*, " to feel the slightest sympathy with a movement in favour of suppressing the language in which everyone has hitherto expressed himself, in order to adopt an artificial dialect which exists mainly on paper, and which is not the natural speech of any one body of persons throughout the whole of Norway."

On reflection, however, it would appear rash to refuse to a movement, which numbers among its adherents some of the most learned and cultured persons in the kingdom, a more respectful and judicial consideration than is embodied in such an opinion as that above quoted. Nor has Sir Edmund Gosse stated the problem accurately : in speaking of "an artificial dialect," and claiming that the Danish forms which the *landsmaal* seeks to supersede are " the language in which everyone has hitherto expressed himself," he begs two important questions, answering them in a way which is at least extremely disputable if not entirely erroneous.

The true position can perhaps best be made clear to British readers by means of a possible parallel nearer home. Scotland and England having now been united so far as the monarchy is concerned since the days of James I, the official language in both countries is

[1] See note at end of chapter.

English.   Scotsmen of the upper class take a pride in speaking and writing English exactly like an Englishman, and for the most part succeed in doing so.   Going a step lower in the social scale, we find in Scotland a large proportion of the population who write what appears to be perfectly pure and correct English, but whose pronunciation of the language is not that of an Englishman.   In ordinary conversation such persons will introduce words and expressions which are Scottish rather than English.   Finally, we come to the country folk and working classes who speak what we call " broad Scotch," something which in its extreme form (*e.g.* " a daimen icker in a thraive ") is quite unintelligible to the Englishman without the help of a glossary.   I am not, of course, referring here to the Gaelic speech of the Highlander, which affords no true parallel, and to the preservation or cultivation of which wholly different considerations apply.   Now the average Southerner is at first inclined to regard the Scottish language as a mere dialect of English, and the Scottish gentleman who does not wish to be thought provincial thinks of it, though he may not dare to say so, in much the same way.   But this is not historically correct. Scots and English, like the Scandinavian languages, are obviously akin, but their common origin lies in a past too remote for any but an antiquarian philologist.   Up to the date of the Union, and even later, Scots was the language spoken by the Scottish King ; it was the language in which official documents were written, and if his English subjects thought the speech of King James I provincial, the feeling seems to have been reciprocated, for the King thought an English accent inferior to Scottish, at all events in the pronunciation of Latin and Greek—" certainly their pronunciation utterly fails the grace of those two learned languages." The tongue his highly cultured tutors taught him was not by way of being English, but Scots.

Now, supposing that political changes had terminated the existing union of England and Scotland, it might be argued with force and truth that the latter country possessed a language of its own, with an historical pedigree as distinguished as that of England, which was still spoken by a large proportion of the population, and a movement might easily arise for the official recognition of this language : firstly, as an expression of national independence ; secondly, because of its intrinsic merits ; and thirdly, as a means of facilitating education, by the elimination of a second language which it had hitherto been necessary for the least cultured element in the population to learn before any progress could be made. On the other hand, it would be contended that the chief literary work of Scotsmen, except for a good deal of Burns and a few exercises by other authors, was liable to become less familiar and intelligible if the proposal took effect ; while there would be a certain amount of prejudice on the part of the upper and official classes who had been educated on other lines, and subconsciously regarded broad Scotch as a concomitant of low breeding and deficient culture. In this way a situation might be created almost exactly parallel to that which has characterised the language-reform movement in Norway. The change would, indeed, be faced with far greater difficulties than are met with in the case of the Norwegian movement, since Danish is a language spoken only by a population not considerably larger than that of Norway, whereas the disproportion in numbers between Englishmen and Scotsmen is very great ; while the English language is spoken and understood over a large part of the globe. This, however, need not materially affect the appropriateness of the illustration.

It is not true to say that the *riksmaal*, as the Dano-Norwegian language is termed, is that " in which everyone has hitherto expressed himself." On the contrary, though Norwegians have been taught in their schools to speak it, the vast majority of the population, in their private conversations with one

another, speak something which has far closer affinities
with the *landsmaal*. True, there are many dialects,
and probably few or none of these are really identical
with the generalised Norse of the *landsmaal,* just as in
Scots there are many dialects, but the existence of
these presents no insuperable obstacle to the adoption
of a generalised and universally intelligible Scottish
like that written by Burns. After all, an official
language is always something of a generalisation ; it
has been said that no one speaks a language so neutrally
as to give no clue to the district from which he hails.
The folk-songs, which are almost the only purely
national compositions of Norway during the period of
the Union with Denmark, may be said to be *landsmaal,*
as Scottish ballads or the poems of James I are Scots ;
an attempt to systematise and generalise the language
in which these are composed, and which is spoken by
the peasantry, cannot fairly be stigmatised as the
adoption of " an artificial dialect which exists mainly
on paper, and which is not the natural speech of any
one body of persons." The *landsmaal* is as emphatically Norse as the poems of Burns, which are not, I
believe, in the pure dialect of any one district, are at
once recognised as Scots. And while a form of speech
descending directly from the Norwegian of the saga
period is spoken every day by a large proportion of the
population, it is really difficult to contend that Danish,
pronounced in a special way and interlarded with a
few words and expressions unfamiliar to Danish ears,
is in fact the national language of the country.

The historical development of the question is as
follows : The victory of Danish, during the period of
the union with Denmark, was more gradual than is
generally supposed. At the outset there was no
common form of speech for the whole of Denmark,
and, as each province spoke and, to some extent,
wrote in its own dialect, it was natural, *a fortiori,* that
Norwegians should retain a great many of the special
characteristics of their own language. But in Norway,

too, there were many dialects, and some of these, particularly in the south, approximated so closely to some forms of Danish that the influence of the latter tongue was easily able to make itself felt. The large proportion of Danish officials, and especially of Danish bishops after the Reformation, played an important part in making Danish the written language of Norway. Norway itself had at this time no literature written in the speech of the people ; what she read was Danish, what she was taught in her schools was Danish. Norwegians desirous of a university education travelled to Copenhagen. Copenhagen printed such books as they wrote, and a considerable proportion of their readers belonged to Denmark. The influence of Holberg, a native of Norway but perhaps the most outstanding figure in Danish literature, tended to stereotype a fixed model for the written language which was regarded as common to both countries. The pronunciation, of course, of the spoken language differed always in the two countries ; but in some respects the Norwegian pronunciation was, as might perhaps be expected, more strictly phonetic than the Danish, and we even find a writer towards the end of the eighteenth century contending on that account that the purest Danish was spoken in Norway. By a curious irony, the victory of Danish was most complete, and the Danish written by Norwegian authors was purest, just at the time when the union of the two countries came to an end. This was partly the result of the publication of grammatical works of special merit and partly due to the revival of the art of literary composition among the Norwegians, who had, of course, at this time, for the most part finished their education in Denmark.

Yet traces of a movement for reviving the national characteristics of the Norwegian language are perceptible almost immediately after the separation. In this movement the national poet Wergeland played a prominent part, writing a tract on Norwegian language reform, which is a vigorous plea for the use of

purely Norwegian words and expressions in place of
the Danish. It is clear, however, that at this stage
the advocates of Norwegian were still on the defensive :
Danish and Dano-Norwegian culture banned the Norse
expressions as vulgarisms ; and Wergeland's main
argument is that the most forcible word or expression,
whatever its source, is rightly used. He has no
objection to borrowing, for example, from Swedish ;
language, he pleads, to live must enrich itself from
whatever sources are the most suitable, but Danish
taste would have the written speech stationary rather
than progressive. He does, however, go far enough to
contend in an eloquent passage that a people's own
language best expresses the special characteristics of
the people.

So far, however, Norway was still a bureaucracy, and
the educated classes tended to look down upon the
agricultural peasantry among whom the genuine uncontaminated speech survived in their everyday conversation. There was a cleavage between town and
country, between official and farmer, and this cleft
was only bridged when the romantic movement in
literature and a growing fondness for democracy
focussed attention on the *bonde* and his folk-tales, and
tended to idealise him as the real backbone of the
country.

As soon as this movement began, those interested
in its literary exploitation found themselves in a
difficulty. What the farmer said, particularly on the
subject of folk-lore, was not capable of being reproduced in his actual words. His language was only
expressed orally ; it had no literature. The first
attempt to bring out a collection of folk-tales, that of
Andreas Faye, in 1833, was an artistic failure. The
stories were retold by a number of too sophisticated
collectors, whose efforts, while failing to harmonise
with one another, completely eliminated the characteristics which principally distinguished the legends from
those of a number of other countries. A few years

later the problem was more satisfactorily faced by Asbjörnsen and Moe, who, while writing in the Dano-Norwegian, which alone stood a chance of being intelligently appreciated by the reading public, created by sheer genius a style which to a great extent reproduced the atmosphere and soil from which their material had sprung. But the difficulties with which these collaborators were faced, and the thought which they were forced to address to the question, emphasised the disadvantages connected with the alien origin of the only literary form of the language.

Still, up to now the speech of the peasantry had been generally regarded as a vulgar and corrupt *patois*, which, like the proverbial mule, was " without pride of ancestry or hope of posterity." The honour of demonstrating its real character and thereby founding the language reform movement is commonly attributed to Ivar Aasen, who published, in 1847 and 1850 respectively, a grammar and dictionary of the national language, in which he showed clearly its direct and almost uncontaminated descent from the Norse of the old days of glory and independence. But though the influence of Aasen's work in getting the true nature of the popular speech widely recognised, and thereby paving the way for the *maalstrev* movement, can hardly be exaggerated, it is not correct to represent him as an altogether original discoverer. In a recent lecture, published in *Maal og Minne*, Professor D. A. Seip has been able to show clearly that many philologists before Aasen, even as early as the sixteenth century, perceived the true character of some at least of the native dialects, regarding them rightly as the legitimate offspring of Old Norse, rather than as corruptions of the Danicised language used by the educated sections of the community. It is probably true to say that Ivar Aasen worked out his theory independently, but he appears in fact to have followed a number of predecessors, not only in their grasp of the essential truth but also in their misconceptions. For neither Aasen nor his forerunners recognised as pure Norse more than a certain number of dialects, the rest were believed to have become corrupted under Danish influences. Modern inquiry, on the other hand, tends to establish the truly national character of these more Danish-sounding dialects as well, and the mistake into which Ivar Aasen fell with regard to them had a prejudicial effect on the utility of the form of *landsmaal* which he strove to introduce. It had too narrow a basis for a practical generalisation of Norwegian dialects, and failed to provide a satisfactory bridge for the established *riksmaal* to cross. To some extent, no doubt, the archaic and unpractical character of Aasen's *landsmaal* was also due to the fact that, having to prove his main point, he tended to select those forms which showed the closest affinities to the ancient speech of the country. But in any case the result was regrettable. Danish stood on one side, sharply contrasted with the most extreme Norse on the other, while intermediate forms which could claim as respectable a pedigree, and the existence of which was by no means due to the Danish supremacy, were neglected and discountenanced.

This regrettable tendency to dualism was increased by transferring the question from the sphere of literature to that of politics. Language is a natural growth, and cannot be suddenly transformed by Act of Parliament. The object which the *maalstrever* had at heart, the development of a really national language, was in itself unobjectionable and even desirable ; but the right road was by way of literary evolution rather than of legislative interference. Left to itself, or encouraged by the example of several writers of talent, the *riksmaal*, now that the influence of Denmark had been terminated, would naturally have shed its alien characteristics, and incorporated more and more of the speech of the people. Associated with political parties, *landsmaal* and *riksmaal* naturally faced one another in opposition, and were vigorously attacked and defended by the adherents of each respective form.

The *maalstrever* accused his opponent of lack of patriotism, and in so doing was really mischievous. For he thus accentuated the already deplorable opposition between town and country, and tended to restrict nationalist sentiment within unduly narrow limits. The exponent of *riksmaal* retaliated by asserting the cultural and æsthetic inferiority of the rival form.

There was great force in his arguments, for the associations of *landsmaal* were rustic, and the language appeared incongruous when applied to anything but peasant life, while a tongue which for centuries had been confined to the humbler classes of the community was necessarily lacking in a comprehensive vocabulary and a flexible style.

In spite of these objections, however, the course of political events during the long struggle of democracy against officialdom, and of Norway against Sweden, tended so to foster nationalist sentiment that the *maalstrev* made very considerable progress. It was advocated and used by writers of such outstanding merit as Vinje and Garborg, and the result has been that it now has a definite legal status.

In the elementary schools, the pupils are taught to read both forms of the language, while a system of local option decides which is to be accorded precedence for writing and general study. The traveller through Norway will also observe districts which have adopted *landsmaal* for official purposes, the notices in railway stations, etc., changing from one form to another as he passes through the country.

Meanwhile the *riksmaal*, as was to be expected, cut off from the direct influence of Denmark, has tended to approximate more and more to the rival form. The legislative changes which brought *landsmaal* into the school curriculum led to a still closer rapprochement, since it was found that there was a large number of words identical in both forms of speech which differed merely in spelling, and as this difference was manifestly an obstacle to education, it was removed by a comprehensive spelling reform. At present there is superficially a great amount of confusion, as authors refuse to be bound by the official spelling, and in some instances, of which the work of Hans Kinck provides a good example, make use of intermediate forms of the language. But this state of affairs is almost certainly transitory, and a hopeful symptom of ultimate fusion. The day, if a foreigner may prophesy, seems not far distant when Norway will be able to express herself in a genuine, single, and distinctive national language. To show how small a gulf at present separates the two forms, a short passage from Garborg is appended, in the *riksmaal* and *landsmaal* approved by the Spelling Committee of 1917. It would be easy to find passages which resembled each other even more closely : the sample may therefore be regarded as a fair one.

RIKSMAAL.	LANDSMAAL.
Derfor sier sannheten : den vinner livet som gjör Guds vilje. Vi bygger det gode i oss når vi gjör det gode omkring oss. Med daglige seiervinninger over naturen i oss arbeider vi frem åndsmennesket i oss, det som har sitt liv i sig selv, og dermed det håp som ikke reddes döden.	Difor segjer sanningi : den vinn livet som gjer Guds vilje. Me byggjer det gode i oss når me gjer det gode ikring oss. Med daglege sigervinningar yver naturi i oss arbeider me fram åndsmennesket i oss, det som hev sitt liv i seg sjölv, og dermed den voni som ikkje reddast dauden.

If we now attempt fairly to sum up the question, we must, in the first place, admit that the *maalstrevers* seem effectively to have ousted the alien Danish, and to have played a large part in establishing a real national language, corresponding in all essentials to that spoken by the majority of the inhabitants. Apart from the influence of this movement, it may well be doubted whether the *riksmaal* of the present day would have separated itself so widely from the speech of Denmark. As late as the early years of the present century it was certainly almost impossible for a foreigner to decide, upon linguistic grounds, whether a given document belonged to Denmark or Norway. Now there is no difficulty whatever. If the present state of the language is to be attributed to natural development after separation from its original source of inspiration, why was the change during the nineteenth century comparatively negligible while the last twenty years have produced revolutionary changes? Surely, if we are just, we must ascribe the present state of both forms of language to the work done in the interests of *landsmaal*. Is the change an advantage? A language of its own is not, of course, essential to a nation, but in this case the language was there, spoken in all essentials by a large proportion of the inhabitants, and in these circumstances there is much to be said for allotting it a share in its birthright. Again, as was strenuously contended by Ivar Aasen, if anyone has to learn two languages it should surely be those of the more leisured class, whose opportunities of education are so far superior to those of the masses. But, under the old system, it was the masses who had to learn a form of Danish in addition to their household speech before they could make any progress in education. So much must in justice be placed upon the credit side.

On the other hand, there are districts to which the extreme *landsmaal* is stranger than the alternative form. And there are men, as I know from personal experience, who, though they habitually speak a dialect which seems almost identical with *landsmaal*, nevertheless are not familiar with it as a written language. When the present writer first went to Norway the peasants used to speak of the *riksmaal* as *almindelig skriftsprog* or *bokmaal*—general writing language, or book language. It was what they had been taught to use for purposes of reading or writing, and an attempt to give to their domestic speech a written form was unfamiliar to them.[1] But a difficulty of this kind is perhaps

[1] The converse to this conception appears to me to be more generally held to-day than it was some twenty years ago. Formerly

temporary : it ought not to affect the rising generation.
Perhaps a more serious objection is that the *landsmaal*,
without providing a key to the treasures of the Old
Norse literature, deposes most of the modern literary
masterpieces—the works of Wergeland, Welhaven,
Björnson, and Ibsen, for example—to the status of a
foreign tongue. True, the difference between the rival
forms is so small that the difficulty of understanding
one from a knowledge of the other is not insurmount-
able, but for the proper appreciation of literature, and
especially poetry, it is of immense advantage to the
reader to have a natural acquaintance with all the
nuances of the language. The point, for what it is
worth, is certainly to be placed on the *riksmaal* side
of the scales. The most formidable objection, however, appears to me to be that though the language
itself cannot fairly be described as artificial the movement can. Language should be a spontaneous growth,
and attempts suddenly to control and direct its development are to be deprecated. As Björnson pointed out,
the *riksmaal*, whatever its ancestry, was entrenched by
centuries of use among all the cultured people of Norway, and an attempt suddenly to supplant it rather
than gradually to lead it into more national channels
was doomed to failure. The truth of this seems now
to be established since, with all the legislative approval
which it has gained, the *landsmaal* has only succeeded
in affecting and modifying its rival in the way advocated
by Björnson, and has thereby strengthened its position
instead of, as the extremists desired, driving it out.
For an established literary language has the advantage
of flexibility and power of growth and development ;
it plays ju-jitsu with its opponents, and by seeming to
yield makes its final victory more assured. The
landsmaal, having existed, so far as it did exist, as an

the peasantry seemed far more used to speaking in *riksmaal* than
they are now. The dialect forms are no longer regarded as
" incorrect " and unsuited to polite conversation, even where
riksmaal is habitually used in reading and writing.

actual language only on the lips of people of small literary culture and limited vocabulary, has to borrow from its rival to express complicated ideas, while from the circumstances of its creation it lacks the right to claim as its own any words which it may happen to adopt. The whole logical position of a man who says to a fellow-countryman speaking the tongue he learned at his mother's knee, " you are not speaking Norwegian," depends on imposing an embargo on all words of extraneous origin ; this position he abandons if he gives himself free leave to borrow. But a language which has grown up naturally is entitled to incorporate effective words and phrases from the speech of any and every country, and the more it develops the more surely it lives. The ultimate victory therefore rests with *riksmaal*, which, when the final blending takes place, will be able to trace its progress by insensible degrees, and say " Plus ça change, plus c'est la même chose." Yet, however unwisely the nationalist language reformers may have proceeded, however intemperate their utterances, and however exaggerated their demands, the fact remains that all Norwegian is now recognisably different from the speech of other Scandinavian countries, that words and phrases are no longer banned because they are not Danish, and that for this real progress the *maalstrever* deserves his share of the credit.

It may still be inquired, however, whether the result attained has been worth the energy displayed by the contesting parties and the confusion involved in bringing it about. Is not all this fuss likely to be regarded by the outside world as displaying a certain childishness ? Does it not tend to obscure more real and solid claims to national individuality ? Grant that there is more sense in it than in the somewhat analogous Celticism of the Irish Free State, for an approximation to *landsmaal* is at least the living speech of a large proportion of the population, and the two forms of the language are sufficiently near to one another to render eventual fusion possible. But are we not driven to think of it, in these days of gigantic problems, only to be solved by concentrated thought and virile effort, with a rather pitying smile ? Language is not of the essence of nationality ; some nations have managed quite well with no distinctive speech of their own. Its main advantage to a nation is the opportunity it affords to her citizens of absorbing without effort the thought of the great minds to whom she has given birth in the past, and this advantage *landsmaal* cannot claim. While it provides no key to Old Norse, it is equally remote from the speech which was used at Eidsvold, or that in which national prophets such as Wergeland, Björnson, and Ibsen left their message to posterity. It may, of course, be urged by the *maalstrever* that the use of the Danish language in Norway recalls a humiliating period of the national history. The facts which it represents are, however, a matter which no childish game of " let's pretend " can alter. It is more profitable to think how, after centuries of dependency and torpor, Norwegians yet retained so large a measure of manly determination that alone and unfriended they forced their claim for independence on the ally of the great Powers of Europe. This was a great victory : it matters little whether we call it *seier* or *siger*. Again, in 1905, Norway proved decisively that her sons had outgrown tutelage, and were entitled to be regarded as men. Having become men, they should put away childish things.

NOTE

For the benefit of those who have not read it, a translation of Ibsen's satire on the *maalstrev*, in *Peer Gynt*, is appended :

> " Blooming in the east afar
> Lie the coasts of Malabar,
> Subject to the cultured touch
> Of the Portuguese and Dutch ;
> There, in scattered tribes, as well
> Native Malabaris dwell.

Now a mongrel speech and base is
Used by all these ruling races,
But ere modern times began
'Twas the great orang-utan
O'er the forest reigned supreme,
As he chose could fight and scream ;
Just as Nature's hand designed,
So he roared and so he whined,
Yelled, with none to say him nay,
In the realm that owned his sway.
Ah, but then the foreign yoke
Came, and marred the speech he spoke :
On the ape descended quite
Twice two hundred years of night :
And, you know, so long a sleep'll
Make a slow and backward people.
Mute the forest's primal howl,
Never now is heard a growl ;
'Tis by human speech alone
We must make our fancies known.
What oppression of the free !
Whether Dutch or Portugee,
Native-born or hybrid race,
All are in this evil case.
I have striven to protect
Our primeval dialect,
To restore it, and to preach
General liberty of screech ;
Screeched myself, to show the ways
It was used in tribal lays.
Still my art is underrated.
Now, I think, my case is stated."

CHAPTER IX

RELIGION AND EDUCATION

THE Lutheran Church of Norway is pre-eminently an established, State-controlled Church. The King is *summus episcopus,* and all ecclesiastical appointments are theoretically in his hands ; practically in those of the Ministry, advised by a Department of State—the Church and Education Department. With regard to such appointments the views of all interested parties are ascertained, but the bodies and individuals consulted have merely advisory powers, and their recommendations are not infrequently overridden. The Government has been known actually to disregard the views of the Church Department ; indeed, the immediate cause of the conflict between the Conservative and Liberal elements in the Church, which still embitters the religious atmosphere of Norway, was the appointment, in 1906, of a theological professor of advanced views, who was chosen by the Michelsen Ministry in the teeth of departmental advice.

Superficially, the State Church occupies a peculiarly strong position. The overwhelming majority of the population gives to it, at any rate, a nominal allegiance : nonconformists of all persuasions barely muster 3 per cent. of the nation. Feeling against the establishment is practically non-existent : upon a referendum held in 1913 on the question of disestablishment only 17 per cent. of the electorate took the trouble to vote at all, and of these only an insignificant minority was in favour of change. This apparent strength of the Church is, however, quite unconnected with the doctrinal and theological views of its adherents. It is endeared to national sentiment as an essential and traditional part of the old Norwegian culture ; it is therefore everywhere desired that it should still be national. On the other hand, it seems probable that there would be a good deal of secession but for purely geographical obstacles. As Dr. Anton Fridrichsen points out in a recent article in *Kirke og Kultur* (No. 5, 1924),

" Geographically it is of importance that in our extensive, thinly populated, and poor country the possibilities of establishing lasting communities outside the Church are very limited ; it is no attractive task to set up free churches in Norway."

Beneath this external conformity there exists, in fact, a remarkably wide cleavage of opinion. The Church is the one institution in the country to which the principles of democracy have not as yet been applied. The clergy, appointed by a single central authority, and, until recently, trained for their calling in one theological faculty, represent for the most part an advanced critical standpoint. There is not, as with us, a variety of patronage to suit the tastes of the masses, who have inevitably progressed more slowly or not at all. Yet Christianity in Norway, ever since the pietistic movement of the early eighteenth century, has depended to an exceptional degree on the work of lay teachers and preachers drawn from the ranks of the people, and, from the first, largely in conflict with the official priesthood. During the enforced leisure of the long winter evenings many a *bonde* has directed his thoughts to religious matters, and has not infrequently felt himself called upon to give to his countrymen the benefit of his meditations. Revivals under the influence of lay preachers of this type have had a tremendous influence upon the religious thought of the masses ; of such the work of Hans Nielsen Hauge, which marked the end of the eighteenth and beginning of the nineteenth century, is only one outstanding example. The opposition between such men and the official pastors of the Church has been more or less marked at different times and in different districts, but the movement as a whole has been definitely anti-clerical. The religious views of large sections of the population have therefore been, to an exceptional extent, under the influence of self-taught men without theological training.

At the present time some of these lay preachers are said to be excessively young. In this connection,

Dr. Fridrichsen tells an amusing story of the wiser practice of an old bishop who was begged by two youths to allow them an opportunity of submitting a trial sermon. He appeared to acquiesce, and suggested 2 Sam. x. 5 as a suitable text. On returning home they looked up the passage and found the words, " Tarry at Jericho until your beards be grown, and then return."

In these circumstances the divergence of views and beliefs between clergy and laity has tended to be exaggerated. Wide as is the gulf here in England between stationary and progressive Christianity, the line of cleavage has not run, to the same extent as in Norway, sharply between priest and congregation. The conflict has therefore, since approximately the beginning of the century, been peculiarly intense. The close connection with America, brought about by emigration, has gone far to substitute the influence of that country for that of the earlier German pietism, with the result that the non-progressive party has become increasingly opposed to the established Church. The question has, moreover, been to some extent affected by the general advance in the direction of democratic control. The principal victory of old-fashioned orthodoxy has hitherto been the establishment, in 1907, of the *Menighetsfakultet* (Congregational Faculty), for the training of theologians on conservative lines ; up to that date the education of candidates for the priesthood was exclusively in the hands of the Theological Faculty at Christiania (Oslo) University, which, indeed, continued for some little time longer to monopolise the qualifying examination.

It is doubtful whether the distance between the modern advanced theologian and the peasant who adheres to traditional orthodoxy is as yet fully realised. The last generation has taken strides actually far longer than those which separated the early Lutheran from the mediæval Catholic, or even the Christianity of Olaf Tryggvason and Olaf the Holy from the heathen cult which preceded it. The ordinary layman of any

cult or creed is really but little interested in details of
dogma or ritual. The religious needs of which he is
conscious are in fact two only : he desires some power
or powers to whom he can appeal for supernatural
assistance in the affairs of this world, and an assurance
of personal survival, for himself and his loved ones,
in the next. These human cravings have been catered
for by religion from the days when Odin and Thor
were worshipped almost down to the present time ;
but they both depend essentially upon the supernatural, and a creed conditioned by modern criticism
and modern science, however great its advance towards
final truth, does not respond to these instinctive
spiritual demands.

The whole essence of religion, as the average man
views it, has therefore recently undergone a revolutionary change ; its appeal is of a different character,
and addressed to a different type of mind.

A striking instance of the extent of the change
which has come over the religious thought of Norway
of late is given by Dr. Schjelderup's recent plea for
the complete abolition of the Theological Faculty at
the University (Lecture to the Student Association,
7th March 1925). Education and the Church have
hitherto been so closely connected in Norway that, as
already indicated, a single Government Department pre-
sides over the affairs of both. " It was," admits Dr.
Schjelderup, " theology which gave rise to the Univer-
sities." But the present position, as this particular
theologian views it, is that the faculty is forced into the
impossible position of serving two masters. Scientific
teaching at a University, he says, requires a completer
freedom from the bands of orthodoxy than the Church
can concede. " The Church, which is bound by its
confession, cannot, of course, permit its future priests
to be trained by teachers whose science involves a
complete breach with ecclesiastical doctrine. But
neither can the University permit its students to be
educated by teachers whose science is fettered or settled

by confessional considerations." Dr. Schjelderup's case is not, of course, unassailable; it has, in fact, found but little support; but his argument is here cited to show how far the advanced theologian has now travelled from a position hitherto accepted as a matter of course.

Equally striking is the smallness of the change which took place during all the preceding centuries. The ancient heathenism of Norway struck deep roots in the soil which have only gradually and recently been eradicated. That the Norseman of the Viking period was a careless sceptic, who believed, like Kjartan, in the *Laxdaela Saga*, or Arnljot Gelline in the story of Olaf the Holy, principally in his own might and main, is a theory which has all the facts against it. Such cases must have been altogether exceptional. The vikings were, no doubt, impressed by the superior culture of the lands which they raided, and their mythology was probably to some extent enriched with features borrowed from Christianity, but this did not go to the root of the matter. The strenuous resistance offered to the missionary efforts of such men as Haakon the Good, and the drastic methods which the two Olafs found necessary, show how keen was the adherence to the old faith.

Above all, this is proved by the extent to which, in spite of all available substitutes, it survived. Bishop Bang, in his *Norske Kirkes Historie*, describes cases in Telemarken, the latest as recent as 1858, where ancient wooden images of gods received offerings exactly in accordance with primitive heathen custom. Another instance is given by Professor A. Bugge in *Norges Historie*, vol. i. p. 172. On a farm at Voss, he says, a very ancient barrow was being excavated in the year 1909. The farmer remarked that this barrow was inhabited by *garvôren*, the tutelary spirit of the estate, and that it had been customary to kill a beast in his honour whenever a death occurred on the farm. The archæologist asked whether this practice had long ceased, and received the reply, " Oh, we slaughtered a beast for him, right enough, when my father died ! " This was said quite seriously by a man little over forty years of age. But, indeed, Nature in Norway is of a type to evoke and encourage superstitious beliefs, as anyone will admit who has spent a night alone in a tent upon the high fjeld.

The transition to Christianity, though strenuously opposed, made, in fact, singularly little difference. The compulsory mass conversions carried out by Olaf Tryggvason were a perfectly logical stage in the process. Converts and missionaries alike accepted the existence of the powers worshipped by their opponents. In their conflict with Norwegians in Ireland, heathen Danes tried the experiment of praying to St. Patrick. On the other hand, Thangbrand, Olaf's missionary in Iceland, replied to an opponent, not that the latter's belief was absurd, but that " Thor would be but dust and ashes did not God *allow him to live.*" Conversion was the transfer of spiritual allegiance to a leadership represented as more powerful and therefore helpful. The most effective of all arguments was therefore a king of magnificent physique, with a distinguished military reputation, offering battle as an alternative to baptism. The fact that he could defeat you gave good reason for supposing that your gods were unequal to the task of resisting his.

To make the change easier, there were presented to the convert as equivalents for his abandoned deities the innumerable saints of the mediæval calendar. The experiment was therefore worth trying ; if the new powers failed to render the required assistance, one could always return surreptitiously to the old. Certain reservations were at first not infrequent. Cases occurred where a child would be kept back from baptism as a sacrifice to the old gods, or where a toe or finger would be bitten from a new-born infant, with the notion that some part of him should be conceded to Odin or Thor, while many converts, like Helgi the Lean, remained

" mixed in faith," and returned to the old allegiance in
an emergency.

There is, as I have pointed out in an earlier chapter,
a suggestive parallelism between the political and
religious policy of the second Olaf.   On the one hand,
we have the King, as a central and supreme authority,
endeavouring to supplant the old local aristocracy ;   on
the other hand, one supreme God set up in place of
many.   The resemblance is not fanciful or superficial ;
it really illustrates a very important factor in the
question.   Local kings and chiefs owed some of their
distinction to claims of divine descent ; in resisting the
Christian God, as in resisting the King, they were
asserting family claims :   moreover, they, under the
old régime, had themselves officiated as priests, and to
see their functions in the religious sphere handed over
to alien clerics must have roused feelings much akin
to those which Erling Skjalgson felt on being subjected
to the authority of a royal bailiff both of whose parents
had been thralls.   It was therefore natural that the
same qualities were required for the establishment of
Christianity as for the centralisation of the national
Government.

These qualities the second Olaf possessed, though he
lacked the attractive personality of his earlier namesake.
He was hard and tactless, but far more of a statesman
and an organiser than Olaf Tryggvason.   He realised
the value, both to Church and nation, of laying solid
foundations.   Where he extirpated heathendom, unlike his predecessor, he seems usually to have stayed
until a church was built and a priest installed, and he
was the first King to have a code of Christian law
accepted all over the country by the different *things*.
The task of church-building was the more rapidly
carried out since the earliest churches were of wood
(*stav-kirker*), and were based architecturally upon the
heathen *hof* or temple, which indeed was probably in
some cases simply appropriated and modified to the
requirements of the new religion.   This kind of build-

ing, indeed, was a late development under the old
régime, and was probably itself modelled upon Christian
churches met with by the vikings in Great Britain and
Ireland.

But though the change of religion was now complete,
it was still largely external. When, after his death,
the King became St. Olaf, the patron saint of Norway,
the country was virtually provided with a new national
god ; it is certain, at any rate, that in many respects
Olaf replaced Thor, was prayed to in the same emergencies, and was even credited with many victories
over trolls and the powers of evil of which Thor had
been the original hero.

" What in our old laws is called Christianity," says
Bishop Bang, " is really a series of external ecclesiastical
ordinances. . . . In the missionary practice of that
time but little was asked about a real living religious
faith and a new Christian life. The important points
were two things : first, that one should submit to
baptism ; and secondly, that one would conform to
ecclesiastical institutions and perform ecclesiastical
duties." In most respects, life went on very much as
before. The old gods assumed the guise of various
saints, and conferred their old names on devils, whose
existence was officially recognised. At the so-called
" ale-feasts," which continued to be held, the beakers
were emptied to Christ, the Virgin, and St. Michael,
instead of, as before, to Odin, Njörd, and Frey, as
described by Snorre in the saga of Haakon the Good.
Some of the more barbarous practices and vices were
condemned, and, under the influence of Christianity,
thraldom gradually ceased to exist, though this did
not involve any recognition of the equality of men in
the sight of heaven. On the contrary, social inequality
pursued the Norseman to the grave, for the Borgar-
things Kristenret prescribes separate quarters in the
churchyard for the free yeoman, the two classes of
freedmen (*leysingjar* and *frjalsgjafar*), and the mere
thrall, with penalties for encroachment on the resting-

place of a superior class. The release of a thrall, which made very little practical difference to his relation to his employer, was probably encouraged mainly as a benevolent action by which the master laid up treasure in heaven.

During this first stage of Christianity, the Church of Norway was in practice a purely national one. The priests were largely dependent upon their congregations, and the bishops upon the King, who appointed them to their sees. The ecclesiastical code (*Kristenret*) was drawn up by the King, and accepted by the popular assemblies in precisely the same way as every other law. The technical control of the archbishopric, first of Bremen and then of Lund, made no practical difference to this state of affairs. The first important change in the status of the Church took place when the Papacy created the archbishopric of Trondhjem, a step which was arranged in 1152 and finally authorised two years later.

By a curious paradox, the creation of a Norwegian archbishopric went far to destroy the independent, national character of the Church. The papal negotiator, the Englishman Nicholas Breakspear, afterwards Pope Adrian IV, seized the opportunity of bringing Norway more directly under the control of Rome. The three joint Kings, Eystein, Inge, and Sigurd Mund, were all extremely young, and do not appear to have realised how much control they were giving up. The new position of affairs is well brought out by the instruction to the new primate contained in the papal letter founding the archbishopric, " Super omnia studium tibi sit apostolicæ sedis decreta firmiter observare, eique tamquam matri et dominæ tuæ humiliter obedire " (*Norges Gamle Love*, vol. i. p. 440).

The greatest advance in the power of the Church took place some ten years later. After the death, in the civil wars promoted about this time by the nobility, of the three joint Kings, and of Haakon the Broad-Shouldered, son of Sigurd Mund, the aristocracy felt themselves sufficiently powerful to elect to the throne Magnus, son of Erling Skakke, whose title was invalid according to all principles of succession recognised at the time. To fortify his position, Erling, who was now the *de facto* ruler of Norway, approached the arch-bishop of Trondhjem and procured his son's coronation, thus giving to Magnus the support of the Church, and a sort of hitherto unrecognised title by divine right, as " the Lord's anointed." This step was not achieved without an unprecedented concession to the ecclesi-astical power. In an extraordinary document, the authenticity of which has been frequently challenged, but which is now generally admitted to be genuine, King Magnus Erlingson purports to convey the kingdom to St. Olaf (*i.e.* in effect to the Church), and to exercise his sovereignty as a sort of feudal vassal or viceroy of the deceased King. The most important clause of this remarkable document may be translated as follows :

" To God on this day of the glorious resurrection (? Easter, 1176) I assign myself with the kingdom for ever, and to the glorious martyr King Olaf . . . (I assign) the kingdom of Norway : and over this kingdom, as the hereditary possession of the same glorious martyr, I will preside under his lordship, as his deputy and his tenant, so far as pleases God."

In other words, while the Church in Norway was now subject to papal control, the King was henceforward to be dependent on the Church, as the representative of God and St. Olaf, for his title to the crown. The consequences of this surrender might have been disas-trous to the political independence of the country, had not a new claimant to the throne arisen sufficiently versed in the subtleties of ecclesiastical controversy to be able to advance an alternative theory of monarchy. With the purely political aspects of King Sverre's long struggle with Magnus Erlingson for the possession of the throne of Norway I have dealt in an earlier chapter. The genuineness of his claim to be a son of

Sigurd Mund has been continually disputed, and no final certainty on the point can, from the nature of the case, ever be reached. But whether this claim were true or false, there can, I think, be no doubt that Sverre really regarded himself as an instrument sent by God to wrest the kingdom from the usurper Magnus, and to restore a new order into a country bled white by the long period of civil war which had so long devastated it. His repeated references to the case of David and Saul make this an almost irresistible inference. In accordance with this theory he advanced the contention that kingly rule (his own, *bien entendu*) was by divine ordinance, and that resistance to it was equivalent to heresy.

Sverre's case was not only advanced with great controversial ability, but was an extraordinarily clever modification of Erling Skakke's policy. As in the case of Magnus Erlingson, a claim by divine right was brought in to bolster up an otherwise doubtful title ; but by his appeal to God himself over the heads of Pope and Archbishop alike the King made himself independent of ecclesiastical support, and escaped the necessity of agreeing to the humiliating conditions to which Magnus had been subjected. It was inevitable, however, that so direct a challenge addressed to the growing power of the Church should have brought Sverre into collision with its rulers. From the papal ban he for a time escaped by the use of a forged bull, but, though his unique abilities enabled him to attain the distinction of being the first King of Norway for a long time to die in his bed, it is clear that by the time of his death both parties to the dispute recognised the advisability of compromise.

This compromise was effected by Sverre's son and successor, Haakon, as his saga tells us, " according to the advice which King Sverre had given before he died." The basis of the settlement was approximately the *status quo* before the coronation of Magnus Erlingson. Under the succeeding Kings of the dynasty founded by Sverre, the relations of Church and State were subject to some fluctuations, but, though the Church attained at this time to the zenith of its influence, the Crown, on the whole, retained supremacy. This was especially the case under Haakon V, who secured the independence of the royal chapels from episcopal control, by placing them under a separate jurisdiction, exercised by the *magister capellarum regis*, who was virtually a royal official endowed by papal sanction with episcopal powers. By this step the Crown secured to itself a loyal Church on which to fall back in case of ecclesiastical opposition. Except in this respect, however, Haakon V was as good a friend to the Church as he was a zealous Christian. It was due to his initiative that partial translations of the Bible from the Vulgate into Old Norse were made, and the Church suffered no more than the nation at large from the aspect of his centralising policy with which they were immediately concerned. The extent, however, to which the Church retained throughout a national character has an important bearing on the hold which it still continues to have upon the hearts of the people.

On the whole, the period beginning with the foundation of the Trondhjem archiepiscopate, and ending in the middle of the fourteenth century with the Black Death, marks the highest point in the prosperity of the Norwegian Church. It was during this period that the history of education in Norway began, with the establishment of the Cathedral Schools. The tremendous percentage of the Norwegian clergy who perished from the ravages of the Black Death says volumes for the fearless and unselfish zeal with which they carried out their ministrations among the stricken populace. But for this very reason the plague left behind it an enfeebled Church, which was powerless to resist the purely political interference of Queen Margrete in her machinations for the Union of Kalmar, or of the later foreign Kings under that Union. Nor had it time or opportunity to regain its former vigour before, in 1536, the Reformation was thrust upon Norway by a royal edict from Denmark.

The change produced by this step was not nearly so great as might have been expected. The illiterate masses of the people, though they speedily adapted themselves to external conformity, were not deeply affected. Education, except for a minimum of elementary instruction at the hands of the *klokker* or sexton, was lamentably neglected. The change was mainly concerned with questions of dogma and to some extent of ritual, matters above the heads and outside the real interests of the peasantry. What was principally felt at first was the loss of the saints, and for this want the people compensated themselves by a greatly increased recourse to witchcraft and sorcery. This was not only the age of prosecutions for such offences, it was also the era of the " Black Books " with their recipes of charms and spells, and of the common practice of such forbidden arts. In Lecky's *History of Rationalism* great stress is laid on the iniquity of superstitious prosecutions for witchcraft, but it seems to me that the author overlooks the extent to which those who suffered from them were, in fact, morally guilty of the charge laid against them. They believed, equally with their accusers, in the possibility of such interference with the order of Nature, and they did their best to achieve such interference. In any case, despite persecution, the practices in question persisted and increased, and it was eventually not the spread of religious ideas, but the growth of general scepticism, which extinguished more or less simultaneously both crime and punishment. Religion remained superstitious, and recourse to magic was, in fact, the natural outlet for superstition deprived of any authorised means of satisfying its needs.

In the first century of the Reformation the emphasis was laid entirely on dogma. In accordance with the doctrine of justification by faith inculcated by Luther,

the early preachers were concerned only to ensure
that the beliefs of their congregations were strictly
orthodox. The Christianity which they taught thus
tended to be completely divorced from life ; and while,
no doubt, the peasantry readily accepted all that they
were taught, to the limited extent to which it was
intelligible, their real attitude to the excessively long-
winded disquisitions to which they were forced to
listen must have closely resembled that of Tennyson's
"Northern Farmer" :

" An' I niver knawed whot a meäned but I thowt a 'ad summut to
saäy,
An' I thowt a said whot a owt to 'a said an' I coom'd awaäy."

The parish clergy of Norway, during the seventeenth
century, were a class apart. It was the common
practice for the successor to a living to marry the
widow of the deceased incumbent, to remarry after her
death, and eventually to pass on his surviving wife to
his successor at his own demise. A living was therefore rather a close borough, and the large families
which this system produced tended to form a sort of
clerical caste, members of which were in occupation
of benefices over most of the parishes in the country.
They were educated abroad, and used the Danish
language in preaching and writing, a fact which must
have accentuated the remoteness of this new form
of native aristocracy from the uneducated masses to
whom they were supposed to minister. In a sense
they were learned and industrious ; many of their
sermons, especially funeral sermons, must have taken
hours to deliver ; but most of what they said must
have been as unintelligible to the majority of the
congregation as well could be.

They had their own attitude towards popular superstition. When the sexton of Fjellberg, in 1669, was
confronted by a white-bearded apparition, which
directed him to sing a psalm and fall on his knees
before the pastor of his parish, the bishop delivered a

solemn judgment to the effect that this was an illusion of the devil, since (1) good apparitions always prescribe prayer rather than psalm-singing ; (2) to fall on one's knees before the priest would tempt him to the sin of pride ; and (3) angelic visitants are always young and clean-shaven, and *quotiescunque angelus barbatus apparuit, diabolus apparuit* (see Professor F. Bull's article in *Samtiden*, part 6, 1923).

Under these conditions the Norwegian peasant provided himself with a creed and solved his spiritual difficulties in his own way. Superficially, he was now a Protestant, but the folk-tales collected by Asbjörnsen and Moe in the nineteenth century show clearly how little the blend of pagan and mediæval Catholic ideas which preceded the Reformation was modified by centuries of Protestant preaching. When we consider the influences to which the people were subjected from the end of the seventeenth century, it may be assumed that before that date the survival of older forms of belief had been even more strongly marked.

During the eighteenth century religion in Norway was affected by two very different movements, which, originating in Germany, found their way to the North through Denmark. They were in many points diametrically opposed ; but they had this in common, that they were concerned with life rather than faith or ritual. From this time date most of the octagon churches to be met with in Norway, a form suited to give to the pulpit the commanding position which it now assumed. The first of these movements was Pietism, of which the principal exponents were found outside the State Church. The Church, indeed, for the most part discountenanced the movement, while the Pietists, in their zeal for the individual life, tended to depreciate the value of institutional religion and ecclesiastical ritual. While the reaction from a barren orthodoxy was undoubtedly healthy, the drab Puritanism of the movement gave to religion a gloomy and unchristian ugliness. It also sowed the seeds of that antagonism between independent preachers and the official clergy which plays its part in the conflict of the present day.

The clergy, however, were not unaffected by the spirit of the age. The point of view of the seven Romsdal priests, known as the Pleiads (*Syvstjernen*), headed by Thomas von Westen, was essentially that of the Pietists. And during the reign of Christian VI (1730–46) the movement was temporarily fashionable in the Norwegian Church, though its new adherents did not fail to persecute the unofficial preachers, from Herrnhut and elsewhere, with whom it had originated. From this time dates the decree which was afterwards used with effect to silence the Haugian revival.

The best work of the movement was undoubtedly the impetus it gave to popular education. From the introduction of confirmation in 1736 dates the spread of a general knowledge of the art of reading. In 1739 an attempt was made to introduce a scheme of compulsory education, but in spite of the efforts of the clergy this was for a time largely ineffective. The peasantry could not be induced to see the necessity for it, while the class of individuals employed as teachers was sadly lacking in the necessary qualifications. There was a proverbial saying, " You wouldn't be a schoolmaster if you were fit for anything else." In spite of these obstacles, however, the majority of the population was soon sufficiently educated to read, and the improving literature of the time, in the form of homily books (*hus-postiller*) and the like, had a great influence on popular religious ideas long after its spirit had passed out of fashion with the official clergy.

The vogue of Pietism within the Church was, however, of short duration, and towards the close of the eighteenth century Norway began to be affected by the characteristic Rationalism of the period. While, however, the influence of Pietism had been greatest among the simple and superstitious masses, that of Rationalism was for the most part confined to the official classes,

where it assumed the form of religious indifference,
and to the clergy trained in Copenhagen University,
where, about 1780, this spirit came to prevail in the
Theological Faculty. The situation in the Norwegian
Church accordingly showed features of resemblance to
that which divides it at the present day. There was
a violent cleavage of opinion between the devout
laity and the official clergy. The homes of the former
were filled with the pietistic literature which, with the
education necessary to read it, was the legacy of the
previous movement, while in the pulpit religious
teaching was so completely subordinated to ethical
that the spiritual hunger of the congregations could
find no sustenance in that quarter. The clergy, indeed,
showed a praiseworthy zeal for education and enlightenment. In the dissemination of useful knowledge in
matters relating to the well-being of their parishioners
they played a leading part : but information on questions of health and pamphlets on improved methods
of agriculture now took the place of the tract and the
homily, with the natural result that the religious
instincts of the people turned elsewhere.

It was in these circumstances that the movement
started by Hans Nielsen Hauge succeeded for a time
in almost completely supplanting the influence of the
Church in the minds of the peasantry. Hauge, the
self-taught son of a *bonde*, from 1796 to 1804 conducted an anti-rationalistic revival throughout Norway.
While his teaching was, on the whole, of a pietistic
cast, it took a more healthy attitude to everyday life,
and was altogether of a more manly and practical
character. With untiring zeal, in speech and writing,
he conducted his short but epoch-making campaign,
travelling to the remotest ends of the country, and
stirring to the depths the starved religious instincts of
the people by his irresistible eloquence. His activities,
however, aroused the bitterest animosity in the ranks
of the regular clergy, and in 1804, by an application
of the anti-conventicle decree of 1741, he was arrested

and thrown into prison, whence he only emerged, ten years later, a broken and ruined man, who passed the final years of his life in retirement.

But the seed he had sown had fallen upon fruitful soil. Unlike most revivals, his work had permanent results. When, with the rise of democracy in the nineteenth century, the *bonde* came into his own, Haugianism, or at least sympathy with the independent lay preacher, was the spiritual aspect of the victorious struggle with bureaucracy. Hauge's religious standpoint suited the devout among the *bönder*, while the peasant revivalist was felt to stand in the same relation to the State-appointed clergy which the agricultural democracy occupied as against the other officials. The movement which ended in the establishment of popular local government in 1837 gave to the hitherto suppressed religious revival a fresh opportunity. Lay preachers of the Haugian persuasion appeared once more throughout the country, and in 1842 their position was recognised by the repeal of the law under which Hauge's activities had been brought to an end. Ultimately the influence of the movement permeated to the Church itself, and in the somewhat pietistic revival among the official clergy inaugurated by Professors Gisle Johnson and Carl Caspari about the middle of the nineteenth century, the services of the Haugian lay preachers were enlisted on the side of the Church. It was this change in the official attitude which led to the establishment of the Home Mission (*Indremissionen*), which, originally created as an auxiliary to the Church, now represents the opposition of the lay preacher's evangelical orthodoxy to the advanced theology of the university-trained clergy.

The growth of democracy necessitated revolutionary reforms in the educational system of the country. Hitherto popular education had been confined to the bare elements necessary to prepare the youth of the kingdom for confirmation. But if the *bonde* was to be entrusted with the responsibilities of political and administrative power, it was essential that his training should be placed upon a broader basis. This was particularly necessary since upon the cultural side the puritanism of the Haugians had exerted its least satisfactory influence. The fine old culture of the country folk, already threatened by changing economic conditions, was not only neglected, but deliberately discouraged; and but for the fact that the spirit of the age now fortunately directed to it the attention of such men as Asbjörnsen, Moe, and Landstad, the traditional links with the past might have been irreparably broken. Still less was this narrow and gloomy religion capable of creating a new culture to take its place. If the peasant was to be fully qualified for the great national rôle he was now destined to play, it was necessary that education should bring home to him the value of many things which his religious outlook tended only to obscure and to belittle.

This want was fortunately realised, primarily by the followers of the Danish preacher and poet, Grundtvig, who endeavoured to supply these cultural elements by the establishment of popular high schools (*folkehöi-skoler*), in which the literary and historical treasures of the national past were given a prominent place in the curriculum. They met with great opposition, and from want of State support most of the original schools of this type were eventually discontinued, though the movement was indirectly of great importance, and many such schools have since been revived under happier auspices. In competition with these voluntary and discountenanced *folkehöiskoler*, county schools for young men (*amts-* now *fylkes-skoler*), on a more severely practical basis and with different instructional methods, began to be established with State support about 1875.

The elementary educational system of the country was also subjected to legislative reform. Under the law of 1860, the hitherto extremely limited range of studies was considerably extended, and school-houses were provided to replace the ambulatory system which had hitherto prevailed. The system in force at the present day, however, dates substantially from 1889, though the principal Act has since been modified by various additions of later date. This law completed the transference of popular education from the hands of the Church to those of the people, for, though the Department of State which deals with these matters is still the Church Department, elementary education is now a branch of the democratic local administration of the country.

As in the case of the local government law generally, somewhat different provisions are applied to urban and rural districts. In towns only, for example, is there an advisory school council (*skoleraad*), which consists of the whole teaching staff of the locality. In the case both of town and country, the Church is only represented by one clergyman on the local school board (*skolestyre*) of each educational *kreds* or district. The teaching profession contributes one male and one female teacher to the board in the case of the larger towns or districts, in other cases only one teacher, who may be either a man or a woman. The remaining members of the board, except for certain special cases, such as industrial employers who have established elementary schools of their own, consist, in the rural districts, of members of the district council (*herredstyre*), and, in the towns, of representatives directly elected by the popular vote of the locality. The decision of all administrative questions rests, broadly speaking, with the school board, while financial matters are the province of the district council, whether urban or rural.

Education is compulsory between the ages of 7 and 14. A departmental committee set up by the Church and Education Department in 1919 reported strongly in favour of compulsory free continuation schools, with a three years' course—at any rate in urban districts. The objects of such schools are defined in the bill drafted by the committee as being " to further the pupil's general education and development of character, to prepare the young for the calling which they choose in life, and to make them good citizens." At present, many such schools are in existence, as well as technical schools connected with various trades and industries, but attendance is so far optional.

The subjects taught in the public elementary schools comprise religion, both forms of the Norwegian language (see Chapter VIII), writing, arithmetic, history, geography, natural science, largely based on instruction in matters of health, drawing, singing, and physical exercises, while appropriate handicrafts for boys and girls are taught with the approval of the local authority. Owing to the comparative scarcity of dissenters, the question of religious instruction has not until recently given rise to the difficulties with which it has been surrounded in England. Nonconformists may, however, obtain exemption for their children from the religious education imparted at school, and, since the conflict caused of late years by the advanced views of the younger clergy, there has been a demand for the extension of this provision to include members of the established Church as well. Feeling on this subject, indeed, runs high, as is shown by the fact that a young priest has lately taken proceedings against a prominent member of the community, who is said to have publicly accused him of " instilling deadly poison into the breasts of candidates for confirmation."

With regard to secondary education, the question of maintaining closer continuity with the course of the elementary schools has recently engaged close attention, with satisfactory results. Particular importance is also attached to the proper training of teachers, who have to pass a qualifying examination. There are at present six public and six private colleges devoted to this object. The Education Department's Report for 1921 complains, however, of the dearth of qualified teachers, which it connects with shortage of suitable housing accommodation. " It will take some time," says the report, " for the deficiency of teachers to be made up, without a considerable extension of training colleges." The Norwegian people have, in fact, fully awakened to the importance of education in all its branches, and, in 1920, a strong commission was appointed to go into the whole question. Even the needs of defectives have not been neglected, and there now exist three schools for the deaf, two for the blind, and three for the mentally deficient, directed by the State at the public expense. By a law passed as long ago as 1881, the education of all these classes of so-called abnormal children was made free and compulsory, though for a time the administration of the schools remained in private hands.

While education has been thus satisfactorily transferred so largely to the hands of local elected authorities, the organisation of the Church has remained more centralised. The growing cleavage between the religious views of clergy and congregations has naturally stimulated a demand for a larger measure of local and popular control. So far, however, there has been no further advance in this direction than is implied by the creation, in 1920, of the *menighetsraad* or Congregational Council elected by the parish. This body has important administrative functions, but in regard to such matters as the appointment of the bishops and clergy its powers are only advisory. The general meeting of all Church members in the parish (*menighetsmötet*) is called by the Council when occasion arises, or when not less than twenty parishioners demand it. It has a power of decision in such matters as the introduction of new authorised hymns and forms of prayer, and an advisory voice on many other questions.

It is fortunately unnecessary to enter in detail into the dangerous and difficult question of the merits of the controversy between the adherents of conservative and liberal theology. The problem is not confined to Norway, though it is hoped that the historical background which has been sketched has indicated the reasons for the special intensity of the conflict in that country. The religion of the masses is naturally inclined to be superstitious and bigoted, influenced as it has been to so large an extent by self-taught lay preachers without theological training. The clergy, on the other hand, have until recently been drawn from a single source of supply, which has, during the present century, inculcated modernist views of a type which the laity of any country would be slow to accept. To give way altogether to the clamour of the uninstructed would be to check the growth of a living organism and alienate intellect from the service of the Church; on the other hand, the conservative Christians can claim for their faith a closer approximation to that of many preceding centuries and perhaps a greater power to satisfy the cravings to which the religious instincts of mankind have hitherto given expression. The liberal theologian is entitled to claim that truth must not be stifled or shunned, and that the attitude of those who deliberately turn a deaf ear to modern criticism would have led, had they happened to be born in heathendom, to persistence in obstinate and invincible error. At the same time, there is a deep wisdom in the policy indicated by the words, " I have fed you with milk, and not with meat : for hitherto ye were not able to bear it." It is useless and dangerous to progress too fast. The harmonising of the apparently irreconcilable views at present prevailing must be a matter of time, patience, and mutual tolerance. It is stated that already the conservatism of the Congregational Faculty of Theology has shown considerable modifications. As regards the Old Testament, at any rate, the teaching of the Faculty is fully in conformity with modern criticism, and when the theory of verbal inspiration is to this extent undermined the essential difference of principle is abandoned. In England, less than fifty years from the persecution of Colenso, many of the authors of *Foundations* sat in high places. Such progress cannot surely be condemned as slow or disappointing. *Magna est veritas, et prævalebit.*

CHAPTER X

NORWAY AT SEA

IT was as a maritime race that Norwegians first made themselves known to the outside world. Norway, indeed, seems created by providence for the training of seamen. The imperfect internal communications of the country, its long indented coastline sheltered by the islands and reefs of the Skjaergaard, and the fact that its inhabited districts are to so large an extent confined to the valleys of rivers which terminate in the sea all tend to make the sea a natural highway for a considerable proportion of the population. It is, at the same time, necessary to bear in mind that the maritime activities through which alone a country so remote from the general life of Europe could come to be known to the outside world were primarily confined to a single class and to certain districts, and that the majority of the population, through all stages of Norwegian history, remained a race of simple, self-supporting agriculturists.

As is elsewhere pointed out, it was the development of a landed aristocracy, as a result of the sanctity and prestige attached to a few old families by the rest of the community under the system discussed in the next chapter, pp. 244 *et seq.*, which gave the first impulse to the viking movement. The mere undistinguished worker on the land could for a long time wring a sufficient subsistence from the soil. But if the ancestral holding, where the original homestead stood by the mound where the founder of the race lay buried, was to be preserved intact in a single line, it soon became necessary for the younger members, and the collateral branches of a stock which had learned to be proud of the position of leadership which the consensus of the neighbourhood conceded to it, to seek their fortunes in a different way of life. The sons of a chieftain were taught from infancy to regard themselves as superior to the humble tillers of the soil around them ; not for them the menial tasks of the farm ; but not all could hope, on their father's death, to share in the succession, if the whole family was not soon to sink into a condition of poverty quite incompatible with the social prestige to which they had grown accustomed. A warlike career, which simplified the problem by imposing a healthy check on the growth of the population, was the simplest solution, and the pursuit of such a career in foreign lands was naturally the method most popular with the head of the family, who wished to be left to develop his estate in peace. War in the neighbourhood would lead to inconvenient reprisals.

The viking movement, then, was in no sense a national movement. It was the work of independent individuals, mostly of the upper class, who took ship with a trusted band of followers to seek their private fortunes after the manner of the prince in fairy tale. It must also have been, so far as Norway is concerned, a much older and more gradual development than the accepted data of history would lead us to believe. Historians have, I think, been inclined to draw too slight a distinction between the shares borne by Denmark and Norway respectively in this epoch-making event. The movement is usually presented as a sudden and simultaneous display of naval activity on the part of both these countries, dating from the last few years of the eighth century. In the case of Denmark this picture is substantially correct and the sudden outbreak easily explained. For the Danish viking movement was primarily the result of the pressure of Charlemagne, about this time, on the neighbouring Saxons, some of whom actually took refuge within the confines of Denmark. In its earliest stages, as was natural, the principal objectives of the Danish freebooters were restricted to the north-western coasts of Charlemagne's Empire.

With Norway the case is different. All that we know of the earliest social and economic conditions in that country suggests a gradual and not a sudden development of the kind of life which was led by the

vikings. The pressure of a hungry land on a growing
population, and the rise of an aristocracy dependent
for wealth, authority, and prestige upon the practice
of war, had in this case far more to do with the movement than the activities of Charlemagne. The earliest
recorded raids by the Norse vikings were the work of
individuals, who were most unlikely to feel any personal
concern in the conquest or oppression of the Saxons
or to be actuated by national or political motives.
Their field of operations was, moreover, about as far
removed from the limits of the Empire as could well
be conceived. And it is not without significance that
when the Danes, about 851, first encroached upon the
territory subjected to Norwegian hostilities, the members of the two races, so far from making common
cause, at once turned their arms against each other.

With everything pointing to an independent and
gradual development of Norse viking activity, we
should, I think, hesitate long before accepting a theory
of sudden and united action on the part of Danes and
Norwegians. It must be remembered that the history
of those lands with which Norwegians came most in
contact was very imperfectly documented, and that
in such places as the Orkneys and Shetlands, the
Scottish Hebrides, and the north and west coasts of
Scotland many raids could take place, many thralls
and much property be carried off, without any record
surviving. It is suggestive, in this connection, to
examine the first recorded instance of a viking raid
on the coasts of England. Under the date 787 appears
the following entry in the Anglo-Saxon Chronicle:

" In this year Beorhtric took Eadburh, King Offa's
daughter, to wife. And in his days first came three
ships of Northmen from Haerethaland. And then
the reeve rode thereto, and would drive them to the
king's vill, for he knew not what they were, and
there they slew him. Those were the first ships of
Danish men that sought the land of the English race."

The learned men of Denmark and Norway have contended with amusing ferocity on behalf of their respective countries for the dubious honour of having murdered this unfortunate and misguided official. The merits of this controversy are beside the present point, which is that this entry clearly was not made until the importance of the viking movement had been impressed upon the chroniclers by later developments. "First ships," "first came," are expressions which imply that other occurrences of a similar kind had taken place by the time the matter was recorded. Apart from the sack of Lindisfarne and Monkwearmouth (793–4), England was left undisturbed for nearly another half-century. And there is reason to believe that, had it not been for the serious outbreak of Danish raids which began about 833, we should now know nothing of the fate of King Beorhtric's port-reeve. The silence of history affords no conclusive argument against the existence of Norse vikings at a considerably earlier period.

But we are not left in a realm of mere conjecture, or compelled to argue merely from the inherent probabilities of the case. The picture of social life in the early Viking period which the poem called *Rigsthula* gives us, represents thraldom as an institution so time-honoured that the author of the poem treats the class of thralls as the oldest feature of the civilisation he depicts. Yet the men and women here described are clearly not of Norse stock, and the researches of archæologists forbid us to believe that they represent an indigenous race. The conclusion is therefore irresistible that these thralls were foreign captives and their descendants. The maritime associations of such features of the old heathen mythology as the ships *Skidbladnir* and *Naglfar* seem also to carry the history of Norwegian shipping to a remote prehistoric past. But there is surer ground than this. The responsibility of Norsemen for the sack of the monasteries in Eigg and Tory Island, reported in various annals

for the year 617, is perhaps uncertain. But Dr.
Jakobsen's researches into the place-names of the
Shetland Isles make it almost certain that there were
Norwegians here in the early part of the eighth
century, and this view is corroborated by the existence, in the time of Harald Fairhair, of odel tenure
in these islands and in the Orkneys, for such rights
are clearly based on a presumption of immemorial
possession, and it is for this reason that the system
was never transplanted in the later Norse colony
in Iceland. From the evidence of Dicuil, a Celtic
monk, who wrote in 825, it is demonstrable that Irish
Christians had progressed as far as the Faroe Islands
nearly a hundred years (*in centum ferme annos*)
before that date, and were, as early as 795, so firmly
settled in distant Iceland that not only anchorites,
but ordinary "clerici," were in the habit of travelling
to and fro. That these men, however venturesome
and regardless of their own lives, would have pushed
out into unknown seas even so far as the Faroes, in
the unseaworthy skin curraghs of the time, without
pressure of the same kind as had, by Dicuil's time,
brought about the evacuation of those islands, is
hardly credible.

There is, indeed, reason to believe that in one
respect a new development took place in the Norse
viking movement about the date to which its com-
mencement is ordinarily assigned by historians. It
is by no means certain that the Irish monks, whose
migrations Dicuil records, were directly attacked.
The Celtic population which the Norsemen found later
on in Iceland left, according to Ari the Learned,
"because they would not live with heathen men,"
not because they were assaulted or disturbed. But
the raids which marked the close of the eighth century, and the beginning of the ninth, were almost exclusively directed against Christian religious centres.
Lindisfarne, Monkwearmouth, Iona, and the monasteries of Ireland were at this time sacked and plundered.

The systematic way in which such institutions were now singled out is in itself evidence that the Norsemen had some previous knowledge of their existence, but that they had previously been left more or less undisturbed. This, perhaps, is the real clue to the synchronised activities of Norway and Denmark. The conquests of Charlemagne did not provide a common political motive, but his forcible conversion of the Saxons and his destruction of heathen symbols was an irritant to religious susceptibilities which could be felt by Norwegian and Dane alike.

A desire for plunder alone will not explain this departure. It was not only to the inmates of comparatively wealthy foundations that the vikings were a terror : lonely hermits upon barren rocks, like the holy man of Scellig Michil, did not escape the same fate. Another fact of undeniable suggestiveness is also apparent from the Celtic chronicles of the period. The strongholds of Irish Christianity were not only destroyed and plundered, but the invaders seem deliberately to have substituted their own pagan cult for that which they displaced. It was from the high altar at Clonmacnois that Aud, or Ota, as the Irish termed her, wife of the viking chief Thorgils, uttered her heathen oracles. Thorgils himself, we are told, " usurped the abbacy of Ard Machar," in other words, discharged upon that sacred ground the functions of a *gódi* or priest of the cult of Odin. Indeed, this practice was so widely extended as to point almost with certainty to deliberate policy.

In the Irish chronicle entitled *The War of the Gaedhil and the Gaill*, these occurrences are given the complexion of fulfilment of a prophecy which is represented as containing the following passage :

" Gentiles shall come over the soft sea ;
They shall confound the men of Erinn ;
Of them there shall be *an abbot over every church* ;
Of them there shall be a king over Erinn.

There shall be of them an abbot over this my church,
Who will not attend to mattins ;
Without Pater, and without Credo,
Without Irish, but only foreign speech."

The Norsemen appear to have gone even further than this, and actually made proselytes to their own faith. The chronicles mention men of Celtic and Christian origin who threw in their lot with the heathen, and even transcended their worst excesses. The suggestion that these so-called Gall-Gaedhil, or Irish foreigners, were of mixed race, or even, as Skene suggests, Scots from the Hebrides and Galloway, cannot, I think, be maintained. By 856, when these men are first mentioned, the Norsemen had hardly been in possession of the country long enough to have produced a sufficiently numerous progeny capable of bearing arms. And the annals make it clear that the Gall-Gaedhil were renegades from the Christian faith, in which the children of Norse fathers were hardly likely to have been nurtured. On the whole, then, I am of opinion that there was a definitely religious side to the earliest recorded raids by the Norsemen, and that it was this new feature, synchronising with the activities of Denmark, which brought the deeds of Norwegian sea-rovers to the notice of the cloistered historians of the period ; but that maritime warfare had been practised by this people at a far earlier date is, I think, demonstrable.

From first to last, unlike the Danes, the Norwegian vikings confined nearly the whole of their attention to the British Isles. Their path, in the earlier stages known to history, was uniformly by way of the Orkneys and Shetlands, through the Hebrides, to Ireland. Up to the battle of Clontarf, in 1014, Norsemen were in control of all the important centres in Ireland, and a considerable Norwegian element continued to exist in that country for a long time afterwards. The Hebrides were a Norwegian possession till 1266, and the Orkneys and Shetlands till 1468, when they were merely pledged as security for part of the dowry of the daughter of the King of Denmark and Norway who was married to James III of Scotland. The right to redeem these islands was tentatively asserted as late as the reign of our King Charles II. At one time the mainland of Scotland north of the River Oichil was a Norse possession, and Caithness and Sutherland were subjected to Norwegian influences for a long while. In England, Northumbria was predominantly Norse, while a large part of the rest of the country, as is well known, was in the possession of the Danes.

The commercially important part, therefore, of what may be called the colonial empire won by the Norwegian vikings was in Great Britain and Ireland. A considerable element of the seafaring stock which proceeded from Norway was bound, in the long run, to become fused with our race and to be lost to the mother country. To a certain extent this fusion took place almost from the first. The " pirates " whom King Alfred is said to have recruited to man his newly formed navy against the Danes were doubtless chiefly Norwegians. Others, like Egil Skallagrimson who fought at Brunanburh, were enlisted by Athelstan. At a later date Olaf the Holy fought in his youth for Ethelred the Redeless against other Scandinavians. Of such recruits, doubtless a considerable proportion settled down permanently in their adopted country.

The remainder of the Norwegian colonial empire was commercially undesirable. The Faroes and Iceland were settled by those independent chieftains who could not brook the centralised control of Harald Fairhair. The settlements in Greenland were an offshoot of the Icelandic colony. All these places absorbed a large proportion of Norway's most adventurous seamen, who were therefore eventually lost to the home country. For a long time, indeed, these colonists continued to sail to and fro as traders, but the absence of facilities for shipbuilding was bound in the end to make them more of a hindrance than a help to the maritime development of the commerce of Norway. When, after the ravages of the Black Death, it became impossible to supply Greenland regularly from Norway, that colony speedily became extinct, while the Icelanders of the same period were so unable to support themselves that they pleaded the insufficiency of visiting ships from Norway as an excuse for their illegal traffic with Englishmen and other foreigners, which they found essential to the continued well-being of the colony.

When, therefore, the maritime life of Norway began to develop a peaceful and commercial character, it was from the outset influenced by various circumstances likely to affect it adversely. The existence of a large section of the population bred to a seafaring life is only one factor, and that not the most important, which conduces to maritime supremacy. The possession of colonies necessitates a great deal of traffic by sea, but this is simply a waste of energy if the colonies are not commercially valuable. A large part of the empire won by viking enterprise consisted of settlements of this undesirable character, while the remainder was destined eventually to assist the development of a rival maritime power—our own.

The original impulse which had made Norway great at sea was, moreover, not representative of the people as a whole. It was the work of a particular aristocratic class, which was likely before long to lose its direct interest in seafaring, when its objective was changed from plunder to merchandise, from the noble art of war to the huckstering of commercial pursuits, and even of this class a large part was, almost from the outset, lost to the country.

If we glance generally at the history of maritime commerce we find that the kind of civilisation which has risen to eminence in this department of life has normally possessed certain characteristics which Norway has hitherto conspicuously lacked. The German

Hanseatic League, and the Dutch who supplanted
them, both represented urban civilisations where commerce was the end and seafaring merely the means.
They occupied central positions ; they had access to a
large variety of markets. The same may be said of
Great Britain, a " nation of shopkeepers," inhabiting
a nodal point in the trading system of the world. In
Norway, almost down to the present day, the vast
bulk of the population has been rural and self-supporting. It had little to export ; it stood in no need of
imports. Town life in Norway has always been to a
remarkable extent alien to the genius of the race, and
indeed the development of her few important urban
centres has owed much to the efforts of foreigners.
The country lay remote from all ordinary trade routes,
and those who laid the foundations of her commerce
were intimately acquainted with but one market—the
British Isles.

In these circumstances, the problem which presents
itself to Norwegian historians with regard to the rapid
decline of their country's early sea-power is one of less
complexity than they seem to consider it. The causes
which they assign to the *débâcle* no doubt played an
important part, but the victory, first of the Hanseatic
League and afterwards of the Dutch, was in any case
inevitable. The shipping of Norway is now, and has
been for some time, extremely important, but about
four-fifths of it is engaged in the tramp trade between
various foreign countries, and it could only flourish
under the conditions now widely prevailing, where no
flag-discrimination—as it is called—exists. Norway
has ships and seamen, but she is not, has not been, and
is not likely to become, a natural trade centre.

For some time, indeed, the great men of Norway
continued to participate directly in maritime trade.
To examine a typical voyage of this character is, however, instructive. In the Saga of Egil Skallagrimson,
a ship sails to England loaded with a mixed cargo of
fish, hides, and furs, which are there exchanged for

wheat, honey, cloth, and wine. This is not the action of a professional trader; it is a case of a rich man shopping in a departmental store. There is no attempt to procure the required commodities in the cheapest market; consider, for instance, that wine is purchased in England, whither, in all probability, it must have been imported. The return cargo consists entirely of the luxuries of the upper class; it is probably intended for the personal use of the shipowner. All the commercial ability shown in the transaction is on the side of the English, who provide from many sources a variety of articles suited to the taste of the customer, and receive in exchange commodities all of which can be made the subject of further trading. The voyage is made, not because the Norwegian is addicted to commercial pursuits, but because his country lies apart from the resorts of the European trader: like a backwoodsman, he has to travel a long way to do his shopping. It is easy to see that as soon as English or other foreign traders think it worth while to visit their country, the aristocratic class which has hitherto engaged in traffic of this description will at first be only too pleased. Like King Sverre in his celebrated temperance speech at Bergen, they will feel disposed to thank the foreigner who brings them so many desirable things: most of them will not, like Sverre, even make an exception in the case of the purveyors of wine.

As late as the period when *The King's Mirror* was written, in the middle of the thirteenth century, a trader's life was still a gentlemanly occupation, but in the course of the thirteenth century it ceased to be fashionable. The next stage sees the growth of an embryo trading class in the coast towns, but these were no proud and independent burghers of the Hanseatic or Dutch type, but agents dependent upon the capital of the aristocracy, and doing what had come to be regarded as their dirty work for them. When their patrons diverted their wealth to their foreign competitors, these men were quite unable to keep up to date in equipment or organisation. Their ships were out-classed, their attempts at the formation of guilds discountenanced and suppressed, as by King Eric Magnusson in 1295, a year after the first important grant of trading privileges to their Hanseatic rivals. From the strictly economic point of view of the country as a whole, there was, indeed, much to be said for the encouragement given to the German and other foreign traders, for it meant that both import and export trade was efficiently and, at first, economically handled. The real objection to the policy was, firstly, that it conferred on the foreigners not merely free trade facilities but monopolistic privileges; and secondly, that the importance of sea-power to a country in the situation of Norway was sufficient to outweigh purely economic considerations and even to be worth financial sacrifice.

The provision of ships for the navy continued to rest on the *leding* system established by the earliest Norwegian kings. The country was divided into districts (*skip-reidur*), each of which had to supply a fixed number of warships of a definite size. These ships continued to be built of exactly the same type as those which the vikings had employed at the dawn of history. The local builders neither knew nor would learn any improvement on the old traditional lines, nor were the districts willing to submit to the additional burdens which up-to-date construction would have entailed. In these circumstances it was above all things essential that seamanship and a more useful and progressive form of shipbuilding should be encouraged by keeping the overseas commerce of the country in native hands.

Nothing of the kind was done. The one class which suffered economically from foreign competition was not strong or independent enough to carry its point when King, nobles, and *bönder* welcomed the foreign trader with open arms. The wonderfully organised commerce of the Hansa would probably have secured, in any case, a certain proportion of the trade, but as it was it practically monopolised it. At least a healthy

competition from England and elsewhere might have
kept this development in check, but even this possibility was precluded by Haakon V's deliberate discouragement of the English trade. When, later on,
attempts were made to reintroduce this element of
competition, the German monopoly was too well
established, and the critical moment had passed.

It may be doubted, indeed, whether the mere loss of
maritime trade would have given rise to the bitterness
and discontent which was felt in Norway during the
period of Hanseatic domination. The class which had
developed Norwegian sea-power was no longer interested in it, while, as already stated, the burgher merchant class was small and insignificant. It was the
overbearing and arrogant behaviour of the Germans
after their monopoly was firmly established which gave
rise to popular resentment. The foreigners settled
permanently in the towns, and did not hesitate to
encroach on the domain of internal retail trade. Even
this departure found its supporters among the inhabitants of Norway. There can be little doubt that
the rising of the *bönder* under Herlog Hudfat in 1508
was the direct result of an ordinance forbidding the
Germans to deal directly with the country inhabitants.
At this time, indeed, such a decree must have occasioned
no little disturbance in the established conditions of
internal trade, for the native commercial life of the
time had long been stifled by unrestricted foreign
competition ; the reform was in itself a wise one, but
it came too late.

It was particularly unfortunate that the pressure of
the German monopoly was not fully felt till the time
when the Kalmar Union had begun to exert its hampering influence upon native patriotic effort. The
earlier Union Kings uniformly and deliberately subordinated the interests of Norway to their own political
exigencies : the Norwegian *riksraad* exerted such influence as it possessed, and under King Christopher of
Bavaria temporarily succeeded in setting some bounds

to the Hanseatic monopoly, but its independent power was continually declining, and was, indeed, consistently undermined by the monarchy. Individual nobles, too, like Olaf Nielsson in Bergen, did all they could to make a stand against the oppressive tyranny of the German merchants, but they received no sufficient support from the Crown; and indeed Christian I, who did more than any other king to surrender the trade of Norway into the hands of the Hansa, lies under some suspicion of connivance at the murder of Nielsson by the Germans in Bergen in 1455, since he took no steps to exact the retribution which this lawless action demanded.

Under Christian I, indeed, Norwegian sea-power was reduced to the very lowest ebb. Not only did the Germans in Bergen and elsewhere conduct themselves with a lawless arrogance which excited widespread resentment, but it must be admitted that Englishmen from Lynn and elsewhere were at the same time behaving equally badly in Iceland. Not only did unlicensed traders constantly infringe the Norwegian monopoly in this colony, but they were in the habit of decoying and kidnapping the inhabitants.

The law restricting trade with this colony to the mother country had, indeed, long been a dead letter so far as the English were concerned. A poem written in 1437, in the days, therefore, of King Eric of Pomerania, thus refers to the traffic already in existence :

> " Of Iseland to write is little nede
> Save of Stocke Fish. Yet forsooth in deed
> Out of Bristowe and costes many one
> Men have practised by nedle and stone
> Thiderwardes within a little while
> Within twelve year, and without perill
> Gon and come. . . ."

But by the time of Christian I matters had gone to far more serious lengths. When an attempt was made in 1467 to enforce the law against the English traders, they slew the King's officer, Björn Thorleifson, and seven of his men, and proceeded to devastate and pillage the country. This occurrence led to a state of war between England and Denmark-Norway, in which the latter, through lack of any adequate naval force of their own, were obliged mainly to rely on the activities of free-booters, mostly of German origin, such as Didrik Pining and other less celebrated adventurers of the same race and proclivities.

This development was turned to better account by Christian's successor, King Hans, the first of the union kings to pursue a vigorous and consistent anti-Hanseatic policy. Since there was now no Norwegian maritime commerce to destroy, Hans found he could safely encourage the indiscriminate activities of the German freebooters above referred to, together with those of other pirates, such as Andrew Barton, the hero of a well-known British ballad. Indirectly, even when these worthies were interfering with commerce other than German, their exploits tended to help King Hans in his struggle with the Hansa, since the complicity of Denmark-Norway was not suspected, and the piracies were ascribed, in England and elsewhere, to the League itself. But within a short time hostilities of this kind were mainly diverted to interference with the German merchantmen, for, in 1490, Hans entered into a commercial treaty with Henry VII, and from this time forward to break down the German monopoly by the encouragement of both English and Dutch competition became a definite part of his policy. At the same time he put off as long as possible the renewal of the Hanseatic privileges, and subjected these to every restriction which he felt it in his power to impose. He revived the question of compensation for the deaths of Olaf Nielsson and those who had perished with him in the German riot of 1455, and succeeded in obtaining a considerable sum. By an anti-Hanseatic alliance with England, Scotland, and Russia, and by the formation of an effective Dano-Norwegian navy, he prepared himself for the struggle which marked the close of his reign and which was concluded by the Treaty of Malmö (1512), the terms of which definitely mark a decline in the powers of the League, from which it never again recovered.

The decline of the Hansa, however, did not mean the immediate recovery of Norwegian sea-power. On the contrary, some of the means employed by King Hans in the furtherance of his policy tended to destroy the last remnants of the native merchant service. Trade with Iceland and the north of Norway, which had hitherto been in law if not in fact monopolised by Denmark-Norway, was now thrown open to the English and other competitors; while the Dutch, who about this time were threatening to acquire the carrying trade of the world, were substitutes for the Germans who, though they might be less arrogant and more pleasant to deal with, left no greater opening for the development of the latent possibilities of Norwegian seamanship. The coast towns, indeed, grew and prospered, more especially after the introduction of sawmills early in the sixteenth century had given an impetus to the timber trade, which now for the first time began to rival fish as the staple export of the country. But the newly developed commercial life of these towns was largely in the hands of foreigners, while the carrying trade was almost completely monopolised by Holland. It was practically in Bergen only, as the domination of the Hansa was more and more relaxed, that the nucleus of a native shipping industry, connected with the fish trade, grew up in the course of the seventeenth century. Elsewhere, the only serious rival to the Dutch was, strangely enough, Scotland, which was firmly established in the fjord districts between Bergen and Lindesnes.

At first, indeed, though the revival of trade was welcomed, there appears to have been little attempt to make use of the latent seafaring potentialities of the people. The *riksraad*, in 1490, had forbidden the *bönder* to sail to foreign ports in their own ships, as it

was believed that the practice had a detrimental
effect on agriculture, and the same point of view may
have survived, to some extent, in the following century ;
but it was impossible in the long run to keep the
Norwegian from the sea. During the sixteenth, and
especially the seventeenth century, the bulk of Norway's export trade was under the Dutch flag, but the
personnel which manned the ships, from captain to
cabin boy, became increasingly Norwegian. " The
best seamen belonging to the King of Denmark," says
Molesworth in his *Account of Denmark as it was in the
Year* 1692, " are the Norwegians ; but most of these
are in the service of the Dutch, and have their families
established in Holland ; from whence it is scarce
likely they will ever return home, unless the Dutch
use them worse, or the Danes better " (p. 88). By
this time, indeed, the exodus of Norwegian sailors
amounted to a serious emigration. But as early as
the reign of Frederick II (1559–88), when the exploits of the Dano-Norwegian fleet in the Swedish war
directed attention to the value of sea-power, attempts
were made to check the foreign monopoly of maritime
trade. The export of oak timber was forbidden, and
foreigners were prohibited from building ships in
Norway, or purchasing Norwegian vessels less than ten
years old. Such provisions as these were, in fact,
very generally disregarded, but they show a dawning
sense of the importance of regaining control of an
industry which the character of the country and its
inhabitants seemed designed to foster.

Cromwell's Navigation Act of 1651 probably marks
the turn of the tide. Under this law the carriage of
timber between England and Norway was restricted
to the ships of the two countries. From this time
down to the Treaty of Utrecht in 1713, the Dutch were
engaged in almost continuous war, first against England, then both England and France, and finally with
England against France. Meantime, in repeated wars
with Sweden, the value of a powerful navy was con-

tinually brought home to the Dano-Norwegian Government. The building of the so-called " defence ships," a type of armed merchantman equally useful in war and peace, led to a considerable development of Norwegian maritime trade during the last two decades of the seventeenth century. The credit for this policy belongs principally to the Norwegian statholder, Gyldenlöve, an illegitimate son of King Frederic III. His alert and sympathetic mind was quick to realise the value of the Norwegian peasantry both as soldiers and sailors; and, apart from the temporary revival of shipping referred to above, his perspicacity was justified during the Great Northern War by the conspicuous part played by Norway both by land and sea. To this struggle belong the exploits of Norway's great naval hero, the dashing admiral Peder Wessel, better known as Tordenskjold.

It was during the remainder of the eighteenth century, when, except for a short war with Sweden in 1788, Norway maintained a position of neutrality, that the shipping of the country first attained an important development. The supremacy of the Dutch at sea had passed away, while England was almost continuously at war. The opportunity was a great one, and it was utilised to the full. The troubles which began with the Battle of the Baltic in 1801, and came to a head with the seizure of the fleet by the English in 1807, and the period of war with this country which followed it, were therefore a heavy blow to Norwegian prosperity. When peace was restored England had begun to look elsewhere for her timber, and most of the old commercial houses of Norway were ruined. But the recovery of a nation so pre-eminently suited to a maritime life could not be long delayed.

At first the trade had serious difficulties to cope with. In many so-called " privileged " countries, which were supposed both to accord and receive equality of treatment as between Norwegian ships and their own, there was, in fact, a differentiation adverse to Norway,

against which she was not in a position to protest,
owing to the importance of maintaining a valuable
trade connection. To counteract this, it was even
suggested by the Storting that a practice should be
revived which had existed from 1672 to 1819, of
secretly deducting from one-sixth to one-ninth of the
actual tonnage of Norwegian ships in calculating the
tolls and dues which were based upon capacity. But
more honourable counsels prevailed. The principal
difficulty affecting the trade was, however, that the
number of ships was now considerably in excess of the
demand, so that freights were reduced by competition
to a minimum, while expenses, in the hard times
through which Norway was passing, were inordinately
high. To some extent this was counteracted by an
increasing volume of imports and exports, but so long
as the services of Norwegian ships were mainly confined
to carrying to and from Norway, the excess of shipping
over available cargoes was bound to be felt.

The great advance came with the repeal of the
British Navigation Act in 1849, and the adoption of a
similar non-discriminating policy by other countries.
The tramp trade of the world, on which the greater
part of the Norwegian merchant fleet has since sub-
sisted, was thus thrown open. At the same time the
increasing industrialisation of the more important
countries caused the enormously increased populations
to become more and more dependent upon overseas
trade.

The result was that the figures for Norwegian
shipping made a tremendous leap, from a tonnage of
233,497 in 1845 to 1,351,722 thirty years later. At
this point it remained comparatively stationary up to
the time of the Great War ; in 1913 the figure for
comparison was 1,767,405. At the same time, Norway
had now won an extremely high place among the
merchant fleets of the world, surpassed only by Great
Britain, the United States, and Germany, while in
proportion to the population the merchant fleet of

Norway was altogether unrivalled. Probably one reason for the comparative stagnation in Norwegian shipping in recent times lies in the fact that Norway has been much slower than other nations to change from sail to steam. As lately as 1900 the sailing ship tonnage was not far short of double that attributable to steam, while even immediately before the war nearly a quarter of the total tonnage was represented by sailing ships.

The history of Norwegian shipping during the Great War is a subject which deserves more space than can be accorded to it in a work of this kind. As in the eighteenth century, Norway derived great profit from the fact of her neutral position at a time when her most formidable rivals were engaged in hostilities; but it was evident almost from the first that neutral trade in the old sense was incompatible with the conditions of modern warfare. The former distinctions between free goods and contraband, whether absolute or conditional, were all obliterated. The improved facilities for inland transport necessitated a wholly new application of the doctrine of continuous voyage. In the complex conditions of modern industrialised existence it was, moreover, unnecessary to resort to military or naval pressure in order to control the activities of neutral countries. Economic pressure, the refusal of supplies necessary to the life and trade of the neutral, was infinitely more effective. Without British coal, for example, Norwegian steamships were practically immobilised. A similar dependence upon British goodwill affected many other industries with which we are not here concerned. But as a result it became inevitable that neutral Norway should become, in fact, one of our most valuable allies. That she made a virtue of necessity is a truth which should not deprive her of a claim on our gratitude. If we begin to test alliances by considerations of self-interest, or even of *force majeure*, where shall we stop ? The orientation of Norway towards England corresponded to the real

feelings of the vast majority of her people. The great
services which Norwegian shipping performed for us
were carried out with a loyalty and a disregard of
risks which showed no signs of reluctance or con-
straint. The gallant sailors who faced the perils of
the German submarine again and again were not
subject to political pressure or parties to any agreement. More than two thousand of them perished in
the war, drowned or shot without the power of retaliation. Many were repeatedly torpedoed, only to seek
employment once again, almost before their clothes
were dry. The following story, which appeared in
the Norwegian newspaper *Tidens Tegn,* is characteristic
of the spirit of these seamen.

" Once during the war an inquiry was being held
after a loss at sea. A sailor who was giving evidence
was asked if he had been present on any former occasion
when a ship had been torpedoed. Yes, this was the
seventh time he had been torpedoed in the North Sea.
The judge asked him casually whether he was not
nervous when he went to sea again after such an
experience. ' Nervous ? ' ' Yes, I mean, don't you
find it a bit queer to go out again and wait to be torpedoed ? ' ' No, the pay is good, and now I'm used to
rowing half across the sea to the nearest land. One
takes with one no more than the things one stands
up in.' "

In the summer of 1917 a definite agreement was
entered into between the Norwegian Shipping Association
and the British Government, which engaged all the ships
which were not needed by the country itself in the
service of the Allies for the duration of the war. This
arrangement was intimately linked with an agreement
for the adequate supply of coal to Norway by Great
Britain. But even before this time a very large proportion of Norwegian shipping was engaged in trade
between allied ports, and it had suffered severely from
the activities of German submarines from the autumn
of 1916 onwards. In the course of the war nearly

half of the total tonnage existing at the beginning was lost from this cause. Against the very large profits earned by Norwegian shipping during the war must be set the serious difficulties in which the replacement of this tonnage under the circumstances of the time has placed the industry. New ships were ordered at the top of the market which have now to be utilised under conditions of increased competition and a collapsed freight market. This handicap has been increased by the alteration in the exchange, as between Norway and shipbuilding countries such as Great Britain, between the dates of order and delivery. As against the pound sterling, the value of the kroner, which at par is about eighteen, has fallen lower than thirty. The cost to the purchasers, in kroner, is therefore enormously increased. So serious has the situation become, that many contracts have had to be cancelled, even at great cost.

A further difficulty resulted from the entrance of the United States into the war. While America was still neutral an important shipbuilding industry was started by Norwegians in the United States ; indeed the great strides made there by this industry are primarily due to Norwegian initiative. When America came into the war she proceeded to take over these yards and to requisition the shipping under construction in them. The Norwegian shipowners have not found that their claims for compensation in respect of this action have been quickly satisfied. One important claim, indeed, is still unsettled, while another was paid, after arbitration, in February 1923.

Norwegian shipping, indeed, has felt to the full the reaction from the fleeting though unexampled prosperity of the war. Even at the best, it was not allowed to derive the full measure of profit which the exceptional conditions of the time seemed to offer. The lion's share went to the State in the form of taxation. It may be questioned whether the policy of loading this industry with exceptional burdens was not short-

sighted and mistaken. The days have long passed
when Norway could afford to regard with indifference
the prosperity of her carrying trade. A small, self-
supporting nation, with a relatively large export trade
consisting exclusively of natural products, might well
feel that, apart from the necessity of supporting and
recruiting an adequate navy, it mattered little whether
her maritime commerce was in her own hands or those
of others. But at the present day, with a balance
of trade inevitably adverse, the existence of a large
carrying trade is vitally necessary to redress the scale.
While, moreover, to other industries it is possible to
accord the protection of tariffs and subsidies, the prosperity of merchant shipping is incompatible with any
attempt to discriminate in favour of national tonnage.
The trade of the world must be kept open to Norwegian
ships, and this fact precludes the possibility of any
measures on the part of the State calculated to favour
her own flag. The retaliatory policy which these would
inevitably provoke would mean the ruin of a trade
plied so largely between foreign countries. " A fair
field and no favour " is all that the Norwegian shipowner demands, but in the case of so vitally important
an industry, he ought at least to expect that his own
country will not subject him to extraordinary burdens,
but will allow him to earn in good times the profits
necessary to support him through bad. But this has
not been the policy pursued. Apart from the special
contributions exacted from shipping for the revenues
of the country, there are complaints that an intelligible
but perhaps excessive desire for the social welfare of
seamen has resulted in regulations which are a serious
handicap in competition with other nations who care
less how their sailors are lodged and fed. On this
phase of the question much may be urged on both sides,
but the existence of the handicap is undeniable, and it
seems clear that social considerations must be reconciled
with economic if the trade is to hold its place in the
world.

Apart from circumstances connected with the present economic depression and the fall in the freight market, there exist other factors which make the future of this industry particularly difficult to forecast. Partly as a result of the unprecedented sums of capital which flowed into it during the war, increasing from 278 million kroner in 1914 to 1159 millions at the end of hostilities, but partly as a phase in the general industrial change which is affecting the country, the whole circumstances of Norwegian shipping have recently undergone revolutionary modifications. A more or less primitive business, conducted by a number of small owners, has now been organised in the hands of powerful companies on up-to-date industrial lines. The financial depression which has ruined many shipowners has tended to assist this development, since their ships have passed from their possession to fewer but stronger hands. The change in the relative proportions of sail to steam and Diesel motor (the latest development) is also significant : sail tonnage has dropped from 566,000 tons in 1914 to 126,000 tons at the end of 1923, while steam and motor tonnage has risen correspondingly. Partly under the pressure of increased competition, the tramp trade on which the prosperity of Norwegian shipping has hitherto depended has been more and more abandoned in favour of regular line traffic.

In many ways these changes have made the future prosperity of the trade dependent upon qualities differing considerably from those which in the past made seafaring a natural expression of the genius of the people. As was indicated at an earlier stage, the greatness of Norway at sea was not so much the result of commercial aptitude as of the existence of a large section of the population which naturally turned to the sea for a livelihood, and consisted, in fact, of born sailors. Under modern industrialised conditions, where the stoker and engineer have replaced the ordinary sailor, and where business organisation and a quick eye for chances of profit play a more important part than seamanship, it does not seem to follow as a matter of course that Norway can maintain the supremacy she has hitherto secured. Life at sea and on land is beginning to have more points of resemblance than in the days of long sailing voyages under a despotic and patriarchal régime. The class from which the modern ships are manned is finding increasing chances of alternative employment as the industrial development of the country progresses. In these circumstances, the future is difficult to predict.

So far, the omens are favourable. The shipping industry has shown, indeed, a remarkable vitality in face of particularly adverse conditions. Very few Norwegian ships, in spite of the unremunerative state of the freight market, have lately been laid up. Ships lost by the bankruptcy of some owners have merely been transferred to other Norwegian hands. The trade has shown a surprising ability to make use of fleeting chances, such as that afforded by the great earthquake in Japan in 1923. The question of maintaining an adequate supply of men trained to a seafaring life has engaged the close attention of those interested, who have sought to solve the problem by the provision of training ships, and the supply of schools for the officers. Above all, the vital importance of maintaining a pre-dominant position at sea under existing economic circumstances is being more and more impressed upon the mind of the nation.

If Norwegian shipowners have maintained their position so well during the last few critical years, there seems every reason to hope that the worst period is over. To some extent, no doubt, they have been helped by the depressed exchange at home, for they pay in kroner while they earn in pounds or dollars. But shipping must necessarily depend upon a constant and increasing flow of imports and exports ; with the development of industry and the revival of settled industrial conditions its prosperity increases. As the countries of the world grow more and more interdependent and less self-supporting, the chances for maritime trade improve. It is therefore to be expected that an industry which has shown such persistence and resourcefulness in adversity will continue to thrive, and that the "honour and might" which "white sails" have brought to Norway[1] will be no less conspicuous in an era of steam and petroleum.

[1] " Vor aere og vor makt
Har hvide seil os bragt."

(Our honour and might
White sails have brought us.)

CHAPTER XI

THE BONDE

As the Norwegian historian O. A. Johnsen rightly contends, " there is actually only one class in the country which is Norse in the full signification of the word, and that is the class of the farmers (*bondestanden*)." With a community of free and equal tillers of the soil, Norwegian civilisation began in the dim unrecorded past on which only the excavations of the archæologist can throw a partial and intermittent light. From this community developed the society, no longer equal but sharply divided into classes, which we know from the early *Edda* and the prose sagas. Once more equal but still free and independent, preserving the national language and the national traditions, the rural population survived centuries of foreign domination, until in the nineteenth century it came once more into its own as the heart and kernel of Norwegian democracy. The younger urban civilisation, however national it may seem to-day, grew up under foreign influences and absorbed many alien elements, and the great industrial change which is coming over the country to-day must not be the work of this section of the population alone if Norway is to retain her national identity and continuity with her historic past.

Between the idolised figure of nineteenth-century romanticism and the earth-bound boor of the present day realist, between the radical who fought and triumphed over bureaucracy and the almost reactionary conservative who is to-day the most uncompromising bulwark against the advance of Bolshevism, there would appear superficially to be little in common. But the fact is, that while schools of literature and of politics change, the *bonde* remains perennially the same, and by his very immobility produces this illusion, just as mountains seen from a moving railway carriage appear to change their form and position.

Having regard to the extremely small proportion which the cultivable soil bears to the whole area of the country, it might be expected that agriculture, as a means of livelihood, would play but a limited rôle in the national economy. Remarkable as it may seem, however, farming in one form or another not only occupies a larger proportion of the population than any other industry, but actually produces a larger aggregate income. Until recently, indeed, almost the whole of the inland population was engaged in agricultural pursuits, while even on the coast a considerable amount of farming was practised in combination with other means of livelihood. But, even in these days of rapid industrial development, the workers on the land constitute about 40 per cent. of the total population, and neither shipping, fisheries, the timber trade, nor the modern industries provide by themselves so large a share of the national income. The soil, though scanty, is remarkably fertile, more so in fact than that of most European countries. This was noticed by the anonymous author of *Animadversions* upon Molesworth's *Account of Denmark as it was in the Year* 1692. " It is observable," he says, " that where the ground is fit to be till'd, it yields a greater crop than the soil of the richest countries." This is as true to-day as it was in the seventeenth century.

One is tempted to describe the Norwegian farmers as a race of peasant proprietors. Holdings are small ; more than 90 per cent. of them have less than 10 hectares of cultivable ground. The vast majority of the farms are freehold. Yet to translate the term *bonde* by " peasant " is to misrepresent the true state of affairs. A whole nation, once sharply divided into classes, has really been absorbed into this category, and the equality and lack of social distinctions which strike the English visitor are the result of external pressure and other historical influences, and are, perhaps, more apparent than real. Many farms have been occupied by a single family for a length of time which would throw the pretensions of most of our county families into the shade, and in at least one instance there existed in Gudbrandsdalen in quite recent times a *bonde* who asserted his descent from King Harald Fairhair, his lineage being widely accepted as genuine. Pride of race exists in no small degree: the apparent equality which strikes the stranger is largely the effect of similarity of occupation. It has been assisted by levelling down in the period of Danish domination and by a wise levelling up in more recent times; but there is a suggestive truth in the observation made by that distinguished artist, Erik Werenskiold, with regard to a district where he was engaged in making studies for his illustrations to Asbjörnsen's *Folk and Fairy Tales*—" here petty kings still dwelt on the large farms, and the cottars (*husmaend*) were their thralls."

The aristocratic element in the agricultural population is, indeed, claimed by Björnson, in a famous speech, as a reason for the special strength of the Norwegian democracy. " The aristocracy," he says, " is absorbed in the people, and thereby imparts to it its own nobility. Therefore to the present day the work of our democracy has been stamped with the qualities of a chieftain (*hövdingepraeget*)."

The characteristic system of land tenure which developed naturally out of prehistoric conditions and has persisted to the present day tends, in fact, in the absence of countervailing influences, to produce not only independence but aristocracy.

The old theory that the organisation found in the country at the dawn of historic times was the result of successive incursions of Teutonic tribes in military formation is now to a great extent abandoned or modified, and is indeed disproved by archæological evidence, which tends to show an unbroken continuity of race and culture reaching back indefinitely into prehistoric times. At the earlier stages, the population was extremely thin and scattered, and its numbers seem only gradually to have increased. It consisted, in fact, of a number of independent families, each of which owned and cultivated a single estate in common.

Manifestly, this primitive arrangement could not continue unmodified for many generations. It would, indeed, be possible to accommodate the head of a family and most of the descendants who were added in his lifetime ; such a practice appears to have been common in the saga-times, and traces of it are perceptible in Norway at the present day. But collaterals would speedily be forced to find fresh land for themselves—a task which in a thinly populated and undeveloped country would for a long time present no special difficulty. There were two possible lines of development. A sort of village community might arise, cultivating a large area in common, either in joint ownership, or with separate intermixed holdings, or a combination of several such systems. In many districts this in fact took place, and the arrangement continued well into the nineteenth century, when legislation was introduced to effect an economical redistribution. But the most characteristic development in Norway was what is known as odel tenure. This is a system of inheritance to landed property which is founded on the primitive idea of family ownership and seeks to preserve continuity of family possession with due regard to the practical difficulties which arise. All male heirs of the same degree are theoretically entitled to share in the succession, either jointly or by subdivision. In practice, however, it is evident that joint ownership of a limited estate would speedily become unworkable, while constant subdivision would soon lead to the disappearance of any inheritance worth having. It consequently became usual, at an early stage, for a single heir to succeed to the ancestral property, thus preserving the integrity of the estate while the remaining claimants were compensated in other ways. The real object of the system was in fact to prevent the alienation of such an estate to strangers—an object which was secured by giving other members of the family a right of pre-emption when the sale of the property was in question, and a right to redeem, on easy terms, for some time after any transfer to a stranger had taken place.

The obvious effect of such a system, even in cases where a certain amount of joint ownership persisted, was to place the direct line of the original ancestor in a privileged position. So long as agriculture was the only available means of livelihood, the head of the family was surrounded by an increasing body of collaterals, who cleared separate holdings for themselves but were in an altogether inferior position. The peculiar sanctity with which family continuity was regarded was enhanced by the prevalence of ancestor worship and the fact that the chief of the family exercised priestly functions in the local religious ceremonies and sacrifices. Probably there was originally an intimate connection between the odel system and a deceased ancestor, real or hypothetical, who was regarded as divine. At any rate, some such reason is required to account for the remarkable persistence in Norway of a system which in other countries was confined to an early and primitive stage of development.

There is a passage in *Norges Gamle Love* which is specially illuminating in this connection. King Haakon V, in 1316, is explaining how he has been asked for rulings on certain doubtful points connected with odel. The inquirers state that some witnesses, though unable to comply strictly with the technicalities of the law, yet appear to make out a satisfactory case, " tracing clearly their line of ancestry to the burial mound and to heathendom." This was, in fact, far more than the existing law required by way of title, and appears, therefore, to be a relic of primitive custom. May we not see in this evidence that odel was originally a title based on immemorial possession by a family whose right to the estate was ultimately traceable to an ancestor assumed to be divine, who was really the thing possessed in common by the family as a whole, and in the interests of whose cult it was deemed essential, at any sacrifice, to preserve continuity ?

On such a point it is difficult to speak with certainty, for, of course, the introduction of Christianity swept away any conscious application of such a motive. But the fact remains that in historic times, and even at the present day, there is a remarkable consensus of opinion, which is quite disinterested, in favour of preserving continuity of possession in the family. And it is equally certain that as early as the eighth century the odel proprietors represented, not the general mass of the freeholders, but a landed aristocracy invested with a jealously guarded social prestige and constituting the natural leaders of local opinion. In the old poem, *Rigsthula*, which divides the Norse society of its day into three classes—the jarl, the karl, and the thrall—it is only to the first of these that the enjoyment of odel inheritance is attributed. In the passage in question it is, moreover, emphasised as one of the most important of aristocratic privileges, so that its omission elsewhere can hardly be accidental :

> " Bade him inherit
> The odel acres,
> The odel acres,
> The ancient dwellings."

From the fact that one of the sons of the middle-class *karl* is given the title of *hauld*, which in the laws of Northern and Western Norway is equivalent to odel proprietor, the most that can be deduced is that the barriers between the classes were not impassable. But, having regard to the fact that in Southern Norway the word was used generally of the free *bonde* without any such special significance, it may well be that no technical or legal meaning should here be attached to the term. In another Eddic poem, *Hyndluljód*, the *hauld-born* are given a most exalted and even divine pedigree, while the care taken in the early laws of Norway to distinguish odel land from other forms of freehold property, such as *kaupajord*—purchased estate—and *föng*—acquired estate—by insisting on an unbroken succession for many generations, shows that the class which enjoyed it in historical times was a proud and select one. Indeed, a common root appears to connect *adal*—noble— and *odal*, so that, as Stubbs has said (*Constitutional History*, vol. i. p. 57), "primitive nobility and primitive land-ownership thus bore the same name." This could hardly have been the case had odel rights been widely enjoyed by the middle class, since, as Gilbert tells us in *The Gondoliers* :

> " When everybody's somebody,
> Then no-one's anybody."

It was, in fact, as a result of the odel system that the militarism of the viking age developed. The tastes of the upper class described in *Rigsthula* are purely war-like ; they acquired land for the prestige which it conferred upon them, but were not in the least interested in its cultivation.

If the estate was not to be subdivided to the point of extinction, wealth, and preferably more land, must be secured to compensate those excluded from the succession, or the younger members of the family must be encouraged to make their own fortunes by the predatory life which was in those days practically the only method open to them. It is perhaps not without significance that *Rigsthula* makes the future king the youngest of the jarl's large family. A solid block of elder brothers would, no doubt, exert a very considerable influence to make the youngest of the series shift for himself, and the founder of a new title might well be a younger son reacting to such a stimulus. To encourage a taste for a predatory life on the part of superfluous members of the family was thus a natural result of the system : they could in this way either win estates for themselves, which would occupy their attention, or be killed, which equally solved the difficulty, or they might take permanently to the career of a pirate and cease to bother about the land altogether.

Warlike tastes were also encouraged among the

landed aristocracy, because only in the event of war did
they, at first, enjoy any superior authority apart from a
barren social prestige.   The old estates fell into the
hands of a minority, because only so was it practically
possible to ensure continuous family possession.   But
the remainder of the free community continued to
enjoy equal rights with them.   It was only the necessity
for defence which gave authority to the hersir, the jarl,
or the king.   Before the *things*, or common meetings,
all free men were theoretically equal.   Even at the
comparatively late date when any codified law existed,
rebellion against a king or other chieftain who proved
aggressive or tyrannical was not only conceded as a
right, but enjoined as a duty.   It was only in wartime
that the necessity for a leader gave any individual
authority over his fellows.   He had on such occasions
to justify his position ; and war, therefore, naturally
became his speciality and his delight.

Out of this militarism developed the third class of
the community described in *Rigsthula*, the thralls.
The description given in the poem leaves no room for
doubt that these men were of alien stock, and now that
archæological researches have disproved the existence
of any aboriginal race in Norway distinct from the
Nordic,[1] it seems certain that the class was mainly
drawn from captives secured in early viking raids.
Elsewhere I have given my reasons for believing that
the Norwegian viking movement originated at a date
far earlier than that usually assigned to it by historians.
In any case, the institution of thraldom as a factor in
the cultivation of the land existed from the earliest
period of which we have any record.

After the introduction of Christianity the emancipation of thralls went on apace ; but, from the smoothness
and rapidity with which this change was carried out, it
may be inferred that it caused little practical change
in the relations of employer and employed.   The

[1] Except for the Lapps of the North, who hardly enter into the
question.

thralls must have mainly been the property of the
military aristocracy, and these men, whose wealth
depended upon plunder in foreign lands, and who were
seldom directly interested in farming, can hardly have
been exacting task-masters. As the viking movement
came to an end, and thralls had to be acquired by
purchase rather than by capture, the system presumably
lost any economic advantages it may once have possessed. There were probably many employers who,
like Erling Skjalgson, permitted their thralls to earn
money to purchase their freedom on plots of their own,
realising that there would be nothing for the liberated
thrall to do but to go on exchanging his labour for the
right to occupy his holding.   Socially, the freedman was
hardly superior to the thrall, the sharp line was drawn
above them. Even in the grave the two classes of
freedmen, *leysingjar* and *frjalsgjafar*, were affected by
this inequality, and had their burial-ground apart from
that destined for the poorest of the free *bönder*.

The effect, in the long run, of the gradual emancipation of the thralls was rather to depress the status of
the lowest class of free labourer than to elevate that of
the thrall.   There is a deep underlying truth in the
remark of Erik Werenskiold quoted earlier in this
chapter, which compares the *husmand* to the thrall.
For the emancipated thrall, bound to one spot by the
possession of a dwelling which he was permitted to
occupy in return for work done for the owner of the
estate, was essentially the same as the modern *husmand*.
He was originally known, however, as a *kotkarl*, while
the term *husmand* was at first applied to a rather
different class, the more independent hired workman,
who was restrained by no family or domestic ties, and
who was consequently to some extent his own master,
moving from place to place and obtaining shelter *in
the houses* of the locality.   In the supposed interests
of agriculture, early legislation forbade the practice of
receiving such potential labourers into dwellings owned
by others, and endeavoured to force them to work for a

standard wage where their services were in demand. The result was to fix them in dwellings of their own, and as these were only obtainable on the same terms as those applying to the *kotkarl*, the distinction between the two classes of agricultural labourer was obliterated.

But the name *kotkarl* disappeared, for the whole class adopted the title formerly enjoyed only by the more fortunate and independent, and thenceforward *husmand* meant substantially what it means to-day, in the typical cases, viz. a labourer, who, but for a negligible wage on the one hand and a negligible rent on the other, in effect exchanges his labour for his holding.

It is, at first sight, rather difficult for an Englishman to appreciate the objections to this system which have given rise to widespread agitation and political action. The arrangement sounds fair enough. The young married labourer requires a house and a small holding, but has no capital but his power to work. The farmer needs this work, and can provide house and plot. Where he does not himself build the house, this belongs to the labourer, and, being made of logs, can easily be removed and set up elsewhere at the conclusion of the tenancy. The terms of occupation and employment vary, but life-tenancies are not uncommon, and the work demanded is frequently only occasional, and confined to busy seasons. In any case, the lot of the *husmand* appears to be superior to that of many an English labourer, occupying a tied cottage merely as a condition of his employment, and working exclusively in the service of his landlord, with little spare time for independent attention to his own affairs. I cannot help feeling that much of the discontent which has arisen is due to historical reasons which have made the *husmand* a despised class, conscious, in a land of few class distinctions, of a galling social inferiority. As the *husmand* is, historically, the liberated thrall, he has inherited much of the contempt formerly applied to this class. Readers of Björnson's tale, *En glad gut,* will remember that it strikes the *husmand* as quite fair and natural that his son should not be placed as high in the school examination preceding confirmation as his abilities deserve.

The view that this social inferiority constitutes the real grievance is supported by the fact, emphasised in the Report of the *Husmaends* Commission of 1920, that the relations between employer and employed play but a subordinate part in the agitation conducted by the *husmaend*. What they demand is to become owners of their holdings, and thus rise to a position of greater social equality with the peasant proprietors around them. " When the *husmaend* all over the country," says the Report, " put forward a demand for a new ' *husmand* law,' no doubt a very important reason for this is the desire to obtain better rules for the relation between *husmand* and landlord at the time of engagement and at its cessation. . . . But it is not this in the first place. . . . It is the *husmaend's* desire to become owners of the holding they occupy which runs as the red thread through all proposals from the *husmaend* for the amendment of the law." In other words, a healthy social ambition, rather than resentment at oppression or unfair treatment, is at the bottom of the movement ; hard cases under the old system are merely put forward as a makeweight. This ambition the State has thought it politic to gratify to a considerable extent. Its assistance has hitherto taken the form of instituting a special bank for the provision of loans on easy terms to those who would purchase their holdings. The committee of 1920 proposed further steps in the same direction. But it is clear that their decision was based on grounds of general policy rather than consideration of any essential hardship involved in the *husmand* system. " It has, in fact, appeared to the Commission," runs the Report, " that this desire of the *husmaend* to become themselves owners of their holdings is an expression of a happy social development, which the community must endeavour to support and help on so far as this can be done without encroaching on the vested interests of others." Potential communists are, in short, to be converted to the stable conservatism associated with landed property. This is probably a wise programme, but it must not be interpreted as a reflection on the Norwegian *bonde* as landlord and employer.

The *husmand* problem is, however, steadily decreasing in importance, and bids fair, before long, to settle itself. Partly this is the result of the steps already taken to promote peasant ownership. Partly it is the result of the modern industrial development, which provides young married men from the country with other sources of employment. Emigration, principally to the United States, has played its part. But it is to be noted that there has been from the farmer's side an increasing unwillingness to continue the old system. Land has become more valuable, and labour-saving machinery has made the assistance of the *husmand* less necessary. From all these causes, the numbers of *husmaend* in Norway are rapidly sinking into insignificance, and what was, until recently, an important social question seems likely to find its own automatic solution.

As the aristocracy became enriched by the viking period and the commercial development which followed it, they purchased much additional land, and leasehold tenure became common. This development, however, probably did not affect the ancestral odel properties so much as freeholds of other kinds, which were more easily alienable. The exodus to Iceland which resulted from Harald Fairhair's policy brought about an immense increase in Crown lands, which were available for distribution as well as for leasehold occupation. As time went on, a great deal of new ground was cleared, and farms established in the clearings; but a decree of King Magnus Lagaböter makes it evident that the occupant of such a *rudstadr*

was not a freeholder, but a tenant either of the Crown
or of some other landlord (*Norges Gamle Love*, vol. ii.
p. 485). As the power of the Church developed, much
land passed into its hands ; this included odel property,
but probably of comparatively recent origin, rather
than that of the old aristocratic families. We have
seen that as late as 1316 it was quite customary to
trace an odel title back into heathen times, while in
the worst period of foreign oppression, in 1548, the
Danish nobles complained of the obstacles which the
existence of such rights opposed to their rapacious
exploitation of the country. In spite of the growing
preponderance of leasehold tenure, the odel system
continued to survive, and it is to a great extent to this
fact that the *bönder* of Norway owe the degree of
independence which they maintained. It was a complete bar to the introduction of feudalism, and in
days when the peasantry of most parts of Europe had
sunk to a condition little better than serfdom the
bonde of Norway was always able to assert himself
to some purpose ; while in some cases he could claim,
like Trond Lauperak in 1762, " Frederic is King in
Denmark, but I am King in Bjerkreim."

Yet the situation of the present day, where freehold
is the rule and leasehold tenure the quite insignificant
exception, is of comparatively modern origin. In the
middle of the seventeenth century, leaseholders outnumbered freeholders by more than two to one, and
barely a quarter of the cultivated land of the country
was in *bonde* ownership. The principal grievances of
the tenants were inability to obtain long leases, which
were indeed not recognised by the old law, and the
extortionate premiums for renewal to which they were,
in consequence, subjected. The Black Death, which
devastated Norway in the middle of the fourteenth
century, considerably improved their position for a
time by reversing the previously existing conditions
of supply and demand. Land was common and
tenants were scarce. From this occurrence dates also

the first stage in the obliteration of class distinctions among the *bönder* which the oppression of Danish nobles and Danish officials was destined to complete. Many of the old aristocratic families were wiped out, others were ruined and sank into the position of simple farmers. Owing to scarcity of labour the prouder *odels-bönder* were similarly forced into equality with the hitherto despised leaseholders. To the foreign adventurers whom the Union, especially after the Reformation, placed in power, the native rural population was simply a nation of peasants, though they discovered that this point of view was mistaken when they attempted to treat this independent people, with its aristocratic leaven, with the oppressiveness which could be practised with impunity on the Continent. There were repeated risings ; officials were not infrequently ejected or slain. The *bonde* was always ready to defend ancient national law and custom ; he was also prone, in spite of every discouragement, to carry his grievances to the King in Denmark, over the heads of his hated representatives. He had courage, determination, and independence enough : the one thing he lacked was cohesion over the whole country. A wider horizon, or the existence of a national as opposed to a local leader, would on many occasions have broken the Danish yoke and brightened this page of Norwegian history. As it was, the *bonde* managed to retain some degree of individual liberty, but the Union continued.

The crisis which turned the Norwegian farmers once more into proprietors dates from the years following the Treaty of Copenhagen in 1660. The period of war with Sweden, of which this was the close, had displayed the worthlessness of the Danish nobility, while the heroism of the King during the defence of Copenhagen immensely enhanced his popularity and led directly to that strange event, the reaction to autocracy. By the fall of the nobles, the Norwegians were freed from the class which had hitherto oppressed them, though for the moment another event prevented them from fully realising the benefit of the change. Impoverished by the Swedish wars, Frederick III began in 1661 an extensive sale of Crown property in Norway. In the meantime a new wealthy class, mostly of foreign origin, had grown up in the Norwegian towns. The Crown tenants, therefore, suddenly found themselves transferred to the tender mercies of commercial speculators of the worst type. The oppression was great, and the protests it aroused universal and loud. Both the Crown and the *bonde* learnt the lesson. In the case of the former it was reinforced by the splendid service of the Norwegian troops in the war which followed the fall of Griffenfeldt in 1676. In 1684–5 appeared a series of royal decrees which made the worst extortions of the new landlords from thenceforth impossible and rendered the ownership of large tracts of land no longer lucrative. The landlords began to sell ; the tenants to buy. About the same time there was a new sale of Crown property, and now the purchasers were the former tenants. In the course of less than forty years the situation was completely changed, freeholders being in a majority among the native farmers, and up to the present day the movement has been in the same direction. Nowadays, as we have seen in the case of the *husmaend*, small ownership is a policy which has not only the approval but the active support of the State.

During the democratic movement of the nineteenth century the *bonde* came into his own. Literature flattered him, folk-lorists rediscovered him, politicians courted him. His hitherto despised dialects became the basis of a national language with a definite legal status. Finally, in 1896, he provided himself with the one thing he had hitherto lacked, a nation-wide organisation—the *Landmands forbund*—to promote his special interests. Since 1920 he has had his own political party. There are signs, however, of difficult times ahead. The *bönder* comprise, as we have seen, all the classes of the old Norway of which *Rigsthula* tells us—jarl, karl, and thrall. For a time there was no other true Norway. Now all this is changing. The future threatens to lie in the direction of industrialism. A new Norway is arising, not less national than the old, to challenge the old way of life.

At the same time the *bonde* class is confronted with a literary reaction. The modern realist, who is frequently of *bonde* stock, and ought therefore to know what he is talking about, represents him as brutal, mean, suspicious, secretive, grasping, obstinate, and ignorant. So long as such charges come merely from the towns one has only to remember the ancient and irreconcilable opposition between town and country, which are in many respects like two different nations. But when a writer born and bred in the country districts repeats and amplifies them, what is a poor Englishman to say on the other side ? He may, indeed, point out how the realistic school of literature in almost every country shows a marked *penchant* for the disagreeable, and displays a capacity for observing more evil in a single house than the ordinary man meets with in a lifetime. But obviously a foreigner cannot speak for the whole of Norway. Even within the confines of our own little island, it would be difficult to find a common denominator for the rural inhabitants of Cumberland, Essex, Yorkshire, Dorsetshire, and Wales, and it is necessary to remember that the barriers and distances separating different parts of Norway are of an infinitely more formidable and isolating character. One feels there must be a germ of truth in the indictment as applied to some districts. At the same time, it may be pointed out that when an Englishman who has lived in Norway says, as he almost invariably does, " What perfectly delightful folk the Norwegians are," he is usually referring to the farmers and fishermen of a western fjord district, *i.e.* to precisely those people whom writers of the school of Hans Kinck depict as little better than the beasts that perish. I hesitate to adopt the unflattering conclusion that a very inferior Norwegian surpasses in charm the best that this country can produce, and prefer to think, in conformity with my personal experience, that the picture is prejudiced and even libellous.   And in this view I believe I should have the majority of Anglo-Norwegians with me.   Obstinacy, so far as it exists, is really an aspect of the self-reliance forced upon the Norwegian farmer by the comparatively isolated conditions under which he works.   Without a good deal of firmness and a determination to insist on his rights, it is difficult to see how the *bonde* could have maintained his independence under the conditions of the Danish Union.   A family which has lived for many generations on a single farm naturally, and in many cases rightly, supposes that it is qualified to manage its own affairs.   It may tend to be conservative, and to pay too much respect to tradition; but in a world convulsed with Bolshevism and unsettled by the breathless progress of mechanical invention, so stable an element in a population is eminently healthy.   As a matter of fact, what strikes a foreign observer at the present day is that the Norwegian farmer has been all too quick to avail himself of modern developments. He buys much which he formerly made, and made much better than the factory which now supplies him.   His domestic architecture, especially, is losing much of its old charm with improved facilities for manufacture and transport.   The old type of house, roomy and comfortable, with its roof of natural turf laid on birch bark, and its walls of solid, round logs weathered to a rich chocolate brown, seemed as much a part of the unchanging landscape as the fjeld which towered above it.   The tall, modern structure, glaring with white paint and filled with ugly machine-made furniture, seems a regrettable change for the worse.   But it is certainly evidence of a disposition to move with the times.

As to the alleged secretiveness of the *bonde*, I can well believe that, like others who are continually forced to bargain with their neighbours, he is none too anxious to disclose his private finances. But I am bound to say that I have found him only too ready to state how much this or that improvement cost him. The price of everything is a topic of absorbing interest to him, and it is possible that one farmer may develop a not unnatural reticence as a defence against his neighbour's rather pronounced inquisitiveness. That the *bonde* is grasping does not correspond with my experience. In main tourist routes, or when the farmer is a returned emigrant from America, different considerations doubtless apply, but under normal conditions the tendency is to ask a standard price. Of course these prices have risen enormously in recent times. Prices in any community are ultimately what the highest bidder is willing to pay ; " spoiling the market " is everywhere possible, but it is, I think, a slower process in Norway than elsewhere. It is not an unheard-of thing for the Norwegian peasant to protest against, and refuse, over-payment, though no doubt this engaging characteristic is becoming rarer. Again, when a sporting lease falls in, and those agencies which of late have competed with the private individual have attempted to seduce the owners of the rights from their old allegiance, cases have occurred where the latter have offered to renew on much less remunerative terms with an old lessee with whom they were on friendly terms. In other respects, the striking and surprising honesty of the Norwegian *bonde* has been the subject of remark by almost every Englishman who has had to do with him. Almost every book written about Norway, as well as the evidence of individuals, might be cited in confirmation of this trait.

Since the *bonde's* whole theory of life depends upon the cohesion of the family, harmonious domestic relations are perhaps to be expected. His remarkable kindness to animals is, however, a sign of essential goodness of heart and evidence of a high standard of civilisation. His past record also shows that, compared with persons in a similar walk of life elsewhere, he is mindful of high things and by no means indifferent to culture. When the Church in Norway was at its lowest ebb, the real religious life of the country was largely carried on by lay preachers of the *bonde* class, of whom Hans Nielson Hauge is the most brilliant example. During the long period when Norwegian literature seemed dead, it was this class which maintained continuity with the cultural traditions of the past, through its ballads and orally transmitted folktales. Until quite recently, too, it was common for a good deal of reading aloud to be carried on, side by side with the practice of all sorts of useful handicrafts, during the long winter evenings. To this day the farmer is an assiduous newspaper reader, and on more than one occasion I have known him felicitously cap a literary quotation. But indeed it is difficult to condemn as unenlightened a class which in fact carries on, and that efficiently, so much of the local government of the country, which includes such matters as education. Another proof of enlightenment is to be seen in the extent to which the principle of co-operation has been adopted by Norwegian farmers. For the sale of dairy produce, indeed, co-operative creameries have for a long time been in general use, while to a certain extent of late years the same principle has begun to be extended to the marketing of eggs and meat. There are also co-operative purchasing societies for the supply of manures and agricultural machinery. These could boast, in 1921, a total membership of about 75,000. Finally, the farmers are beginning to combine to sell their timber on the same principle, thus escaping the exploitation to which they were formerly exposed at the hands of the urban timber merchant.

The whole tenor of the Norwegian farmer's existence, indeed, tends to make him efficient and versatile. On every holding all branches of farming are carried on together, though the cultivation is usually subordinate to the stock-rearing and dairy-farming, and the produce mainly used to feed the cattle. The crops are by no means sufficient at present to feed the population of the country, though it seems to be the ambition of the *bonde's* political party to make them so. Yet each individual farm is, as a rule, more or less self-supporting. Besides the farm proper, and the remote upland pastures where the cattle are removed and tended from *saeters* in the summer, there is a considerable area of forest, which provides work in the winter, and connects the *bonde* with the important timber trade of the country. On the coast the farmer is also a fisherman and the fisherman a farmer, for this also is an industry mainly carried on at seasons unsuited to agricultural work. The *bonde* thus represents in his own person almost every side of the old way of life on which Norway throve before the recent industrial development.

The family system under which these varied resources are exploited ensures that the work is efficient and that everyone is, so to speak, born and bred to his job. Some shrewd remarks appeared recently in one of the English reviews as to the effects of increased longevity on the British landed system. In old days, said the writer, the landowner normally died in the early 'forties, and was succeeded by his son, aged a little over twenty, who had all his life been brought up on the estate. Now the old man dodders on to eighty or ninety, during the last ten years or so being quite incapable of giving the estate the attention it requires, and is succeeded by a middle-aged stockbroker or colonel, who knows nothing whatever of agricultural matters. In Norway, an ancient and widely prevalent custom renders the interests of the land independent of the advance of medical science. When the farmer's eldest son marries, his parents, like Laertes in the Odyssey, retire into the background. The farm is handed over to the young couple, under a contract which ensures to the old folks house-room and a sufficiency of food; and while the parents continue to live on the place and lend a hand according to their capacity, the active management and the financial responsibility pass to the son, who has naturally been kept from infancy in close and unbroken touch with the property. Under circumstances which now, alas! are passing away under the influence of improved communications, these isolated family microcosms became skilful at all manner of incidental crafts outside the strict work of the farm. " In the country," says an eighteenth-century writer, " there is no use for hatter, shoemaker, tailor, farmer, weaver, ropemaker, carpenter, or joiner . . . since all these handicrafts are learned and practised in every farmhouse by every lad who aspires to be a good man." The same, with little modification, might have been said until quite recently; and the Norwegian peasant still retains to some extent an inherited aptitude for turning his hand to anything, which stands those in good stead who are forced to leave the country as emigrants.

Division of labour is dear to the heart of the political economist. But man does not live by bread alone, and the character of the race is perhaps of more importance to a nation than economic considerations. Modern specialisation too often sacrifices wisdom to wealth. If a nation is to have an opinion and play a part in every emergency which may arise, instead of learning to depend on individuals, whose brains likewise may be atrophied by a few more generations of mechanically controlled existence, such an element as the old-fashioned Norwegian *bonde* must be encouraged and sedulously preserved. At present Norway is alive to this, and agriculture is given a full measure of encouragement. Since 1900 it has had, thanks to the initiative of the *Landmandsforbund*, a special department of State to guard its interests. Large sums have been voted for the encouragement of agriculture and the development of hitherto uncultivated tracts. Nor is the scientific and technical side neglected. There are at present no less than 131 special schools dealing with various aspects of farm life which are administered separately from the general educational system of the country, not by the Church and Education Department, but by the Department of Agriculture.

But at present Norway is still imbued with nationalistic ideals; the danger will come when she begins to realise that the interests of industry, as opposed to agriculture, are really international. If industrial development continues to progress, as appears likely, a time may come when Norway will adopt a less exclusively national attitude. It is then that the farmers, and all those who see in them a necessary element in the nation, will have to hold together. Past history, however, suggests that a class which has preserved Norwegian independence and freedom through the difficulties which now lie behind it, should be equally able to assert its claims against whatever may threaten it in the future.

CHAPTER XII

INDUSTRIAL DEVELOPMENT

THE keynote of the situation in Norway at the present day is transition. Of course, owing to the world-convulsion produced by the war, the same thing could be said with a great deal of truth of a large number of other countries. And no doubt, here as elsewhere, the events of 1914 to 1918 have played their part; but in Norway there are, at the same time, many aspects of the passing of the old order, and the consequent confusion and uncertainty prevailing, which must be attributed to quite different and indeed mutually independent causes. In the field of language, for example, a change, ultimately for the better, seems to be taking place, which at the present moment is marked by an apparently complete chaos. Highly educated, and indeed literary, Norwegians constantly confess that they have no clear ideas as to how to spell; indeed, the so-called " obligatory " forms of spelling differ from others principally in the fact that practically no one makes use of them in their entirety. But this most noticeable aspect of the prevailing transition rests upon causes wholly peculiar to itself, which are dealt with in another chapter. Its existence at the present moment is a mere coincidence.

Another change, due no doubt to a great extent to the indirect influences of the war, is the increased and increasing interest in sport in urban circles. The peasantry, indeed, have always hunted and fished, and I maintain, in spite of the disparaging comments of many English writers on the subject, that many of them show the true sporting instinct extremely highly developed; but the wealthier inhabitants of the towns have, until very recently, left interest in these matters mainly to the foreigner. The new fashion, which seems to have come to stay, is due, according to the best information available, partly to pro-British enthusiasm developed during the war, partly to the absence, during the same period, of English competitors, and, finally, to the temporary wave of prosperity which arose in the progress of the campaign, and enabled many in whom a taste for sport was latent to gratify it. Or, again, one might instance the sweeping changes in the civil legal procedure of the country which are contemplated, and have only been delayed by the present financial stringency. This is a matter which would deserve more particular mention but for the fact that the transition has not yet been carried into effect, so that while it seems useless to explain the existing system, it would be premature to describe that which will ultimately replace it.

These, however, are merely examples, selected at random, to illustrate in how many different spheres of life in Norway a great change, coincident in point of time but independent in its causes, is now to be observed. In addition to such subordinate matters there is, however, one main group of changes which are traceable in one way or another to a common cause— the fact that Norway has now at last come, late in time, into the grip of an industrial revolution. This is a form of transition through which we ourselves have passed at an earlier date ; we are familiar with the power exercised by developing industrial life to modify the habits of centuries and to produce bewildering changes with a rapidity which seems to increase like the velocity of a falling body. Yet the industrial revolution of Norway has features of special interest, not only because the fate of our ancestors is here being re-enacted before our eyes, but because the process of transition is affected and modified by external developments which had not come into being when we and other industrial communities underwent this tremendous change in our whole organisation.

In England, the change, rapid and impressive as it was, had yet to be comparatively slow. The stages, so well sketched by Mr. G. M. Trevelyan in his *British History in the Nineteenth Century*, by which coach replaced pack-horse, railways succeeded coaches, and petrol-driven transport modified and supplemented steam traction, marvellously rapid though they were, yet had to take place, accompanying the general trend of the movement. Most of the machinery whereby the necessary capital became a fluid and an international force grew gradually out of the altered conditions. The revolution, again, was born when mechanical invention was in its first crude stages, and adequate communications had yet to be constructed, in a community where labour was disorganised and almost all power was in the hands of employer rather than employed. A large proportion of the population was ignorant and illiterate, unaccustomed and unable to enlarge its mental horizon beyond the immediate outskirts of its villages. Popular government on a wide franchise followed gradually on the industrial revolution; it did not precede it. The result was that the system with which we are familiar, and through which our swarming populations maintain their existence, was able to establish itself on solid foundations before the growth of those forces which now seek and threaten to disintegrate it.

Norway, faced for the first time at the present day with a somewhat similar development, has to deal with it under altogether different circumstances. The latest mechanical inventions, the most recent scientific discoveries, are within her knowledge, ready for immediate application. The remarkable delay in her industrial development is due, not to backwardness or ignorance, but to natural causes. Having no coal, she has had to wait till the advance of electrical science rendered possible the utilisation of her practically inexhaustible water resources, not as a direct motive force, but to create electrical power. To some extent also, for the development of easy communications is a necessary and important element in breaking down old ways of life, petrol and the motor-car have played their part. In spite of remarkable engineering skill, the development of railways in Norway has been and must be slow and local in its effects. The country as a whole is too difficult and the obstacles too formidable for a rapid growth of railway communication. More than twenty years ago the traveller north of Trondhjem found the railhead at Sunnan, on the shores of the Snaasen Vand, only a few miles from Stenkjaer at the head of the Trondhjem Fjord; and there, in spite of much labour, it remains to-day. But in another way rapidity of communication has been immensely improved. In days which most habitual visitors to Norway remember as comparatively recent, the commonest means of getting about the country was by the time-honoured method of driving a horse and the curious single-seated vehicle known as a cariole in slow stages between posting stations or *skydsstationer*. Now, even on roads whose steepness, narrowness, and unsatisfactory surface seem eminently unsuited to such modern modes of progression, motor-cars running to a fixed time-table are everywhere to be found, the fare on which works out at little more than twopence a mile at the present rate of exchange. Even on by-roads, or at times which do not fit in with the services of these *rute-biler*, numerous privately owned cars are to be found which can be hired at extremely cheap rates. The development has had a revolutionary effect on the life of the inhabitants. The change has been both good and bad. The bright side of it is that it tends to break down the barrier hitherto existing between town and country, to which I have previously had occasion to refer. But there is another side. In recent times, now, alas! passing away, what struck the visitor particularly about the Norwegian peasant was his versatility and handiness. On the isolated farms everything necessary to domestic and agricultural economy was home-made. The long winter evenings were spent in the practice of all manner of useful crafts, to the accompaniment in many cases of reading aloud, which exercised the brains of the workers simultaneously with their hands. Now everything, or almost everything, is bought ready-made.

This has not only involved a great sacrifice of picturesqueness, in such matters as furniture and domestic architecture, but tends also to modify, greatly for the worse, the resourcefulness and capability of the rural inhabitants. It is but an indirect result of the industrial revolution, but is none the less important.

But we are concerned more particularly with the direct changes and their special aspects.

The first great peculiarity of Norwegian industrial development is, as already stated, that the mechanical and scientific side of the problem is from the first in a state of up-to-date development. Norway, indeed, has—in a sense—known all about industrial life for a long time. The saw-mill is as old as the sixteenth century, and there existed until the nineteenth century a considerable number of quite important iron-works, which only ceased to be profitable with the general introduction of coal-smelting in other iron-producing countries. Mining, too, has been carried on for a long time. The silver mines of Kongsberg have just celebrated their tercentenary (in 1924), and the copper mines of Röros are nearly as old. It was merely the lack of the coal on which the modern factory has primarily depended which made industrial life in Norway comparatively unimportant until the twentieth century. The next important contrast which Norway presents to England in the matter of industrial development is political. As has already been pointed out, our modern democracy is a product of the industrial revolution. The upheaval found a country accustomed to regard differences of wealth and social status as part of the necessary and immutable order of things. The new system became firmly planted, population increased with gigantic strides, the new-born masses felt their strength, used it, and attained to power. In Norway, on the other hand, Nature and circumstances combined to create a full-blown democracy while the old order was still in full swing.

This democracy developed early, and was for a long

time a model of all that popular government should be. It found, perhaps, its best expression in the system of local administration introduced about 1837, which familiarised the inhabitants of every district with the tasks and problems of government. Where the population was so sparse, and so innocent of class distinctions, everyone soon learned to feel his share in the common responsibility. Under agricultural conditions, Nature forced upon men of the working class the amount of leisure necessary to the development of thought and ideas. But to-day that democracy shows symptoms of that reaction to despotism which seems characteristic of the final, or overripe, stage. The extremists of one party turn hopefully to Moscow and the tyranny of the Soviets; those of the other cast envious glances at Mussolini and the Fascisti. The Communists talk of hanging opponents to the lamp-posts; the Die-Hards dream of treating them with castor-oil.

In industrial circles, both employers and employed are most thoroughly organised on up-to-date lines into perpetually conflicting forces, and have reached the stage arrived at by other communities after the system had attained to full and healthy growth, before they have really had experience enough fully to understand the conditions of this form of national existence.

Popular government has, in fact, reached that advanced stage which some think the final one before industrialism is much more than born.

As the late Lord Bryce pointed out in his work on *Modern Democracies*, the claim of organised groups within the nation to settle by mutual conflict or even agreement matters with which the whole community is in fact concerned, is a factor which, while it appears to grow naturally out of popular government, is really quite inconsistent with it. In England, indeed, those concerned in industry constitute so large a proportion of the community that it is not at once obvious that the will of these organisations and that of the community as a whole are or may be two different things. But in

Norway, in spite of the strides which industry has made of late years, the vast majority of the nation, while it is made to feel the distress occasioned by the war between Capital and Labour, stands altogether outside the struggle. It is somewhat in the position of the neutral in the late war, who suffered much from the actions of the belligerents, but was not directly involved in the conflict. It is therefore not surprising that one of the most interesting points in the industrial struggles which have been so lamentable a feature of recent Norwegian history consists in the efforts of the legislature to arrive at some effective means of mitigating their effects on the community. An attempt to describe these experiments, to estimate their success and diagnose the causes of failure, may therefore be of interest to readers in our own country.

The most permanent result of legislative interference in the matter has been the Law concerning Industrial Disputes of 6th August 1916. This law, after providing for the registration of all organisations, whether of employers or employed (unorganised labour is outside the law), draws a clear distinction between the two main forms of industrial dispute. A dispute as to whether a tariff agreement, entered into between the respective organisations, constitutes a binding contract, or generally as to its interpretation, is treated differently from all other differences of opinion as to the terms or conditions of labour. The first may not be settled by recourse to a strike or lock-out, but must be brought before a special Labour Court, constituted for the purpose, whose decision, subject to a limited right of appeal to the Supreme Court on subordinate points, is final. In cases under the second head there must be no recourse to the weapons of strike or lock-out until an opportunity has been given for a public conciliator (*riksmaeglingsmand, kredsmaeglingsmand*) to intervene. This official, upon receiving notice of the failure of negotiations between the parties, must forbid cessation of work until he has had an opportunity of attempting to effect conciliation, if he is of opinion that the general interest will suffer from such cessation. The matter then comes forthwith either before a district conciliator (*kredsmaeglingsmand*) or the national conciliator (*riksmaeglingsmand*), the latter exercising control over the former, and having power to take the negotiations in any particular dispute into his own hands.[1]

Only after the breakdown of such official efforts at conciliation can recourse be had to the weapon of strike or lock-out. On the failure of such efforts the conciliator may issue to the public a report on the whole affair, thus mobilising the forces of public opinion in favour of the right side. For the breach of a tariff agreement, or for an unlawful strike or lock-out, the Union responsible is liable to pay compensation, while the individual members of its council who bring an unlawful cessation of work into operation, or contribute to its continuance by resolution or otherwise, or supply it with funds whether from the Union or by independent collection, are liable to pecuniary penalties.

As an illustration of some phases of the practical working of this law, the history of the great lock-out of 1924 may be of interest. Under the terms of a tariff agreement arrived at in the iron industry in the previous year, it was agreed that wages should be lowered 5 per cent. from October 1923, if the official index figure for the cost of living for the previous month was as low as 232. The figure in question at the time was 230, and, though it was widely stated that this was both temporary and for various reasons did not represent the true state of affairs, the wages were lowered in accordance with the agreement. The workers at once struck ; the matter was taken before the Labour Court, whose judges are a nominated body

---

[1] The application of this expedient is an idea which seems to have grown naturally out of the legal procedure in civil actions between individuals, which in Norway always begins with the attempt of the local *forliks-kommission* (Conciliation Commission) to bring the parties to agreement.

in whose appointment the larger organisations on both sides have a voice, and the strike was declared illegal. In spite of this it continued, and, as the whole matter was one concerned with the interpretation of a tariff agreement, the Employers' Federation was not in a position to meet it with a general lock-out. Meanwhile, however, negotiations for a new agreement had been proceeding in the dock and transport workers' branch of the industry. Into this agreement the employers, admittedly because of what had happened in the iron industry, stipulated for the insertion of fixed guarantees on the part of the Unions concerned for the future observance of tariff agreements. On this point the negotiations broke down, and in January 1924 a dock strike began. In view of these events, ostensibly on the question of guarantees, but actually, as everyone agreed, on account of the unlawful strike in the iron industry, the Employers' Federation declared a general lock-out, which came into operation towards the end of February, and involved, taken together with strikes by which it was answered, some 60,000 workmen in a very large number of industries. This state of things, in spite of the close and constant attention of the public conciliator, lasted until the end of May, when the dispute was settled on terms regarded, at any rate in communist circles, as a defeat for the workmen.

These facts can scarcely be said to be encouraging. The disturbance to industry could hardly have lasted longer had the law not been in existence, and the victory appears to have rested with those who had recourse to the drastic weapon of a general lock-out. The influence alike of Labour Court and of conciliator appears to have been infinitesimal. The former was defied, the latter ignored, and industrial war on the old lines raged, with disastrous results to the community.

It is not surprising, therefore, that pleas began to be heard for the reintroduction of another experiment on the same lines—compulsory arbitration. This ex-

pedient had already been tried in Norway as a temporary measure, but its former history is not altogether
calculated to inspire confidence. It has been well
pointed out that the normal use of arbitration is to
settle a dispute once for all, after which the parties
in many instances never come in contact again. In
the case of arbitration in industrial disputes no reasonable person expects that the award given will be
permanent. The cost of living and other essential
factors change with extraordinary swiftness, and even
if the duration of the award is very short, it is more
than likely that before it runs out one if not both
parties will be quite reasonably dissatisfied with it.

In these circumstances employer and employed are
tied together for a fixed period under conditions which
lead to increasingly embittered relations. Intelligent
observers have come to the conclusion that the growing
sympathy with the extreme communists which may
be noticed among the industrial workmen of Norway
owes much to the temporary and spasmodic endeavours
of the community outside to impose a legal check
upon their power of collective bargaining. The history
of the experiment shows a curious fluctuation in the
opinions of Capital and Labour with regard to it. Its
earliest advocates in Norway, in 1901, came from the
side of the workmen, but when in 1909 a committee
appointed to consider the question issued a majority
report in favour of it, in cases where the interests of
society as a whole were threatened by a dispute, the
Labour representative was in the minority. In 1913,
when the introduction of a law for compulsory arbitration was proposed, a joint committee of employers
and employed decided unanimously against it. Thenceforward, up to 1916, every proposal to introduce such
a law was met with protests and threats of a general
strike from the side of organised Labour. The law was
nevertheless passed, and so long as the good times lasted
appeared to have the approval of the employers but
not of the employed. After the slump set in in 1921

the tables were turned. In 1922 the renewal of compulsory arbitration was carried with Labour support against Conservative opposition.

The inner meaning of this curious state of affairs seems to be this : in times of prosperity, with the strike chest full, organised labour prefers recourse to industrial war, while the employers will find any award better than a cessation of work at a time when they can obtain what prices they choose. In bad times, on the other hand, Labour is not in good fighting trim, and will accept arbitration as a temporary expedient, while employers find it better to let their works lie idle for a time than to face the risk of a possible adverse award.

The rest of the community, while it also tends to change sides, is on the whole steadily in favour of compulsory arbitration. Consisting, as it does in Norway, very largely of small farmers, when prices are high it sides against the workman, since a rise in his wages tends to make everything more expensive ; but when times are bad it wishes to fill the pockets of the workman to increase his purchasing power. In both cases, therefore, the outside community largely rallies to the ranks of the advocates of arbitration. To these motives must, of course, be added the fact that the interests of the community are, *ex hypothesi*, adversely affected by strikes and lock-outs.

It must be admitted that in practice the expedient of compulsory arbitration has sometimes worked quite well. In many cases, while the law was in operation, the mere fact of its existence was enough to bring the parties to terms, and the labours of the official conciliators were appreciably facilitated and rendered fruitful ; but whether in normal times the modern industrial workman would permanently and passively submit to the award of any tribunal seems a question to which the experience of the iron strike does not suggest an encouraging answer. It must, indeed, be remembered when we are considering legislation which makes illegal the use of the workman's principal weapon—refusal to work—that it is but a reaction to methods tried in the past and found ineffective. Experience up to date tends to show that a strike cannot be prevented by calling it "illegal," it will, on the contrary, merely be more subversive of society and difficult to control from the fact that those who take part in it have been forced into defiance of the law. A prominent Norwegian Communist, Professor Edvard Bull, sarcastically asks in a recent article " how long the normal form of strike in this country will continue to be the ' illegal,' as the case is now." This is significant.

Like every interference with the liberty of the subject, compulsory arbitration can only be defended as the lesser of two evils. If, as seems to be the case, it tends to promote Bolshevism and discontent in a growing class of industrial workers, it may well do more harm to the community in the long run than a few strikes and lock-outs. But perhaps the gravest objection to it comes from the employers' side. An award depends upon the possibility of enforcing it. Now, while it is perfectly easy to compel employers to observe certain regulations and adopt a certain scale of payment, it is quite another matter to force a recalcitrant workman to work. The sanctions for an award are therefore unequal, and this inequality works to the prejudice of employers rather than employed.

Industry in Norway has, in fact, in spite of all efforts at legislative control, been hampered by continual and extremely serious industrial war. Apart from the effects upon not yet fully established industry of these perpetual conflicts and stoppages, there is another factor peculiar to the country, the influence of which upon the question deserves serious consideration. Norway's industry, taken as a whole, depends upon the exploitation of her water-power, and this is severely controlled by what are known as the Concession Laws. The application of these laws is not confined to waterfalls and water-power, but extends, broadly speaking, to all the important natural resources of the country, forest tracts, large peat-bogs, etc. It is, however, with the provisions relating to industrial water-power that we are here immediately concerned. The acquisition of important sources of water-power, or of electrical energy developed thereby to a greater extent than 500 h.p., except by the State or the municipalities, is made subject to a concession by the Crown. This concession is not granted for a longer period than fifty years, with a possibility of extension for a further ten years. In the case of a concession of electrical power to a foreigner, the period may be still further curtailed. At the termination of the period the property, with all plant and accessories, reverts to the State without compensation.

I confess that the policy embodied in the Concession Laws originally seemed to me to be unwise and short-sighted. To this view I was led by statements similar to that made in a recent article in a leading Norwegian newspaper, which states that " it was principally the fear of foreign capital which was the reason for this legislation." This fear undoubtedly played its part both in the passing of the laws and still more in their administration, and to this extent the policy certainly appears to be open to serious criticism.

It is difficult to see the harm which foreign capital— or, indeed, a measure of foreign management—subject to the laws of the country, could do when such capital is, *ex hypothesi*, to be sunk in works and plant which will ultimately revert to Norway. We hear, indeed, in our own country, some hard things said about international financiers, but there is reason to doubt whether the dangers apprehended from this development of in-dustrialism are not, to a large extent, exaggerated. The fact that a large amount of the capital of one country is invested in another is, or should be, a con-siderable guarantee of the peaceful and friendly relations of both, while external pressure or interference is most unlikely in the case of a State which is sufficiently civilised to manage its internal affairs with reasonable efficiency. If other nations had a large interest in Norwegian waterfalls, would they be in a position to exert more serious pressure than they can at present? A recent writer in the interesting Norwegian periodical, *Samtiden*, in advocating the stiffening and extension of the Concession policy, says some hard things about the pressure put upon his country by both England and Germany during the war. But it is to be observed that such pressure was wholly independent of financial control of Norwegian industries. The withholding of necessary supplies or the boycotting of products are methods open to foreign countries under existing conditions. The first was exemplified by the action of England during the war, the second by Spain and Portugal when they felt injured by the effects of the prohibition policy—and in both cases the objects sought were attained. The case of the Norwegian fisheries during the war, though this industry is perhaps less affected by modern developments than some others, is instructive. During the Napoleonic wars, while Norway was still neutral, it would have been exceedingly difficult for England to have prevented the export of fish to her enemies. The whole of the apparatus of fishing was at that time home-made and self-supporting. But, during the late war, the position was altogether changed. The modernisation of the industry involved the use of petrol-driven boats and imported nets and other appliances, and of these necessary adjuncts we had the control. It was therefore possible for us, as in fact we did, to threaten to withhold these essential supplies if fish were exported to Germany. The fact is that a nation which embarks on industrial development is at once debarred from keeping itself to itself. Industry is essentially international. The whole point of the revolution is that it enables a nation to support a vastly increased population by manufacturing, with

the aid of machinery, far in excess of its own requirements, and exchanging the surplus in foreign countries
for supplies unobtainable at home. The disadvantage
is that the industrial nation is inevitably to some extent
dependent on the wishes of the foreign vendor and
purchaser. The receipt of capital from another country
is, on the other hand, analogous to the importation of
necessary supplies and raw material, and it seems to
the present writer that Norway has far more to gain
than to lose or to fear from the adoption, under reasonable safeguards and the protection of her domestic
laws, of such a policy.

But, while the fear of foreign domination has had a
good deal to do with the adoption of the policy under
consideration, the principle of the Concession Laws is
also defended upon grounds for which there is a great
deal more to be said. There are, in the first place,
reasons apart from the possibility of domination by
foreign capital which render the presence of an excessive
number of foreign traders in the country undesirable.
The regrettable lack of mutual understanding between
town and country which exists in Norway, and to which
attention has previously been drawn, is attributable, to
a large extent, to this cause. The development of the
timber trade which contributed, during the sixteenth
and seventeenth centuries, to the growth of the coast
towns, was attended to a very great extent by an
influx of foreigners, under which the urban civilisation
of the country lost its national outlook and character.
During the eighteenth century an important native
merchant class grew up, but this, in the period of
depression which followed the Napoleonic wars, was
almost completely ruined and extinguished. During
the nineteenth century the intrusion of a foreign
element began once more, and with the development
of industrial life would, if allowed to proceed unchecked,
most probably again assume undesirable proportions.
One of the most pressing political tasks at the present
day is to break down the barrier hitherto existing

between town and country, and this can only be accomplished if the composition of the towns is approximately as national as that of the rural districts. A true national spirit can only be maintained if town and country are united in a common patriotism.

Still more important is the preservation of the agricultural population. As is elsewhere pointed out, this is the real backbone of the country. It consists, to an extraordinary extent, of that most stable element in a nation, the small proprietor, working his farm with little or no extraneous help, and practically self-supporting. Industry, it is felt, cannot be allowed to progress unchecked at the expense of this most valuable and characteristic class in the community. In the conditions of industrial unrest at present prevailing, these considerations apply with even greater force. The effects on the rural community have also to be considered from the point of view of the poor law and contributions to unemployment. After the lapse of the time necessary to acquire a local settlement, the collapse or reduction of an industrial undertaking employing a large number of workmen is calculated to throw an intolerable burden upon an otherwise sparsely populated district. But apart from this, it would be a calamity were the rural population to be enticed from their healthy and nearly self-supporting labours by the apparently more lucrative rewards of mechanical industry, or if the conditions of their existence were disturbed by the accumulation in the hands of commercial undertakings of the timber and other natural resources on which they have in part depended. In regard to water-power, it is felt that the local population should have an adequate share in the benefits to be derived from its development. But besides this, it is considered desirable that the rapid development of this new way of life, with all its revolutionary effects on the habits of the nation, should be controlled and even retarded for a time by the imposition of reasonable restrictions.

The reversion to the State of the natural resources utilised needs no justification. The ultimate prosperity of the industry based on Norwegian water-power depends entirely on the relative cheapness of this factor in production. It is the one advantage which the Norwegian has over the foreign manufacturer, and to part with it irrevocably at a time when its possibilities are only beginning to be realised would be the height of folly. The preference shown by these laws for the State and the municipalities has also much to be said for it. Development of water-power schemes by the local authorities tends to keep a fair share at any rate of the benefits derived from them in the hands of the district primarily concerned, while possession by the State, in a country of great distances and imperfect communications such as Norway, facilitates on the whole the economic development of a well-thought-out and comprehensive scheme. The only danger lies in a too extravagant expenditure of public money, and the temptation afforded to local and national Governments not to rest content with the provision of the power, but to compete in the commercial use of it. Of extravagance, under the stimulus of temporary wartime prosperity, both State and municipalities have undoubtedly been guilty ; of State and municipal participation in industry there has been so far comparatively little trace. In the special circumstances of the war the extravagance was, moreover, pardonable ; it was natural to take advantage of the sudden access of wealth to construct works of permanent value to the country ; but under normal circumstances there is something to be said for throwing the cost of development upon private concessionaires and waiting for the ripened fruit to fall into the hands of the nation. In considering the development of water-power for the production of electricity, it is necessary to distinguish sharply between the employment of that power in industry and the supply of electricity for the normal private and domestic needs of the inhabitants. Against

State or municipal participation in the former there is a very strong case to be made, but this side of the question has in fact, in Norway, been left almost exclusively to private enterprise. The most that can be said against the Concession Laws in this respect is that they provide an opportunity for indulgence in such socialistic experiments. In practice that opportunity has not, as yet, been seized either by State or municipalities. The use which the municipalities, in particular, have made of their privileged position under the Concession Laws has been very considerable ; but the object in view has not been the industrial use of the power, but the distribution of electricity to the general consumers of the district. This side of the question they have almost been forced to take up, because such distribution over a sparsely populated rural area is not a proposition likely to commend itself to the commercial instincts of a private undertaking. They may have gone too far, but the temporary prosperity of the war, and the scarcity, during the same period, of oil and other alternative sources of light and heat, together constituted a temptation which it would have been difficult to resist. There is, however, a touch of irony in the thought that the preference given to State and commune by laws aimed to some extent at the exclusion of foreign capital should have led to the result that these privileged institutions have been forced into recourse to foreign loans, which have been used to develop the unproductive rather than the productive side of water-power, and constitute, therefore, a more permanent burden of indebtedness to alien resources. If financial dependency on external powers is a thing to be dreaded, Norway would seem, to this extent, to have exchanged the frying-pan for the fire.

Regarded solely from the point of view of industry, the Concession Laws are undoubtedly an impediment to its immediate progress. During the war the capital of Norwegian investors would probably have been more usefully invested had it not been so largely debarred from playing a part in the development of water-power. But the deliberate intention of many of the wiser advocates of these laws was not to stimulate industrial progress, but to apply a brake to it. A due regard for the interests of the agricultural population was unquestionably sound. All lovers of Norway would regard the advance of Norwegian industry with something like dismay if it entailed the speedy or even the eventual disappearance of the small landholder who has made the country what it is.

There is also a feeling that the change from agriculture, and the other traditional sources of livelihood, to modern industry is a new and dangerous experiment over which it is essential for the State to retain control, at least in the present early stages. From this standpoint the suspicion of foreign capital may perhaps be really justified. It is not so much that it is foreign as that it might be an uncontrollable flood. To prevent the sudden and unmanageable growth of a possibly dangerous monster, it is important for the owner to keep its nourishment in his own hands. So long as it is an open question whether Norway should or should not become industrialised, the prejudice against foreign capital may be regarded as reasonable. As a matter of fact, this opposition to foreign capital, which to some extent played a part in the legislation, shows some signs of yielding to the economic pressure of the post-war situation. Two articles have very recently appeared in the Norwegian newspaper, *Tidens Tegn*, which is generally sufficiently Nationalist in its views, advocating the granting of concessions to foreigners under suitable conditions. "Are we to use our water-power or not?" asks the writer. "If we are to do so, we cannot for the time being get away from foreign capital; without its help it is hardly possible now to start great industrial undertakings here. And the danger from these undertakings is scarcely so great as is generally believed. The greater part of the returns of the business will remain in our country, and no lasting subjection to the foreign yoke can be imagined under the existing right of reversion."

The suspicion of foreign industry here referred to is to some extent bound up with a general fear of large trusts and combinations. The Norwegian historian, Dr. Jacob Worm Müller, has lately delivered an address on this subject which attracted much attention. Though he expressly dissociates himself from those who would keep foreign capital out of the country, the antipathy he shows for undertakings affiliated to large international combinations, even when the management and the labour employed is exclusively Norwegian, seems to some extent based on the fear he repudiates ; for in such a case the foreign influence exerted seems confined to that of the capital engaged. The problem resolves itself into two parts, the question of trusts and combinations generally, which in Norway as elsewhere has attracted the attention of the legislature, and the question of businesses which are in effect branches of large international combines. Both these matters are of too general application to be dealt with in a work of this kind. The fact that they have excited notice in Norway is merely mentioned to illustrate the stage of industrial development at which the country has arrived. It may be added, however, that in industrial circles the feeling seems to be that there has hitherto been too little combination in Norway, and too much cut-throat competition. This may well be true, since individualism and a tendency to put the parts of the country before the whole are characteristic of Norway generally.

Norway is at present still at the parting of the ways. Voices are still to be heard urging a return to the old simple ways of life, crying, The evils of industrialism are many and our complete independence is much. That is at least a point of view with which many who felt affection for the old Norway and cannot understand the new will feel the deepest sympathy. By industrial development it often seems that a nation stands to gain the whole world and lose her own soul. But the probability is that the movement has acquired too much impetus to be stayed, however much we may desire it. It only remains to estimate its probable chances of ultimate success.

The difficulties and disadvantages have already been pointed out. The industrial movement has to wrestle, during its first inexperienced and nursling years, with disintegrating forces serious enough in the case of countries whose industry was firmly based under an easier régime. Norway is a poor country suffering at present from crushing taxation and exceptional financial stringency, yet a large section of national opinion has hitherto seemed determined to rely on her own resources. The population is losing its old versatility under the influence of factory-made supplies easily obtainable along improved lines of communication. The population is also small, and its growth does not keep pace with the industrial development, so that, though at the present time there is a surplus of labour, for reasons connected with the world-convulsion of the war, in normal times the expansion of industry is handicapped by a shortage. There is much cause, in fact, for doubts and questionings; but not, I think, for despair. When it has weathered the storm, and even in the process of weathering it, Norwegian industry will possess several solid advantages over other industrial countries.

Norway starts with all the slowly won experience of those countries at her disposal. Her equipment does not require to be perfected from stage to stage. Her political difficulties, though more serious to her, are such as much of the outside world is encountering and endeavouring to solve with her. Delays are not wholly against her, for the commercial use of electric power is a matter still in its infancy. By the time the battle is won, the resources can in all probability be far more profitably employed. Above all, the utilisation of water-power in industry possesses advantages and

amenities which the users of coal can never enjoy. With
" white coal," as the source of power is termed, there
will be no " black country." Nature remains to a great
extent unpolluted. The worst features of urban industrialism need not, and will not, exist. According
to recent statistics, considerably more than half of the
industrial plants of Norway are situated in rural
districts, where the workman is in close touch with the
country, and can employ his leisure in rural pursuits.
There is no necessity to cluster round the source of
supply, for the power generated is so easily transferable
that its export, at any rate so far as to Denmark,
is already a practical question. And if industry in
Norway is born in an era of organised strife between
Capital and Labour, it is also born in a time of much
social legislation, which perhaps made exceptionally
rapid strides in Norway from the fact that until 1905
the interests of the legislature were so largely domestic.
Compared with his confrères in other lands, the industrial worker in Norway should enjoy happy and
healthy conditions of existence, which should tend to
make him contented. Add to these advantages that
the source of power is practically unlimited, remarkably
cheap, and quite inexhaustible. If the day ever comes,
as presumably it must, when the coal of the world is all
consumed, that day will still hear the waterfalls of
Norway roaring over their precipices. However many
mistakes may be made as the industrial revolution runs
its course, the permanent resources of that industry will
not have been wasted, but will continue undiminished.

The development of industry also assists in the
solution of a problem which has, in the past, been
extremely serious. The old conditions of life were
quite incapable of maintaining anything like the whole
of the population. From the earliest times down
almost to the present day a large proportion of the
population has been forced to emigrate. In recent
times the region specially favoured by Norwegian
emigrants has been the United States, particularly

Wisconsin and Minnesota. Here there is in some places so large a Norwegian element that newcomers do not always find it necessary to learn to speak English. I have come across men who have returned to Norway, after an absence of some years in America, unacquainted with any language but their own. Such men will tell you that they practically never had the occasion to use any other. But, as a matter of fact, of those who go out only a small proportion returns, and of these too many have lost the engaging characteristics of their race and become Americanised. One learns, indeed, instinctively to shun and to suspect the Norwegian who addresses one in fluent and nasal American ; there are brilliant exceptions, but for the most part the native honesty of such men has been sacrificed on the Yankee altar of " success," and their love of country is changed to outspoken contempt for the primitive virtues of the land of their birth. Small wonder that the State of late years has set itself to discourage a tendency which drains away her most enterprising and useful citizens, or returns them in a form so deteriorated. But, though the development of hitherto uncultivated tracts has done something to check the flow of emigration, such an expedient can only be temporary. The development of industry is the only known way of enabling a country to support a population indefinitely in excess of its natural resources. Here, it is true, there lies a danger, for the tendency is for the industrial population to develop with a rapidity out of all proportion to the agricultural, and this provides an additional reason for going slow while the economic creed of the industrial proletariat remains so unsound. But if the population is to be retained in the mother country, there seems no alternative to the stimulation of industrial life with such precautions as may suggest themselves.

And in spite of all the handicaps under which it has laboured, the growth of these industries based on water-power has, in fact, been astonishingly rapid.

The electro-chemical factories have already a world-wide reputation, and it has been stated that during a part of the war the French depended for 90 per cent. of their ammunition upon the nitrates of Norway. Electric smelting, again, though the technical perfection of the method for commercial purposes is still to be attained, seems to have a promising future. And these are only instances of the multifarious uses to which the available power is being, or can be applied. Meantime the benefits of the main plant are not confined to the factories, but are cheaply shared by the surrounding population.

The very fact, of which I spoke at the outset, that so great a transition from the old ways of life is noticeable, and that the formerly peaceful solitudes of Norway now echo to the clamour of industrial strife, shows that remarkable progress has been made. At the beginning of the nineteenth century the farmer outnumbered the manufacturer by about 16 to 1. As lately as 1865 the proportions were 64·1 to 15·6. The latest figures are 35·9 to 29·7. These speak for themselves. The advance has, in fact, been too rapid. Norway's inhabitants have developed their most admirable qualities from the conditions of rural existence which have hitherto prevailed there. It will take time before the new industrial classes can develop national traditions in any way fitted to replace those which the old way of life encouraged. The economic collapse which has followed the war, by checking the pace of industrial progress, may prove to be a blessing in disguise. The much-abused and perhaps misapplied Concession Laws are probably another. The pace at which an industrial population grows is immeasurably faster than anything which was possible in the old, primitive, self-supporting days. The problems which accompany such a development need time and experience for their solution, and in the meantime the nation should carefully preserve the class which has hitherto maintained her traditions.

Above all, the old mistake must not be made of accentuating the difference between town and country by making mechanical industry a purely urban occupation. The natural resources on which it depends, and which are for the most part necessarily rural, must be shared with the agricultural population. But if due attention is given to these things, and at present this seems to be the case, the outlook gives no cause for alarm.

And, after all, having said so much about transition, a phrase which in itself tends to palliate much of the unrest of the present and to reduce the difficulties to growing-pains, I feel inclined to end on another note. Nothing has so far been said of the somewhat sentimental objection which many feel towards the harnessing of waterfalls for industrial purposes—that it ruins the beauty of the countryside. In fact, I think such objections are to a great extent without foundation. Last year I passed through a place which had, since my last visit, been subjected to industrial development. True, the scheme had failed, owing to Labour troubles, but the new buildings stood, and one could form an opinion of what the change would mean. I had been led to expect a great alteration, but what impressed me most was how much remained, and must remain, the same as ever. If we could recall to England to-day a visitor from the eighteenth century, it may be doubted if he could recognise the scene of his earthly existence. But if anyone were privileged a century hence to revisit Norway, he would, I think, feel comparatively at home. The floor of the valley would indeed hold more and larger buildings than of old; but the salmon would still leap in the unpolluted waters of the same familiar stream. The same forests would clothe the hillsides, where they became too steep for building. And, above all, in an ether pure as of old, dwarfing and confining in impassable limits the proudest advance of industrial civilisation, the mountains would lift their changeless peaks to the eternal snows.

CHAPTER XIII

THE WAR AND AFTER

NORWAY as a completely independent kingdom was almost exactly nine years old when the Great War began. Until 1905 the control of her diplomatic relations with foreign countries had been in other hands : this circumstance was, in fact, the principal cause which led to the dissolution of the Union. While steadily developing commercial intercourse with all parts of the world and with nations now to be divided into two hostile camps, she had remained completely outside the currents of international politics, and had preserved an indifference to such questions which was the natural legacy of her former inability directly to participate in them. This attitude was encouraged by her geographical position. Norway had not an enemy, actual or potential, in the world. During the union with Sweden, indeed, there had existed a considerable suspicion and fear of Russia. When the present author used to visit Norway in the early years of this century, the farmer's stock conversational opening was generally, "Hvad taenker de om Rusland ? " (What do you think about Russia ?), followed by lurid and highly improbable stories of the activities of Russian spies. At one time, indeed, the fear that Russia would endeavour to secure access to one of the ice-free harbours of Northern Norway was sufficiently real to be shared by Great Britain : Palmerston concerned himself with the question from 1836 onwards, and during the Crimean War, in November 1855, a treaty was actually concluded between England and France on the one hand and Norway and Sweden on the other, whereby the territorial integrity of the latter was guaranteed, while Oscar I agreed not to part with any land to Russia, nor even to allow her rights of pasturage or fishing. The territory most in danger at this time was Norwegian, and it is perhaps somewhat astonishing that separation from Sweden should have sufficed to kill the Russian scare. Under modern conditions, however, it seems likely that aggression on the part of Russia would be directed to the annexation of the territory served by the railway running from the Gulf of Bothnia to Narvik, in which region Sweden serves as an effective buffer-state. However this may be, dislike and fear of Russia was, at the outbreak of the war, almost exclusively confined to Sweden, and there was thus no threat from any quarter which could dispose Norway to take sides in the European quarrel.

On the other hand, Norwegian friendships as well as Norwegian commercial interests were calculated to promote a very genuine neutrality. The closest tie of this kind was undoubtedly with Great Britain; this friendship was cemented by centuries of historical association and a similarity of outlook which has led many Norwegians to remark to me that they can understand the mentality of an Englishman even better than that of a Dane or a Swede. Friendship with France, though not of so long standing, was also traditional and almost universal, while Italy has been to many Norwegians almost a second home. But for many years Kaiser Wilhelm had deliberately cultivated and courted Norwegian friendship, and his frequent visits to her shores had drawn thither an increasing stream of German tourists and sportsmen, as well as business men, who had managed to ingratiate themselves with certain elements of the population. In the first decade of the twentieth century, for example, one would meet with more Germans than English in Namdalen during the elk-hunting season. Commercially, Great Britain was before the war Norway's most important market for her exports; but Germany came next, and her position was rapidly improving, while as a source of supply for imports she had already attained the leading place. At the same time, as the war was to demonstrate, the supplies controlled by Great Britain were of specially vital importance. All her circumstances, therefore, combined to dictate to Norway an attitude of strict and genuine neutrality.

In this respect her position differed considerably
from that of the other Scandinavian countries. The
traditional sympathies of Sweden were with the
Central European Powers, and opposed to Russia,
whom she disliked and feared. Among the Swedes,
especially in Court and Conservative circles, there was
a party in favour of active intervention on the side
of Germany, and it is probably only the danger
of complete isolation, with a hostile Russia on her
unprotected flank, which turned the scale. By the
Trälleborg - Sässnitz ferry, Sweden maintains direct
railway communication with Germany, and her most
powerful commercial interests coincided with her
cultural and traditional associations to colour her
neutrality with a decided bias in favour of the Central
Powers. The neutrality of Denmark was, in the
main, a nicely adjusted balance between hatred and
fear of Germany. From the victory of the Allies she
might hope to recover a portion of the territory lost
in 1864 ; but, in the circumstances of the war, her
commercial interests tended to work in the opposite
direction, and the ever-present threat of an invasion
which she knew herself powerless to resist made her,
in fact, more accessible to German pressure than to
the purely economic influences which the Allies could
bring to bear. Her mining of the Great Belt, through
which, during the real neutrality which Denmark
observed in the Russo-Japanese War, the Russian
fleet had been allowed free passage, was an action
as definitely partisan as the closing of the Kogrund
Channel by Sweden.

It is stated by the writer of an article in *The Norway
Year Book for* 1924, that attempts were made by
belligerent parties to induce Norway to throw in her
lot with one or other of them. That this was the
case it is rather difficult to believe. The advantage
to Germany derived from Scandinavian neutrality is
obvious, and the task of persuading a nation whose
sympathies were quite 70 per cent. pro-British to take
up arms against this country must evidently have been

hopeless. On the other hand, there is direct documentary evidence that England desired, and indeed enjoined, Norwegian neutrality. In the Belgian Diplomatic Correspondence published in October 1914 as a British parliamentary paper (Cmd 7627) is included the following telegraphic report from the Belgian Minister in London, dated 4th August 1914: "The Minister for Foreign Affairs has informed the British Ministers in Norway, Holland, and Belgium that Great Britain expects that these three kingdoms will resist German pressure and observe neutrality. Should they resist, they will have the support of Great Britain. . . ." It would thus appear that no serious attempt can have been made on either side to induce Norway to engage in hostilities.

On the other hand, efforts were of course made by both sides to direct and control the channels of neutral trade. Neutrality, of the character which had prevailed in previous wars, was, in the circumstances of 1914–8, no longer possible. That important branch of international law which had hitherto defined the rights and limitations of neutrality was developed at a time when " contraband of war " was an expression capable of easy definition, and when, owing to the imperfections of internal communication, the consignment of goods to a neutral port involved no great danger that any considerable proportion of them would ultimately find their way to an enemy. In the late war, the presumption of enemy destination in the case of imports largely in excess of the neutrals' normal demand was nearly conclusive, and the class of goods which could not afford direct assistance to a belligerent had shrunk to insignificance. This fact is forcibly brought home to anyone who sees the variety of " surplus Government war stock " which has, since 1918, been thrown upon the market.

As these facts dawned upon the parties concerned, lists of contraband were modified in conformity with existing conditions until the " free-list " virtually disappeared. Under similar influences, the doctrine of continuous voyage was extended into the system

of rationing neutral countries to the extent of their
normal domestic requirements, on the well-grounded
assumption that any surplus would find its way to
the enemy. It has been claimed that in this respect
England sometimes went too far, ignoring the fact
that overseas imports in excess of the normal were
actually required to replace supplies no longer obtainable through other channels; but it cannot be contested that from Denmark so large a percentage of
produce was exported to Germany that the home
population went short—fish, for example, being almost
unobtainable in the country, in spite of the quantity
ordinarily procurable. Neutrals inclined to take a
harsh view of British action in this respect should
peruse Admiral Consett's *Triumph of Unarmed Forces*,
when they will realise how far short our methods fell of
satisfying the ideals of the gallant admiral.

The action of Great Britain in dealing with the
Norwegian fishing industry can hardly be condemned
on the score of excessive harshness. It was of course
impossible, by the exercise of sea-power, to prevent the
home products of Norway from reaching Germany.
Yet it would have been easy, by methods to which
no legal objection could be taken, to have brought this
important industry of Norway completely to a stand-
still. The Norwegian fisheries depended upon essential
supplies of gear and other commodities, which it was
fully in our power to withhold. We did not ourselves
want the fish, and for the pickled herrings, of which a
large proportion consisted, there was little or no market
in England. Notwithstanding this, in view of the
friendly feelings subsisting between ourselves and
Norway, it was decided to proceed by purchasing the
Norwegian supply, and this decision was expeditiously
carried out through the agency of a Norwegian who had
previously worked for the German market, before the
Central Powers had realised that any such step was in
contemplation. Under a separate agreement with the
Norwegian Government, the export to Germany of fish
caught with supplies of gear, etc., obtained from us

and our Allies was precluded. During 1916 and 1917 the Norwegian fishermen enjoyed unexampled prosperity under this arrangement ; as indeed was the case to the end of the war, though after 1917 we ceased to purchase the catch, which was taken by the Norwegian authorities with the object of supporting the industry.

Another Norwegian product the control of which was secured by agreement was copper. Norway is for the most part unable to make use of the copper extracted from her own mines, but depends upon import for the manufactured copper which is necessary to her industry. The native copper ore was at the outset of hostilities almost exclusively exported to Germany, where it was used in the manufacture of munitions. From the beginning of 1916 England had practically stopped all imports of copper to Norway. In August of the same year it was therefore possible to conclude an agreement whereby the export of native copper and pyrites was only permitted in exchange for an equivalent in manufactured copper goods—an arrangement which effectively checked the export to Germany, which had no copper to spare. After this date a considerable quantity of Norwegian copper was exported to Great Britain in return for facilities for the importation of manufactured copper, though it is asserted by Admiral Consett that the price which we paid was considerably higher than that at which the Norwegian output could have been secured at an earlier stage in the war.

Most important of all was the arrangement, touched on elsewhere, by which England secured the services of a large proportion of the Norwegian shipping. Here the lever used was our control of the coal supplies, which were essential to this and other branches of Norwegian industry. The power of withholding supplies of coal was also effectively used in other cases—for example, during a dispute with regard to copper in 1917, and, in order to control the export of condensed milk, by refusing supplies to glass-bottle manufactories who worked in connection with the German trade.

For the most part, the necessity for the pressure

exercised by Great Britain was understood and appreciated. Feeling in Norway became increasingly pro-British as time went on. The fishermen talked of "the blessed war," and as outrages by German submarines became more frequent, feeling against the nation responsible grew more and more pronounced. An even greater effect was produced in 1917 by the arrest of the German courier von Rautenfels, who had smuggled into Norway a quantity of explosives, in baggage consigned from the German Foreign Office to their Legation in Christiania. In a somewhat lame attempt to palliate this gross abuse of diplomatic privileges, the German authorities contended that these explosives were intended for use outside Norway ; but a suspicion was not unnaturally prevalent that this was not the case, and that destruction of the Norwegian shipping, which was rendering valuable services to the enemies of Germany, was in fact the object in contemplation. The devotion of Norway to the cause of the Allies, though politically it may have been the result of pressure, was in fact fully in conformity with the sentiments of the population.

It must be remembered that the measures adopted by Great Britain, while they changed the attitude of Norway from one of strict neutrality to that of being virtually a non-combatant ally of Great Britain, were very far from prejudicial to Norwegian prosperity. On the contrary, during the years of the war, commerce and industry developed on a quite unprecedented scale : foreign competition was reduced to a minimum ; fisheries and shipping made unexampled profits ; industry found a ready market, where purchasers were not too particular how much was paid. It is true that the cost of living increased to a greater extent than was the case in other neutral countries, and that, after the entry of America into the war, the difficulty of obtaining supplies led to the introduction of rationing from the end of November 1917 ; while from that date until the conclusion of the Norwegian-American agreement negotiated by Dr. Nansen on 30th April 1918, the situation gave rise to considerable anxiety and some internal unrest. It is also true that the uncertainty of the situation, the expense of measures for the preservation of neutrality, and of encouraging agriculture with a view to rendering the country self-supporting, combined with the high cost of living and rate of wages to bring about heavy taxation ; the taxes imposed on shipping alone absorbed a larger share of the takings than went to the shareholders, and amounted to nearly eight times the sum represented by the total share capital of that industry at the beginning of the war.

Between 1914 and 1919 the national debt of the country was nearly trebled, though perhaps the whole of this increase cannot fairly be attributed to necessary war expenditure. The Government of the time is indeed loudly accused in Norway of reckless extravagance, and an inability, shared by the people at large, to realise that these good times were only temporary. Of the combined national and municipal debts, amounting to some $3\frac{1}{2}$ milliards of kroner at the present time, it is stated that 1050 million kroner consists of money expended on various capital enterprises which are not, and cannot under existing conditions be, remunerative. At the same time, the sum expended by public authorities on the development of water-power schemes for the provision of electricity should not be too hastily condemned. An immediate or even comparatively distant commercial profit was not for the most part the end in view. No one could tell how long the war would last, and the inconvenience and danger of being so largely dependent upon imported resources was every day brought forcibly home to Norway by the action of the belligerents. To make use of a sudden influx of national wealth for the purpose of rendering the country more self-supporting was a wise and a sound policy. It is not fair to judge these power schemes from the purely commercial standpoint of an industrial undertaking. They were largely designed to assist the agricultural population of various districts by the provision from native sources of the light, heat, and mechanical power for which the farmers were otherwise dependent upon the goodwill of one or other of the belligerents. And even if these advantages must for some time to come be paid for in increased taxation, they are none the less in existence, and a time will come when the full benefit will be realised.

But for a time the prosperity was striking. The amount of capital invested in the industry of the country, exclusive of shipping, which showed an almost equal increase, advanced from 390 million kroner to 1535 millions. The people, and even the banks, were altogether unaccustomed to the figures with which they now had to deal. Before the war there were not more than six stockbrokers in Oslo. Now a fever of speculation set in, which, affecting as it did persons hitherto comparatively inexperienced in financial matters, was not calculated to do much permanent good to the country. It was not easy, in the general excitement, to draw a sound distinction between concerns whose prosperity was almost wholly dependent on the continuance of hostilities, and those which could hope, in more normal circumstances, to yield an adequate return. Far less could those developments be foreseen which were to affect businesses which in days before the war were in a sound position, the extinction of markets, the chaos of exchanges, and all the other factors which have afflicted post-war Europe.

There was another difficulty which presented itself to bankers and professional business men. Capital was pouring in ; what was to be done with it ? It had to be invested, and with practically the whole world at war and the result uncertain, investments were to all intents and purposes confined to national industry ; to enterprises, that is to say, peculiarly dependent upon the outside world both for supplies and for markets, and therefore peculiarly sensitive to the economic fate of Europe.

Doubtless there was also a good deal of waste and extravagant living. The capitalist of normal times devotes the bulk of his wealth to productive purposes.

In the striking language of Mr. Keynes, "The capitalist classes were allowed to call the best part of the cake theirs, and were theoretically free to consume it on the tacit underlying condition that they consumed very little of it in practice. . . . Like bees they saved and accumulated, not less to the advantage of the whole community because they themselves had narrower ends in prospect." But the man promoted to sudden wealth by successful speculation has no such habits. Either he continues to speculate, with less satisfactory results, or he spends his unexpected gains in luxury. In the outskirts of Oslo many a staring and pretentious new building is pointed out with the comment, "War profiteer—bankrupt now."

Under any circumstances, however, the economic position of Norway was bound to react in an exceptional degree to the conditions prevailing in the outside world. The real gravamen of the indictment against the Norwegian Government and individual traders is that they did not foresee this, or accumulate reserves in the times of prosperity to meet the coming depression. At the end of the war the country was glutted with stocks intended for export, for which no purchasers could now be found. Apart from the timber trade, fisheries, and shipping, Norwegian industry is dependent, for supplies as well as for markets, on external sources. Its one advantage lies in relatively cheap production through the utilisation of water-power, and this, in times of high cost of living and high wages resulting from the temporary prosperity of the country, was largely neutralised. But the circumstances of post-war Europe affected the commerce dependent upon natural resources as well. The fate of Norwegian shipping has been dealt with elsewhere in greater detail ; here it is sufficient to say that the collapse of the foreign freight market was bound to affect it detrimentally. The timber trade, and the industries dependent upon forest products, slumped in 1921, as a result of competition from Finland and Central Europe, with their depreciated exchanges.

The fisheries were dependent upon imported gear and supplies, which rose in price to an almost prohibitive figure, while important markets, in Russia and Central Europe, were no longer in a position to take supplies. Above all, this industry, and to a lesser extent the shipping trade of Norway also, suffered a crushing blow from the attitude of Spain and Portugal provoked by the prohibition policy, a question of paramount importance in recent Norwegian politics of which more must be said later. Spain and Portugal constitute, in normal times, Norway's most important market for dried cod; but, in retaliation for the exclusion of their wines, these countries proceeded to subject the importation of Norwegian fish to practically prohibitive duties. Shipping was not only indirectly prejudiced by the diminution in Norwegian exports thus occasioned, but, in the case of Portugal, was also subjected to the payment of special dues, five times in excess of those ordinarily demanded. So serious, indeed, did the situation become that in 1923 it was found necessary to modify the prohibition laws to the extent of permitting the import and sale of the strong wines of these countries. The distress occasioned in the meanwhile had, however, been extremely severe.

In these circumstances, it may reasonably be contended that the Liberal Government which was in power during the war, and indeed for some time afterwards, showed a lamentable inability to appreciate the realities of the position. Failure to forecast the effects of post-war conditions might have been pardonable, but it is, to say the least, astonishing that in the election campaign of 1921 Mr. Gunnar Knudsen, the Liberal Prime Minister, could speak as follows : " It is certainly no exaggeration to say that our country's financial position is better than that of any other country in the whole world. At any rate, I know of no other land which is in a better position."

At this time the situation had already begun to tell on some of the Norwegian banks, and at the end of March 1921 a State fund of 15 million kroner was established for their assistance by means of deposits in the banks concerned. In April of the following year a similar fund of 25 million kroner was approved for the same purpose. About the same time a tendency to transfer balances from the smaller banks to older and larger institutions began to be manifested. The bank crisis rapidly developed, some banks stopped payment, and there were disquieting rumours as to the stability of others. In the interests of the commercial life of the country, no less than of the banks themselves, it became evident that drastic steps must be taken. Accordingly, in March 1923, a law was passed providing for the public administration of banks unequal to the strain of resisting the crisis for periods of a year at a time. During the period of administration such banks were to enjoy the advantages of a moratorium, while new engagements were given a priority over old in the contingency of eventual failure. At the same time, the release of old deposits was severely restricted, and the amount so paid out was not permitted in any case to exceed the dividend assured in the event of bankruptcy.

The first result of this measure was to accelerate the catastrophe. To the fears entertained as to the stability of a bank was added the risk of indefinite retention of deposits, and these were increasingly withdrawn with a rapidity amounting in some instances to a run. At the same time, foreign banks became dissatisfied with the position to which the law reduced their claims, and agitated for a State guarantee. This differentiation between natives and foreigners naturally presented considerable political difficulties, though it had the support of the Association of Norwegian Bankers. Eventually, in order to secure the credit of the country in the interests of general trade, engagements arising out of the passage of goods received the required guarantee. A further assurance by the State was found necessary to attract new business to the administered banks, and in April the fulfilment of engagements entered into under administration was guaranteed in the case of banks whose prospects of eventual survival seemed satisfactory. Whatever the demerits of the scheme, it is contended that no equally effective alternative could be found. Many banks were forced to take advantage of the law, the total number in 1923 being no less than twenty-seven, the greater part of them coming under administration very shortly after the passing of the law.

The conduct of Norwegian banking has, in these circumstances, naturally formed the subject of severe criticism. How far this has been justified it is difficult for an outsider to say. There is doubtless great force in the observation that the bank crisis is merely a symptom of the general business depression. When a large part of a nation's trade is ruined, the cumulative reckoning falls upon the bankers. At the same time, that there is an element of truth in some of the criticisms put forward seems extremely probable. The bankers appear to have shared the inability of the nation to forecast the course of events, and to have refrained from applying the necessary brake to speculation while it was in their power to do so. That they put too many of their eggs in one basket, as the saying goes, is probably true, but it was difficult to act otherwise in the circumstances of the time. It is also suggested that they locked up too large a proportion of their resources in long-sighted industrial loans, while their share capital was too small to suit this class of business. So far as the present writer's uninstructed observation goes, the trouble is that there are, or were, too many banks in Norway. Every locality, and many an industry, has tended to rely on a bank of its own rather than on branches of a few nation-wide undertakings. In England the tendency has been more and more towards amalgamation—at one time the title of what is now the Westminster Bank could not be written in a single line on any ordinary envelope, owing to the number of banks which had coalesced in it ; in Norway, on the other hand, diffusion has been the rule. This state of things must, one would think, have promoted an unhealthy degree of competition, incompatible with prudence. There were 132 banks in 1914, and over 200 at the close of the war.

The Norwegian authorities seem to some extent to have shared this view as to the excessive number of banking undertakings. In reporting upon the proposals which eventually took shape as the Joint Stock Bank Act of 1924, the Finance Department expressed itself as follows : " We have had some experience, both during the time of the last Great War and in the earlier period of speculation at the close of the 'nineties, of how times of prosperity tempt to the establishment of new banks, which, in competition with the older banks of the locality, involve themselves in more or less unsafe undertakings. . . . And it can hardly be doubted that still more examples of this kind would lately have been seen, if the liberty to establish new banks had not been checked by the temporary law of 9th March 1918."

The Act of 1924 definitely aims at restricting the sphere of operations of the ordinary banks, and laying down conditions to which all must conform before being allowed to engage in this business. As the committee entrusted with the consideration of the subject recognised, banking, as contrasted with other forms of commercial activity, has " a semi-public character," which seems to render it a proper subject for the special attention and control of the State. The committee, indeed, advanced conclusive arguments against the nationalisation of this form of business, and was, for similar reasons, averse from subjecting it to the Concession Laws, and making the Royal permission a condition precedent to the establishment of a bank. On the latter point they were, however, overruled, and, under the Act, existing as well as new banks are ultimately subjected to the necessity of obtaining such permission. Further restrictions prescribe the minimum amount of share capital, and endeavour to confine the activities of bankers more strictly to banking proper. The managing director of a bank may not carry on any other trade or industry, or belong to the board of any company which does so. To a lesser extent a similar limitation applies to the directors generally. But the principal innovation introduced by the Act is the establishment of a public bank inspectorate to keep an eye on banking activities in the general interest. The law has, of course, been in force for too short a time to allow of any practical experience of its working, or of the improvements which it may or may not effect in the general economic situation.

In the early part of this year (1925) some excitement was occasioned by revelations connected with the affairs of the Handelsbank, an important institution which came under administration in September 1924. It appeared that the Finance Department, under the presidency of the late Prime Minister, Berge, had, without consulting the Storting, deposited in this bank a sum of 25 million kroner in May 1923, with the object of avoiding the shock to the national credit which might follow should this important house be obliged to place itself under administration. In the Liberal Press this action was made the basis of a bitter attack upon the late Prime Minister, which even went to the length of suggesting his impeachment before the *riksret*. At the time of writing the matter does not seem to have been finally disposed of, but from the documents published by the Finance Department it appears that the action criticised was not only supported but energetically advocated by the Bank of Norway and other leading banks of the kingdom, which pointed out that not only national but external confidence in Norwegian banking was shaken, with disastrous results to commerce; and urged that further banking difficulties should at all costs be obviated, adding that it was no exaggeration to say that a general collapse of the commercial and economic life of the nation was in question. It was further, though as the event proved erroneously, stated that the bank's financial position was sufficiently sound to free the step contemplated from any element

of risk. In these circumstances it was thought necessary to take some action, and that quickly. Time
and secrecy were equally of the essence of the problem,
and it was decided, for both these reasons, that the
Storting, even if it sat with closed doors, could not be
consulted. "In these circumstances," says Mr. Berge,
"I considered that I must take the responsibility of
acting as I did. Both I and my colleagues were fully
alive to the seriousness of such a course, but I considered that if there ever was a situation in which a
Finance Minister should act on his own responsibility, it
was present here." The problem is not one for us to judge,
but it must at least be admitted that the Finance Department and its former Minister have a substantial case.

As before remarked, the prohibition question is a
product of the war which has its serious economic
as well as moral aspects, and it is at the present time
perhaps the most important concrete political problem
in the country. It cannot be denied that from the
earliest times down to some sixty or seventy years
ago Norwegians had the reputation of hard drinkers.
Even so early a poem as *Hávamál* contains warnings
against intemperance, and all the older Norse literature
suggests that drunkenness was extremely prevalent.
King Sverre's temperance speech towards the end of
the twelfth century points in the same direction, and
indeed indicates that the situation in this respect must
have become distinctly serious, when a King, who in
other respects was inclined to favour foreign traders,
felt bound to enter a strong protest against the importation of wine through the German merchants.
Under the union with Denmark it can hardly be doubted
that Norwegians shared with Danes the reputation to
which Shakespeare alludes in *Hamlet* :

> " This heavy-headed revel, east and west,
> Makes us traduced and taxed of other nations :
> They clepe as drunkards, and with swinish phrase
> Soil our addition."

In the eighteenth and the earlier years of the nineteenth century the situation was made, if anything,

worse, by the encouragement which the State gave to
private distilleries in the supposed interest of agriculture. Even so virtuous a man as the great lay
preacher Hans Nielsen Hauge distilled spirits. The
natural consequences followed ; and I remember a relative of mine, who visited Norway about 1860, telling
me that the thing which struck him particularly was
the constant drunkenness of everyone, "from the priest
downwards." Brawls, involving the frequent use of the
knife and consequent loss of life, are incidents which
occur everywhere in literature dealing with this period.

It is therefore all the more praiseworthy, and a
curious commentary on all that temperance lecturers
tell us of the demoralising and deteriorating effects
of alcohol upon the race, that the Norwegians, after
a history of this kind, were able, swiftly and suddenly,
to pull themselves together. Under the influence of
men like Kjeld Andresen, whose teaching was remarkably free from fanaticism, and who confined their
efforts to restraining the abuse of spirits while raising
no objections to the moderate consumption of alcohol
in other forms, the country turned over a new leaf.
Private distilleries were abolished, and the temperance
movement, conducted on these unusually moderate
lines, undoubtedly won a large number of adherents
throughout the country.

The benefits derived from the well-known *samlag*
system, which was introduced in 1871, are more open
to question. It seems probable that much of the decrease in drunkenness observable about this time was
the result of the general improvement in the national
habits, and cannot entirely be laid to the credit of the
system. The *samlags* were incorporated societies to
whom the monopoly of the sale of spirituous liquors
was entrusted on a basis of theoretically disinterested
management. The Norwegian scheme differed from
the similar " Gothenburg " system of Sweden, in that
the surplus profits were not employed in relief of the
rates of the municipalities, but devoted to the public
welfare generally. The practical working of the system

has been subjected to considerable criticism, notably by Mr. E. A. Pratt, *Licensing and Temperance in Sweden, Norway, and Denmark,* though no doubt it furthered the cause of temperance in the country districts by confining the sale of spirits to the towns.

From 1894, the establishment of a *samlag* depended upon a popular vote of the local inhabitants, while the Town Council also possessed a power of veto. The grant to a *samlag* of the power of selling spirits lasted for five years only. Under this system of local option the numbers of the *samlags* declined, and in 1914 they existed in thirteen towns only. In these circumstances the consumption of alcohol in Norway decreased, till the figures for this country were almost the lowest in the statistics of Europe. Although from 1907 onwards the consumption increased, at the outbreak of the war there certainly existed no apparent need for drastic legislation.

During the war, however, it was thought advisable to pass a temporary measure of prohibition. The reasons for this were to a large extent independent of considerations of temperance. Partly it was desired to promote economy and discourage luxury ; partly the object was to preserve food supplies normally used in the distillation of spirit ; and to some extent, no doubt, the preservation of public order seemed of special importance in these critical times. The scope of the restriction varied somewhat from time to time, but for the most part it included, besides spirits, wines and other drinks containing more than 12 per cent. volume of alcohol. The prohibitionists were quick to seize the opportunity thus afforded, and exerted their efforts to convert this temporary war measure into a permanent law. In 1917 it was accordingly enacted that a referendum of the whole people should be held in 1919 on the question whether spirits and strong wines should be permanently prohibited. Somewhat to the surprise of many anti-prohibitionists, the referendum resulted in a considerable majority for prohibition, on a poll consisting of rather more than 66 per cent. of the voting population. The proportions for and against the proposed measure were about 63 per cent. to 37. In these circumstances, the legislature felt itself bound to pass a prohibition law, and this was accordingly done on 16th September 1921.

The difficulties with Spain and Portugal, resulting in the repeal of the provisions relating to strong wines, have already been mentioned. Before the passing of the law difficulties of a similar kind had arisen in relation to France, the settlement of which, by a convention binding Norway to import annually from that country a minimum of 4000 hectolitres of brandy or strong wine, considerably delayed the proposed legislation. The import from France was, however, to be utilised for medicinal, technical, or scientific purposes, and was not therefore inconsistent with the law.

This is not the place to enter into the difficult question as to how far the interference with the liberty of law-abiding subjects entailed by such a measure is justifiable. It may be suggested, however, that the decision of the question by a referendum was open to grave objections. The irresponsible, secret votes of men and women imperfectly informed as to the conditions outside their own district are hardly a satisfactory substitute for legislation in the Storting after the expression of all points of view by representatives from every part of the country. It must be remembered, too, that in Norway the cleavage between East and West, and between town and country, is particularly marked, and a large majority of votes polled in districts where local veto has already been adopted does not exclude the existence of extensive districts where a measure of this kind is so universally resented as to leave little chance that its provisions will be respected. The force of public opinion is a far more powerful sanction for a law than the fear of punishment, and where a man's neighbours are inclined to approve disobedience to such a measure, the law tends to fall into contempt. Such has certainly been the case in Norway.

The advocates of prohibition claim that statistics show a reduction in drunkenness. This, however, is strenuously disputed. Such figures, in any case, show periodical fluctuations, and the true cause often differs from that assigned by partisans. It is probable, too, that relatively fewer cases come to the notice of the police under conditions when drinking necessarily takes place in privacy. The figures, however, since 1921, when the prohibition law was first made permanent, hardly seem to bear out the contention of its supporters. According to the Statistical Central Bureau the number of offences for the years 1921–3 are as follows :

1921	.	.	.	35,528 cases.
1922	.	.	.	44,685 ,,
1923	.	.	.	49,019 ,,

These would indicate that matters were getting steadily worse, though the available figures for 1924 show some improvement.

Perhaps a surer test of the efficacy of prohibition is to be found in statistics relating to smuggled liquor, for the villainous alcohol known as *sprit*, which forms the stock-in-trade of the smuggler, is not of a quality likely to appeal to the taste of the moderate drinker. That a larger proportion than one-fifth falls into the hands of the authorities it is difficult to believe, and, indeed, it has been stated that the estimate of the Social Department puts it as low as one-tenth. The quantity of *sprit* confiscated in 1923 amounted to some 400,000 litres of 100 per cent. alcohol. The quantity introduced into the country, and presumably consumed there, cannot, therefore, during this period have fallen far short of the equivalent of 4 million bottles of ordinary 50 per cent. spirit, and was not improbably much more.

In considering these facts, it should be borne in mind that the smuggler in Norway does not, as is alleged in the case of America, cater for the rich. On the contrary, *sprit* is a form of alcohol so noxious that no discriminating palate would tolerate it. The wealthier classes, in so far as they disregard the law, use other methods : the wholesale smuggler caters for the proletariat. And seeing that the coast of Norway is, as it were, created by Nature to facilitate such a traffic, it is hardly surprising that he drives a thriving trade.

Even if we accept the view that some slight decrease in drunkenness is demonstrable, there is much to be set on the debit side of the account. Murders and other crimes of violence, of which this fiery poison is the cause, and which over-indulgence in more wholesome intoxicants seems rarely to induce, are constantly reported in the newspapers, the health of the community is undermined by recourse to this and even more injurious substitutes, while large sections of enlightened public opinion are openly ranged on the side of the law-breakers. When a prohibitionist professor took the unconventional course of lodging an information against his fellow-guests at a commemorative banquet, it was his conduct, rather than that of the accused, which provoked widespread indignation. Doubtless the instinct which prompted such an attitude was right, for the informer's action cut at the roots of that mutual confidence among comrades on which civilised society depends, while the injury to the community caused by moderate indulgence in forbidden beverages is less apparent : but such episodes cannot but tend to bring the administration of the law into contempt.

Apart, however, from the pros and cons to be urged on the moral side of the question, there is a serious economic aspect. The injury to the fishing and shipping industries caused by the disputes with wine-producing countries has already been referred to. But at a time of the gravest financial depression, when Norway groans under a crushing debt and a depreciated exchange, and financiers are at their wits' end to find a way out of the difficulty, the loss to the country of a source of revenue estimated at some 30 million kroner annually, and the immense expense entailed by more or less fruitless endeavours to intercept the smugglers, are matters which throw upon the advocates of prohibition the onus of establishing a much stronger case than they have hitherto been able to make. It was, in fact, the economic aspects of the question which led the Conservative Government of Mr. Berge, in the summer of 1924, to propose the repeal of the law without more ado. Granted, they said in effect, that some slight, very slight, social improvement may have resulted from prohibition, there are times when even the most desirable social legislation has to be subordinated to economic exigencies. The proposal, indeed, led to the fall of the Ministry, but their Liberal opponents were themselves by no means whole-hearted supporters of prohibition ; they merely adopted the somewhat doctrinaire standpoint that a measure inaugurated by a referendum must be disposed of through the same machinery, thus subordinating parliamentary authority to a questionable expedient unrecognised by the Constitution of Norway. For the present, however, prohibition survives, and, as the results of the General Election held in the autumn were inconclusive upon the point, may continue to do so for some time to come. How far the financial position of the country can bear its survival still remains to be seen.

The problem is not a simple one. To increase the burden of direct taxation seems out of the question. The weight of the national and municipal debts suggests that borrowing has reached the limit. The principal expedient tried by the late Conservative Government, the so-called *guld-told*, *i.e.* the levying of duties in kroner at the gold rate, has already been the subject of serious criticism, though there seems no prospect that the present Ministry will endeavour to dispense with it. No doubt the deliberate object of this step was partly to reduce the volume of imports and thus improve the trade balance, but it has inevitably tended to keep prices high, and thus to increase the cost of production and induce labour unrest at a time when not only the strictest economy, but a stimulated industry able to hold its own with foreign competitors, is called for. At the same time a satisfactory alternative policy has not hitherto been found.

The only glimmer of light comes from the fact that there are no other outstanding political questions to distract the attention of statesmen from the economic problem. A short time ago, public opinion in Norway was seriously excited by the Greenland question, provoked by Denmark's assumption of sovereignty over the whole of Greenland, to the detriment, as was feared, of time-honoured Norwegian interests connected with fishing and hunting. The dispute was, however, settled for the present in the course of 1924 by an agreement, to last for twenty years, which, broadly speaking, gives to the Norwegian hunters and fishermen free right of access to those parts of the country where no Danish settlements exist.

It is therefore no longer necessary to enter at any length into the merits of the controversy, which was by no means confined to the practical aspects of the question at the present day. Roughly summarised, the position was that Greenland was discovered and colonised by a Norwegian from Jaederen, Eric the Red, that it became subject to the Norwegian King in the thirteenth century, and that it remained juridically a possession of the Kingdom of Norway, and not of Denmark, through all the period of Union down to 1814. The man who recolonised the old settlements in the eighteenth century was a Norwegian, the missionary Hans Egede, with the assistance of funds raised in Bergen. Though the central office of the trading monopoly was in Copenhagen, questions relating to Greenland were handled by the Norwegian Departments of State, and indeed the only possible title which the Dano-Norwegian Kings could show to this colony was through their sovereignty over Norway.

By the Treaty of Kiel, however, under which Frederick VI purported to resign his sovereignty over Norway in favour of the Swedish King, Greenland, Iceland, and the Faroes were expressly excepted. From Frederick's side this action was in conflict with the provisions of the *Kongelov* of 1665, which provided for the integrity of Norway and her provinces. On the Swedish side the concession was due to ignorance, as is apparent from the report of the negotiator, Wetterstedt, on 16th January 1814. "Although," he said, "Iceland, Greenland, and the Faroes have never belonged to Norway, Mr. Bourke (the Danish negotiator) wished —and I have not considered that I should resist it— that these countries should be specially mentioned in Article 4 of the Treaty."

Norway, as is elsewhere stated, never recognised the validity of the Treaty of Kiel, and the Storting took an early opportunity of protesting against the retention of the Norwegian colonies. In the negotiations, however, connected with Norway's payment of a share in the common debt incurred during the Union (see p. 105), the question of the retention of the colonies by Denmark was used as a make-weight, and, in the conclusion of this matter in 1821, the Storting agreed that all claims on both sides connected with the Union between Denmark and Norway should be regarded as finally settled. From that time to the present day the claim of Denmark to the Norwegian colonies has been generally recognised.

This side of the question, therefore, amounts to no more than a moral claim to special consideration, based on a legitimate grievance. Under the Swedish Union, in respect of foreign affairs, the hands of Norway were tied, but it would be difficult to establish any legal claim, at this distance of time, to the Greenland colony. But there is another side to the matter. The Greenland of Eric the Red, of Egede, and of the Danish administration consisted of a few isolated settlements on the south-west coast. The Danish monopoly has never been held to extend to the vast mass of Greenland generally. In the exploration of other parts Norwegians, and indeed other nations, have played an important part, and off and on the east coast especially, during the whole of the nineteenth century, Norwegian hunters and fishermen have plied their trade unchallenged. Herein lies the real strength of the Norwegian case, which, indeed, in the agreement now arrived at has to this extent been substantially admitted.

This question having been satisfactorily shelved for

the present, Norway is free to devote her full energy to the problem of economic recovery. The solution of the problem depends above all things upon strong and stable government. It is a healthy sign that, during the election campaign of 1924, subordinate questions, even that of prohibition, tended to recede into the background, and party recriminations to a surprising extent gave place to a growing recognition of the importance of co-operation and solidarity among all the stable political elements in the country. As the veteran ex-Prime Minister, Christian Michelsen, emerged from his retirement to point out, in a remarkably statesmanlike and broad-minded speech, "When a ship is in danger at sea, the important point is to secure the safety of the vessel and her crew ; it is of no use to discuss who has navigated worst. . . . If we are to come out of the quagmire, we must stand together. We must therefore learn the simple rule which every intelligent man applies in his private life, that there are differences in the values of life ; the small and unimportant must be subordinated to the great and uniting. And in times like these, to wish to promote these special interests in one form or another shows only how little many in this nation still understand the importance of the great co-operation and the great union which must take place." These were the words of a wise man, and they were not without their effect.

At the same time, the evolution of Norwegian democracy has produced tendencies, characteristic of popular government in all parts of the world, which present considerable obstacles to the attainment of the consummation desired. A fully developed democracy is, indeed, the only conceivable form of government for a nation in which class distinctions play so small a part as they do in Norway. The seeds of democracy were sown as far back as the Constitution of 1814 ; in that respect the bureaucrats of the period "builded better than they knew," and prepared their own downfall. The system of parliamentary government, for example, is to all intents and purposes a single-chamber form :

many important matters, including finance, are decided by the united Storting, and in any case the division into Odelsting and Lagting is only attained by electing for the duration of the Parliament a quarter of the whole membership to serve as a second chamber—the Lagting—which thus tends to reproduce the prevailing popular view, if any, in a concentrated form. And at the present day, with universal male and female suffrage, it would be difficult to imagine a more emphatically democratic form of government than the Norwegian. But, perhaps for this very reason, the system has not failed to develop its typical vices in a marked degree. That these exist is admitted by all ; and though a prominent Labour politician, Herr Inge Debes, has maintained that " the ills from which democracy now suffers . . . are no signs of senility, but infantile ailments—measles, whooping cough—which it will quickly conquer," observation of the conditions elsewhere may lead to the conclusion that they are characteristic of popular government in a more advanced stage of development.

Perhaps the most serious of these is the tendency to substitute for the simple lines of party cleavage, under which parliamentary government grew up, a large number of more or less equally balanced groups, no one of which is by itself in a position to assume the reins of government. That this is the result of a broad democratic franchise is confirmed by the fact that it is among the ranks of Labour that these fissiparous tendencies have specially been evinced. In Norway the evil has been intensified by the application of that logical development of the democratic idea, proportional representation. The effect of this is found to be that while every point of view is represented, none have a chance of a working majority. As the inevitable result, no Government can govern. The reconciliation of discordant elements on which it depends can only be temporary. The difficulty is increased by the fact that, in Norway, general elections take place only at constitutionally prescribed intervals

of three years, and it is not possible, as with us, for a
new Ministry to have the Storting dissolved, and gain,
from a fresh election, the support it needs. It has to
carry on as best it may in a legislature which on most
points is often more in agreement with its defeated
predecessors. Nor are there any by-elections to test
the currents of public opinion or vary the proportions
of parties; for, at a general election, as in the local
Government elections, substitutes as well as members
are chosen once for all.

It is difficult to forecast the means whereby a
remedy will ultimately be found for this paralysis of
government. For the moment, the evil is mitigated by
a large measure of rapprochement between the anti-
revolutionary parties in face of the Communist menace.
The danger of Communism does not, indeed, strike an
outside observer as particularly pressing, so long as a
large section of the population consists of small land-
holders; but the Communists are loud-voiced, and, by
a strange departure from the pronounced nationalism
which has hitherto characterised the people, the extremists have admittedly placed themselves under the
orders of Moscow. The existence of such a party
makes particularly necessary the speedy amelioration
of the economic depression which is the soil in which
such weeds thrive, and encouragement of those stable,
proprietary elements of the population which have
hitherto constituted its strength.

In such circumstances strong government and continuity of policy seem specially called for. The weakness of parliamentary government under present conditions is therefore attracting attention. Elsewhere
in Europe the commonest solution seems to be a
reaction to some form of dictatorship. The rival
tyrannies of Fascismo and Bolshevism have, indeed,
their adherents in Norway, and it is significant that the
Liberal Party, which with a characteristic rigidity of
doctrinaire principle seems now the only unwavering
adherent of democracy, is, as with us, rapidly losing
ground. Yet, in a country where so large a measure

of real equality exists, among a people whose prevailing characteristic is independence, it seems unlikely that such dubious alternatives have much chance of flourishing. The most probable and most hopeful way of escape is that suggested in the speech of Mr. Michelsen referred to earlier—the temporary co-operation of all the stable elements in the kingdom in the face of a a common emergency. This is the traditional method often applied with success by Norwegians, as, for instance, in 1905. In normal times the difficulties of uniting the inhabitants of Norway are greater than in the case of almost any other country ; geographical conditions, traditional antipathies, and that ingrained individualism into which their fine self-reliance tends to degenerate, are factors which keep them apart. But in the face of a common danger, universally recognised, they are capable of showing a united front which carries all before it. Norwegian effort is apt to be spasmodic, but whenever it is really exerted there is no doubt as to the result. It is to such a display of united effort that we should look with hope, rather than to any constitutional changes.

Since these words were written a promising development on these lines has taken place. On 5th January a manifesto, addressed to the Norwegian people, and bearing some 800 signatures, including such names as Dr. Nansen and Christian Michelsen, was published in the press. It called upon the nation to assist in the creation of a non-party association, *Fedrelandslaget*, to co-operate in resisting revolutionary tendencies of every kind, and to present a united front to the difficulties and dangers at present threatening the nation. " We stand," reads the manifesto, " before difficult times. The materialism of the war years cannot satisfy the ideal demands of the age. Everything is stamped with unrest and insecurity and the conflict between new and old has brought revolutionary tendencies into the foreground. But it must be clear to all that those who tread the way of revolution waste time and strength, and that there is no soil in Norway suited to the dictatorship either of the proletariat or of reaction. To preserve our political and economic independence, our association now calls for the co-operation of Norwegian men and women, without respect of political party. The time has come when we must all meet in collaboration about the task of maintaining the authority of the community, and protecting it against every policy based on force." It will be interesting to see how far this movement receives the support which it demands, or succeeds in giving effect to the sound principles on which it is based.

There is, of course, an obvious difference between the circumstances of 1905 and those of the present day. In the former case it had become so clear that dissolution of the Union was the only remedy, that it was comparatively easy for the adherents of all parties to sink their differences and combine for their country's good. An economic crisis raises a very different problem. The remedies proposed are likely to be numerous and varied, while Conservatives, Liberals, and moderate Socialists will probably put their faith in measures which have a genuine and fundamental relation to their differing creeds and standpoints. Abandonment of party tactics is not enough by itself to create a basis of policy. There is, further, a danger that many adherents of the new league will be actuated principally by antipathy to Communism, and may turn into Fascisti after all. Of this tendency the speeches of some of those who have concerned themselves most closely with the league show distinct traces. Hostility to Bolshevism is the aspect of their programme which is, perhaps naturally, more clearly expressed than any other. The situation calls for more than a mere coalition of constitutional parties. Inspiring leadership is also required, and a sound economic policy ; but, as the first desiderata for the remedy are manifestly thrift, self-sacrifice, and industry throughout the population, an organisation which can inculcate these virtues without distinction of party should, at all events, be welcomed as a step in the right direction.

But the vices of Norwegian democracy do not end with a tendency to reduce parliamentary government to impotence through subdivision of parties. It is a paradox of this kind of government that, though impotent to discharge its own proper functions, it exercises the maximum of interference with the liberty of individuals, and that, stepping to power over the prostrate body of a vanquished bureaucracy, it proceeds to become a bureaucracy itself. This is, of course, a phenomenon in no way peculiar to Norway, though State interference and the growing host of officials are the subjects of serious complaint here as elsewhere; but it is perhaps of peculiar importance to a nation whose greatest strength probably lies in individual resourcefulness. By excessive State interference such a quality is not only hampered in action, but permanently atrophied.

Improvident expenditure both in central and local governments is another characteristic tendency which the figures of the national and municipal debts show clearly to exist. Of this, however, less need be said at a time when adversity has thoroughly awakened the public consciousness to the need for crying a halt. And it may be doubted whether in the case of Norway this was not in the main a wartime phenomenon, induced by a temporary prosperity which went to the heads of Government and individuals alike. The financial burden resting upon the rising generation is heavy; it has been calculated that every child in Norway is born with a debt of 1300 kroner. But Norway has won through hard times before, and will undoubtedly do so again.

When all that can be said against Norwegian democracy has been said, it remains true that Norway is a country to which this form of government is peculiarly well suited. In few other countries, if any, is the entire electorate so well qualified for the task of government. Through the very fully developed system of local government which has been in existence now for nearly a hundred years, all sections of the community have been trained to an intelligent grasp of their responsibilities. There is no governing class ; the whole nation plays an equal part. The population is well educated, and being at the same time extremely scattered is inaccessible to the mob-oratory of the demagogue. These circumstances make the success of revolutionary activities extremely improbable, while one feels that even if through any accident an extremist policy came to be tried, its effects, however disastrous, would be less permanently harmful in Norway than in any other country. There is no large wealthy class to be dispossessed, and the common-sense and determination of a people accustomed to think and act for itself would inevitably put an end to any folly before the damage done was irreparable.

The post-war situation is perhaps more gloomy than a neutral nation could reasonably have expected. But much that has been lost, possibly all that is permanently lost, is merely the abnormal surplus of Norway's wartime prosperity. No one who knows the inhabitants of Norway can doubt that recovery and ultimate progress is only a matter of time. It will be, I think, no unmixed evil if the industrial development of the country is for some time retarded. It has hitherto progressed too fast to blend healthily with those qualities which have made the Norwegian character an object of universal admiration. Had the war come later, the results might have been more serious still. An industrial community is far more dependent on economic conditions than a sparse population of farmers, and in economic knowledge and experience Norway has shown herself to be somewhat deficient. A comparison of the exchange in Norway and Sweden draws pointed attention to this fact. Foreign affairs, also, have hitherto not unnaturally been an unduly neglected subject, and Norway must learn to take an increased interest in other nations if she is to prosper in competition with them. Fortunately, the agricultural population, which is still the backbone of the country, has not suffered in proportion to the rest of the community. With the fall in the krone their debts, which are in money, have decreased ; with the rise in prices, their assets, the produce of their farms, have appreciated. The love of the land which they own gives them a patriotism which, if at times too narrow, is at all events a salutary counterpoise to a Communism which looks to Moscow. The spirit which survived centuries of foreign oppression, and the versatility and self-reliance which have distinguished the Norwegian *bonde* in all ages, are qualities too valuable to be endangered by too abrupt a transition to the specialised and cosmopolitan outlook of modern industry. Money is not the only form of wealth to a nation. The change will inevitably come in time ; but it is just as well that it should be slow, and that Norway should continue to look. for some time to come, to the sources of livelihood which have hitherto made her people what they are.

I have referred to the natural lack of interest in external affairs, and suggested that this should be rectified. It is true that the country lies apart from the main currents of European politics, and that, historically, Norway has fared best when she has been content to work out her own salvation unfettered by union or alliance.

The dream of Björnson's old age, a Scandinavianism enlarged into a Pan-Teutonic alliance, seems singularly remote from the politics of to-day. In such a concert, as in the various forms of Scandinavian union which have from time to time been tried, Norway could play but an insignificant part, unworthy of the real ability of her citizens. Even from the scheme of Scandinavian co-operation into which she was enticed during the war, it may be doubted whether she derived any real benefit. But since the war an opportunity has arisen, to which perhaps no parallel can be shown in the history of the world, for nations to play an influential and useful part in controlling the destinies of the world, irrespective of the military or naval forces at their command. Of this opportunity Norway has already made a striking use in the work done by Dr. Nansen in the League of Nations. No better repre-

sentative could have been chosen to bring out the
special genius of the nation than this man who, with
characteristic versatility, has established a world-wide
reputation in a great variety of apparently unconnected fields. Through such men, under existing
conditions, Norway can always exert a great and a
beneficent influence, the more so because, in the
majority of questions which arise, her attitude will be
plainly disinterested. Until recently, influence in
international affairs has rested ultimately upon physical
force, upon great armaments and mighty alliances.
In such circumstances Norway, whatever her material
prosperity, could never have played more than a very
subordinate part. But the future, if it develop on
the lines which alone seem to contain any lasting
hope for mankind, will rest increasingly with the
impartial arbitrator. For such a rôle Norway, from
the very fact that she lies so remote from the storm-
centres of international politics, seems specially qualified. No other neutral nation is in a position equally
fitted to discharge such tasks without fear or favour.
For the moment she cannot be expected to do much
more than to set her own house in order. But when
she has made the inevitable recovery from the collapse
to which she has been temporarily reduced, largely by
circumstances not of her own making, there seems to be
no reason why a people so gifted, so resourceful, so honest,
and so charming should not win for their country a
place in the history of the future which need fear no
comparison with the brightest glories of her past.

INDEX